CANDID EYES
ESSAYS ON CANADIAN DOCUMENTARIES

Even before the creation of the National Film Board of Canada (NFB) in 1939, documentaries dominated Canada's film production; since then, more than any other form, they have continued to be crucial to the formation of Canada's cinematic identity. Surprisingly, there has been very little critical writing on this distinguished body of work. *Candid Eyes: Essays on Canadian Documentaries* addresses this oversight in the scholarly literature with an exceptional collection of essays by some of Canada's best-known film scholars. Focusing on films produced in French and English under the NFB umbrella, the fourteen essays in this book discuss and critique such landmark documentaries as *Lonely Boy* (1961), *Pour la suite du monde* (1963), and *Kanehsatake* (1993). This long-awaited and much-needed volume will be an indispensable resource for anyone seriously interested in Canadian film studies.

JIM LEACH and JEANNETTE SLONIOWSKI teach in the Department of Communications, Popular Culture, and Film at Brock University.

CANDID EYES

Essays on Canadian Documentaries

Edited by Jim Leach and Jeannette Sloniowski

UNIVERSITY OF TORONTO PRESS
Toronto Buffalo London

© University of Toronto Press Incorporated 2003
Toronto Buffalo London
Printed in Canada

ISBN 0-8020-4732-7 (cloth)
ISBN 0-8020-8299-8 (paper)

Printed on acid-free paper

National Library of Canada Cataloguing in Publication

Candid eyes : essays on Canadian documentaries / edited by Jim
Leach and Jeannette Sloniowski.

ISBN 8-8020-4732-7 (bound)   ISBN 0-8020-8299-8 (pbk.).

1. Documentary films – Canada – History and criticism. 2. National
Film Board of Canada. I. Leach, Jim II. Sloniowski, Jeannette
Marie, 1946–

PN1995.9.D6C35 2003   070.1'8   C2002-903319-5

University of Toronto Press acknowledges the financial assistance to
its publishing program of the Canada Council for the Arts and the
Ontario Arts Council.

This book has been published with the help of a grant from the Humanities
and Social Sciences Federation of Canada, using funds provided by the
Social Sciences and Humanities Research Council of Canada.

University of Toronto Press acknowledges the financial support for
its publishing activities of the Government of Canada through the
Book Publishing Industry Development Program (BPIDP).

To Joe, Lisa, and Mick, and to Jenny, Aphra, and Nat

Realist documentary, with its streets and cities and slums and markets and exchanges and factories, has given itself the job of making poetry where no poet has gone before it, and where no ends, sufficient for the purposes of art, are easily observed. It requires not only taste but also inspiration, which is to say a very laborious, deep-seeing, deep-sympathizing creative effort indeed.

John Grierson

Contents

Acknowledgments xi

Contributors xiii

Introduction 3
JIM LEACH and JEANNETTE SLONIOWSKI

Geography and Myth in *Paul Tomkowicz*: Coordinates of
National Identity 13
RICHARD HANCOX

The Days before Christmas and the Days before That 31
SETH FELDMAN

From Obscurity in Ottawa to Fame in Freedomland:
Lonely Boy and the Cultural Meaning of Paul Anka 48
BARRY KEITH GRANT

Images and Information: The Dialogic Structure of *Bûcherons
de la Manouane* by Arthur Lamothe 61
PETER HARCOURT

Linking Community Renewal to National Identity:
The Filmmakers' Role in *Pour la suite du monde* 71
DAVID CLANDFIELD

Dark Satanic Mills: Denys Arcand's *On est au coton*   87
JIM LEACH

Performing the Master Narratives: Michael Rubbo's
Waiting for Fidel   103
JEANNETTE SLONIOWSKI

Hard Film to Define – *Volcano: An Inquiry into the Life and
Death of Malcolm Lowry*   115
PETER BAXTER

Not a Love Story: A Film about Pornography – Tabloid Rhetoric
in Interventionist Documentary   131
JOAN NICKS

Voyage en Amérique avec un cheval emprunté: A Journey of the Mind   148
MARION FROGER

Queer Cinema at the NFB: The 'Strange Case' of *Forbidden Love*   164
JEAN BRUCE

'This Land Is Ours' – Storytelling and History in *Kanehsatake:
270 Years of Resistance*   181
ZUZANA M. PICK

Hyperbolic Masculinity and the Ironic Gaze in *Project Grizzly*   197
BRENDA LONGFELLOW

Sympathetic Understanding in *Tu as crié Let Me Go*   211
JANINE MARCHESSAULT

Filmography   227

Works Cited   231

Index of Film Titles   243

General Index   245

Acknowledgments

We would like to thank William Webster, former Dean of the Faculty of Social Sciences at Brock University, and Lewis Soroka, former Interim Dean, for their support. We would also like to thank Siobhan McMenemy of the University of Toronto Press for her editorial work.

Contributors

Peter Baxter teaches in the Department of Film Studies at Queen's University. He is the author of *Just Watch! Sternberg, Paramount, and America* (1994) and is currently working on a study of the portrayal of gender in contemporary French cinema.

Jean Bruce is an adjunct professor in the Department of Film Studies at Queen's University, where she teaches film and media studies, and popular and consumer culture. Her research centres on melodrama, representations of gender and sexuality, and the culture of food and drink.

David Clandfield is associate professor in the Department of French and the Cinema Studies Program at the University of Toronto. In addition to writing *Canadian Film* (1987) and articles on Canadian film in various journals around the world, he has translated and published research on the French educator Célestin Freinet and the politics of education. He is currently Principal of New College in the University of Toronto.

Seth Feldman, a founder and former president of the Film Studies Association of Canada, has published extensively on Canadian cinema, including a recent work on the documentary filmmaker Allan King. He is also the author of some twenty-three radio documentaries for the CBC program *Ideas*. He is a former Robarts Chair in Canadian Studies, a former dean of Fine Arts and has been awarded the title of Distinguished University Professor at York University.

Marion Froger is the scientific coordinator at the Centre for Research on Intermediality at the Université de Montréal. She is currently a PhD student at the Université de Montréal 'en cotutelle avec' l'Université de Paris I Pantheon Sorbonne (France). Her area of research includes Canadian documentary, Deleuze's philosophy, and the use of new technology in humanties research. She is the recipient of a team research grant from the Fondation Daniel Langlois for 2001–3.

Barry Keith Grant is professor of film studies and popular culture at Brock University and director of the graduate program in popular culture. His books include *Voyages of Discovery: The Cinema of Frederick Wiseman* (1992) and his work has appeared in numerous journals and anthologies. Professor Grant is also the editor of the Contemporary Film and Television series for Wayne State University Press.

Richard Hancox is an associate professor in Communication Studies at Concordia University, where he teaches both film production and film studies, including Canadian documentary and aspects of film, time and memory, space and place. He is an artistic innovator of personal films, including *Moose Jaw: There's a Future in Our Past* (1992) and others, which have been widely screened. Hancox taught for twelve years at Sheridan College, where in the 1970s he was credited for helping to launch Canada's first wave of personal, experimental documentary. He is currently working on a series of films entitled *All That Is Solid*.

Peter Harcourt has taught at Queen's University, York University, and Carleton University. He now lives in Ottawa and writes about film. He is the author of *Six European Directors* (1974), *Movies and Mythologies* (1977), and *A Canadian Journey: Conversations with Time* (1994).

Jim Leach is a professor in the Department of Communications, Popular Culture, and Film at Brock University. His research and teaching interests include Canadian cinema, British cinema, popular cinema, and film and cultural theory. He is the author of *A Possible Cinema: The Films of Alain Tanner* (1984) and *Claude Jutra Filmmaker* (1999) and prepared the Canadian edition of Louis Giannetti's *Understanding Movies* (2nd ed., 2001).

Brenda Longfellow is currently graduate program director in the Department of Film and Video at York University. She is an award-

winning filmmaker who recently premiered a new feature documentary *Tina in Mexico*, which explores the life and work of photographer
and revolutionary Tina Modotti.

Janine Marchessault is an associate professor and chair of the Department of Film and Video at York University. A past president of the Film
Studies Association of Canada, she has published widely on film, video,
and new media technologies in such journals as *Cine-Action, Convergence, New Formations, Public,* and *Screen*. She is the editor of several
anthologies, including *Mirror Machine: Video and Identity* (1994), and co-
editor of *Gendering the Nation: Canadian Women Filmmakers* (1999) and
Wild Science: Reading Feminism, Science and the Media (1999). She is also a
founding editor of *Public*, a journal of art, culture, and ideas.

Joan Nicks is an associate professor in the Department of Communications, Popular Culture, and Film at Brock University, and a member of
the Popular Culture Niagara research group. She is co-editor of *Slippery
Pastimes: Reading the Popular in Canadian Culture* (2002). Her essays have
appeared in *Post Script, Canadian Journal of Film Studies, Textual Studies
in Canada,* and in the anthologies *Documenting the Documentary: Close
Readings of Documentary Film and Video* (1998) and *Gendering the Nation:
Canadian Women's Cinema* (1999).

Zuzana M. Pick is a professor of Film Studies in the School for Studies
in Art and Culture at Carleton University in Ottawa. She is the author
of *The New Latin American Cinema: A Continental Project* (1993) and is
currently working on a book dealing with the imagery of the Mexican
revolution in Mexican and foreign films. Her essay on the documentary
practice of Native filmmaker Alanis Obomsawin appeared in the anthology *Gendering the Nation: Canadian Women's Cinema* (1999).

Jeannette Sloniowski is an associate professor in the Department of
Communications, Popular Culture, and Film at Brock University. Au-
thor of a number of articles on documentary, she is also co-editor of
*Documenting the Documentary: Close Readings of Documentary Film and
Video* (1998), *Canadian Communications: Issues in Canadian Media and
Culture* (2nd ed., 2002), and *Slippery Pastimes: Reading the Popular in
Canadian Culture* (2002).

CANDID EYES
ESSAYS ON CANADIAN DOCUMENTARIES

Introduction

JIM LEACH AND JEANNETTE SLONIOWSKI

Each of the essays in this book deals with a single Canadian documentary and provides a close reading of the film text in its historical, cultural, and cinematic contexts. The emphasis and approaches differ, according to the authors' interests and the films' specific characteristics, but the dual focus on text and context remains constant. In this way, while examining some key films in the Canadian documentary tradition, these essays also raise important questions about how documentary films represent reality and about critical methods that seek to respond to their representations.

There is nothing new in acknowledging the important contribution of Canadian filmmakers to the documentary, although many histories privilege developments in Britain, France, and the United States. However, even those films that have been recognized as Canadian documentary 'classics' have rarely received close critical attention. One of the aims of this book is to fill this gap by providing the first detailed analyses of some of these celebrated films. Other essays deal with more recent films that make use of innovative or controversial documentary approaches. There is no attempt to offer definitive accounts of these films; rather, the essays raise questions and offer some tentative answers.

All the films were produced by the National Film Board of Canada (NFB), although this is, in a sense, incidental to our purpose. There were documentary filmmakers in Canada before the NFB was established in 1939, notably those who worked for the Canadian Government Motion Picture Bureau (1917–41) and itinerant filmmakers, such as the Abbé Proulx, in Quebec.[1] Many important documentaries have also been made by filmmakers working in the private sector. A strong case could be made that in recent years, when major budget cuts have reduced the NFB to a shadow of its former self, innovative Canadian documentaries are more likely to come from outside the Board. However, given the dominant position of the NFB for so many years and its highly effective distribution system, the most widely known Canadian documentaries have been NFB productions. Since these films are readily accessible to interested readers, it seemed best to focus on NFB films, while recognizing that a full understanding of Canadian documentaries will require a consideration of other works – non-NFB films as well as films that will illuminate other aspects of the NFB's history.[2]

The book is organized chronologically, and the essays thus offer a sense of historical developments, although there is inevitably a certain amount of overlap, omission, and disagreement in their accounts. We make no claim to provide a comprehensive account of the history of the NFB.[3] For the most part, Board productions have been workmanlike, never aspiring to anything beyond straightforward educative or simple public service functions. Our focus is on those films that were innovative, aesthetically groundbreaking, or controversial. We do not apologize for this perhaps elitist approach to our subject because we have chosen to write about some of the Board's best and most thought-provoking films.

Many factors come into play in assessing the different strategies adopted by filmmakers working at the NFB, including the interests of the filmmaker, responses to documentary ideas worldwide, Board policy, economic constraints, and the influence of television. Especially since the 1950s, there has been a tension – often productive, but sometimes frustrating – between the idea of documentary 'objectivity,' supported by the Board's social mandate and institutional codes, and filmmakers, often working together in official or unofficial groups, who challenge the cinematic and political implications of this idea.

Documentary has traditionally depended on what Andrew Higson calls the 'public gaze.'[4] In other words, the images on the screen and their arrangement in the editing room must provide an external and supposedly objective viewpoint on the film's subjects. This restriction is necessary if the images are to claim the status of evidence. They must not be contaminated by the subjective points of view with which fiction films normally involve the spectator in the action. However, the 'public gaze' takes on an added meaning when the documentaries are produced by a public institution like the NFB.

When the federal government set up the National Film Board of

Canada, it acted on the advice of John Grierson, who became its first commissioner. An ardent believer in the potential of film as a public service, Grierson had already achieved acclaim as the leader of the British documentary film movement in the 1930s, using sponsorship by government bodies to provide a realist alternative to the spectacle and illusion of popular Hollywood cinema. Grierson was passionately committed to documentary and often contemptuous of fiction filmmaking, claiming that the much-admired technical superiority of studio productions merely covered over the fact that 'the technical splendours of cinema loom gigantically over trivial and contemptible issues' and that they are created by a cinema magnate who is 'more or less frankly, a dope pedlar.'[5] While perhaps rather extreme in his views, Grierson was interested above all in the creation of an informed citizenship – informed, of course, in a particular way.

The 'classic' documentary style which Grierson developed depends on the photographic basis of the film image as evidence of the actual existence of what it shows; it further depends on a commentary that claims the same status of evidence for its argument about the meaning of the observed reality. Although the process of arranging (editing) the images itself provides a kind of commentary on their meaning, the Griersonian documentary employed a (male) commentator whose omniscience and invisibility gave him the authority of 'the voice of God.' The commentary was usually prescripted and the images filmed (or selected from stock footage) and arranged to support the argument.

As the essays in this book make clear, many recent documentaries offer a frankly 'subjective' point of view that places the 'public gaze' of documentary under severe pressure. This development owes much to social and cultural changes that have produced the so-called 'postmodern condition' in which objectivity no longer seems possible and 'reality' is difficult to distinguish from the proliferation of media images that claim to represent it. The resulting tensions within documentary theory and practice can also be attributed to technological factors. As Brian Winston has suggested: 'It is somewhat ironic ... that just as documentarists finally got the equipment to illuminate, as they supposed, the real world of externally verifiable data, that world was denied them and they were instead revealed as the constructors of particular ideologically charged texts par excellence.'[6] The new lightweight equipment that became available in the 1950s enabled documentary filmmakers to get closer to their subjects, but, in so doing, it raised awkward questions about the relations between public life and personal experience. In the Canadian context, this moment occurred at a time when NFB filmmakers were seeking alternatives to the classic documentary style. In the uncertain political situation of the postwar years, Grierson's insistence on the clear distinction between documentary and fiction became increasingly difficult to uphold. The effect was to undermine documentary's claims to moral superiority and even its truth claims. There were some attempts at the Board to adapt to the new circumstances by combining documentary and fiction, but the general impression was that the documentary movement had lost its way.[7]

The films produced by Tom Daly as head of the NFB's Unit B seemed to provide a new direction.[8] Several of the filmmakers in Unit B started out in the animation department established by Norman McLaren, and they brought a willingness to question the relations between image and reality. Using the new equipment, they produced a series of innovative films that firmly established the Board's international reputation.[9] Many of these were made for television, and Unit B is perhaps best known for the short documentaries aired by the Canadian Broadcasting Corporation in 1958 and 1959 under the title *The Candid Eye*. Indeed, many of the Unit B films reveal not only a discerning eye for the aesthetics of film but a new awareness of the immediacy and power of television, which would now be where documentary, for better or worse, found a new home. Many later NFB documentaries exhibit a strong desire to entertain – perhaps a development that occurred as documentaries took their place on the menu of entertainments available to the audience each night.

Although Unit B produced many films that were not part of the *Candid Eye* series, its title was often applied to a documentary approach that became known as candid eye filmmaking.[10] A documentary no longer illustrates a preexisting argument that could be scripted in advance but rather involves a process of observation seeking to understand a given situation. In the Unit B films, the experience of observation reveals the difficulty of disentangling reality from the images and myths that surround it. The filmmakers themselves may end up contributing to these very images and myths. Some critics have argued that despite the new intimacy between the filmmakers and their subjects, the candid eye films passively observe reality from a viewpoint that is essentially voyeuristic.[11] As the first three essays in this book suggest, however, the Unit B filmmakers were very much aware of their own role in shaping their material and often incorporated this awareness in their films.

In borrowing the title of a short-lived television series for a book about Canadian documentaries made between the 1950s and the 1990s, we do not intend to suggest that all these films were directly influenced by this series. Indeed, the makers of the later films studied in this book often positioned themselves in opposition to what they saw as the candid eye approach; but they all raise questions about documentary images and their relations to reality, questions that become even more urgent at a time when computer-generated special effects threaten to undermine all confidence in images that claim to represent reality. The importance of the films lies less in the specific techniques they adopt than in their questioning of some of the basic assumptions of documentary film theory and practice.

As an example of how Unit B's innovations foreshadowed later developments, we might look at the question of the documentary 'voice.'[12] When he came to Canada, Grierson brought with him the methods that had proved so successful in Britain, and they proved highly appropriate to the propaganda needs created by the Second World War. In the wartime NFB documentaries, the voice-of-God commentator is, if anything, even more forceful than in the British documentaries, reflecting not only the urgency of the war effort but perhaps also the influence of the *March of Time* newsreels from the United States.[13]

The authoritative commentary in these wartime documentaries was usually delivered by the stentorian voice of Lorne Greene. In one early film, *Corral* (1954), the Unit B filmmakers eliminated the commentary completely but, more typically, they used it sparingly and trusted it to the quieter voice of Stanley Jackson. Later filmmakers often used their own voices and sometimes appeared on-screen in their own films, thereby decreasing the sense of a disembodied voice of authority, while others attempt to transfer the commentary to the film's subjects through the use of interviews.

None of these practices necessarily make the films less manipulative than the Griersonian approach; indeed, the lack of commentary can be a way of denying that the film offers any point of view at all, making it appear that the filmmaker has merely been a 'fly on the wall,' letting reality just 'happen' in front of the camera, or that the film's point of view is that of the subjects, who speak for themselves. The effects of these films must be carefully determined in each specific case – hence the need for close analysis – but the meaning also depends on the film's relations to documentary traditions and to its historical and cultural contexts.

One context that was extremely important for the NFB filmmakers was the Board's mandate to make and distribute 'national films.'[14] Under Grierson, the NFB set out to produce films that would stress the common interests of people from different cultural backgrounds living in a vast and sparsely populated nation. In this project, the realism of documentary images testified to the existence of the nation and supported the effort to construct and communicate a sense of national identity. The goal was to free the idea of 'nation' from the myths and traditions that made nationalism a divisive force in world politics, although later critics have shown that this was in itself a myth-making operation in which public service often functioned as public relations and propaganda.

The national context is not always in the foreground, but the production and reception of NFB films are inevitably coloured by the vexed question of Canadian identity. In keeping with their abandonment of the authoritative voice-of-God commentary, Peter Harcourt has suggested that the 'Canadianness' of the Unit B films comes through in 'a quality of suspended judgment, of something left open at the end, of something left undecided.'[15] This tentative approach can easily be read as the absence of national identity, but it is rather a way of projecting a sense of Canada as a tolerant and open society in keeping with the emergent politics of multiculturalism that many later NFB films would promote.

The national focus of NFB films was inevitably viewed rather differently by the francophone filmmakers who came to the fore at about the same time as the Unit B films were making their mark (indeed, some of them worked on the *Candid Eye* films). While the move of the NFB's headquarters from Ottawa to Montreal in 1956 encouraged the development of French-language production, the new techniques (known in Quebec as *cinéma direct*) led to a more overtly politically conscious kind of filmmaking. The French-language films that began to emerge in the late 1950s were more explicitly concerned with questions of nation and social justice than the Unit B films, and often suggested allegiance to a different 'nation.'[16]

The new lightweight equipment also led to the production of several low-budget fiction films that encouraged the government to establish the Canadian Film Development Corporation with a mandate to develop a film industry in Canada. Many of the filmmakers who moved into feature film production had experience working at the NFB, and two of the most important films, Don Owen's *Nobody Waved Good-bye* and Gilles Groulx's *Le Chat dans le sac* (both 1964), were made at the NFB. Both of these films began as documentary projects, and this new wave of fiction films was deeply influenced by direct-cinema techniques and practices. As far as documentary filmmakers were concerned, the effect was to blur the boundaries between documentary and fiction and to reinforce the growing scepticism about the possibility of an objective representation of reality.

The rapid political and cultural changes of the 1960s also forced the NFB to reexamine its own documentary practices. Its most prominent response was the Challenge for Change/Société nouvelle program (1967–80), which extended the questioning of the authority of the classic documentary style by putting the film (or video) camera into the hands of the people. This program produced some interesting experiments in social activism, most notably the series of films made by Colin Low with the Fogo islanders in 1967, but was limited by uncertainty about whether the objective was to promote or manage social change.

If these developments began to place a strain on the 'realist' aspect of the NFB's mandate, the 'national' aspect was also disturbed by a growing recognition that the dominant myths of national identity tended to erase cultural differences. On the one hand, there was a call for more recognition of regional interests other than those of central Canada (Ontario and Quebec), where most films were made. Under Grierson, the NFB's 'national' project had stressed the similarities among Canadians in all parts of the country, but the Board now began to establish regional offices to encourage a more diverse representation of the nation. Unfortunately, as the films chosen for this book attest, this initiative was only a partial success, and the films it produced rarely achieved widespread distribution.

On the other hand, the NFB was more successful in addressing the questions of gender, sexual orientation, and race that were raised with great urgency by the new 'identity politics' of the 1960s and 1970s. These questions disturbed traditional notions of both national unity and documentary form. In particular, female directors became more prominent at the NFB, especially in Studio D (1975–96), a women's filmmaking unit established by producer Kathleen Shannon. Although there was no equivalent unit for francophone women filmmakers at the NFB, there were occasional collective projects, such as that produced by Anne Claire Poirier under the title *En tant que femmes* (1975–6).

Documentary as a political tool had been part of Grierson's original vision for the Board, but it is doubtful that he could have envisioned the questioning of patriarchal social structures by feminist filmmakers, of national unity by the Québécois filmmakers, or of Canada's reputation for tolerance in the work of Alanis Obomsawin, a First Nations filmmaker who reveals the racism and injustice suffered by Aboriginals at the hands of their fellow Canadians. Many of the more contentious films, including Obomsawin's, came under attack for their lack of objectivity, but this usually meant that they offered viewpoints that had traditionally been neglected. The 'public gaze' now incorporates a more diverse and fragmented sense of the public interest as well as a greater interest in the effects of social conditions on personal experience.

It has become increasingly apparent that documentary realism and national identity, and the relations between them, are not such straightforward issues as Grierson assumed. The controversies that broke out over many NFB films from the 1960s onward can be attributed at least partially to differences of opinion about the purpose of the Board and of documentary in general. Despite its long record of producing important and ground-breaking films, to which the essays in this book offer only a partial testimony, the NFB has come under frequent attack, not only from those on the political right opposed to the existence of public institutions in a private enterprise culture, but also from left-wing critics who argue that Grierson's reliance on documentary realism and state sponsorship resulted in a tradition that was far from the progressive force that it claimed to be.[17]

The fallout from such attacks has led successive governments to cut funding. Yet the NFB archives, now being digitally preserved, are an important resource and, as the essays in this book make clear, demonstrate that NFB filmmakers have created a major body of work that actively and provocatively engages with these issues. These films can still challenge our critical understanding of documentary cinema and Canadian culture.

We do not propose to summarize the essays in our book since such introductions often seem like superfluous, and even tedious, recapitulations of ideas better engaged within the essays themselves. The writers in this book approach the films from a variety of critical perspectives, from the very formal to the very personal. To some degree their critical approaches match the demands that many of the films have made upon them, as well as their own interests. The films, and thus the essays, deal with issues of nation (*Paul Tomkowicz: Street-railway Switchman*, *Voyage en Amérique avec un cheval emprunté*), myth and tradition (*The Days before Christmas*, *Pour la suite du monde*), biography (*Volcano: An Inquiry into the Life and Death of Malcolm Lowry*), social justice (*Bûcherons de la Manouane, On est au coton, Kanehsatake: 270 Years of Resistance*), pornography (*Not a Love Story*), popular culture (*Lonely Boy, Project Grizzly*), affectivity (*Tu a crié Let Me Go*), sexuality (*Forbidden Love*), and the question of the authority of documentary itself (*Waiting for Fidel*). In a sense, this final question comes up, more or less explicitly, in all the films, and it is thus at the core of the argument in most of these essays inspired by films that have both provoked and entertained Canadian audiences for many years.

In the following essays, we have not provided translations of the titles of French-language films except when it is essential for the author's argument. The English titles can be found in the filmography at the back of the book. Similarly, because many essays refer to the same films, we have included the directors' names only when these are relevant to the argument, but they can be found by referring to the Index.

Notes

1 For a brief survey of the early history of Canadian documentary, see Clandfield, *Canadian Film*, 1–16. See also Backhouse, *Canadian Government Motion Picture Bureau*.
2 For an assessment of recent Canadian documentaries and interviews with several filmmakers, see Steven, *Brink of Reality*.
3 An excellent account of the Board's history can be found in two books by Gary Evans: *John Grierson and the National Film Board* and *In the National Interest*. See also Jones, *Movies and Memoranda*.
4 Higson, *Waving the Flag*, 192–8.
5 Hardy, ed., *Grierson on Documentary*, 53–4.
6 Winston, 'The Documentary Film as Scientific Inscription,' 55.
7 See Morris, 'After Grierson.'
8 For an excellent account of Daly's career at the NFB, see Jones, *The Best Butler in the Business*.
9 For more details on the equipment they used, see Seth Feldman's essay in this volume.
10 In the essays in this volume, the films made for television series will be referred to as *The Candid Eye* films, while the style that developed in Unit B will be designated as candid eye filmmaking, although there will be a few ambiguous cases.

11 See Elder, 'On the Candid Eye Movement,' for an account of the Unit B films that stresses their observational approach. The charges of voyeurism perhaps result from a conflation of the candid eye approach with the popular *Candid Camera* series, but the Canadian documentaries make limited use of the hidden camera.
12 See Nichols, 'The Voice of Documentary.'
13 Ian Aitken refers to the influence of 'the didactic style of *March of Time*' on Grierson in the late 1930s but suggests that the effect was only to intensify qualities already present in his earlier work; *Film and Reform*, 144–5. Ironically, the British wartime documentaries produced by the Crown Film Unit – the successor to Grierson's earlier documentary film units – tended to be much less strident in their approach.
14 The term 'national films' comes from the revised mandate in the National Films Act of 1950, but it is very much in the spirit of the original Act of 1939.
15 Harcourt, 'The Innocent Eye,' 72.
16 See Clandfield, 'From the Picturesque to the Familiar,' for an account of the French-language films that stresses their engagement with the communities that they documented.
17 An outspoken attack on Grierson, stressing his work in Canada, can be found in Nelson, *The Colonized Eye*.

Geography and Myth in *Paul Tomkowicz*: Coordinates of National Identity

RICHARD HANCOX

Mid-winter, 1953, 8:00 A.M. With the satisfaction of a job well done, a robust, 64-year-old man hangs up his parka and sits at a lunch counter anticipating his reward. By prior signal, breakfast has been prepared – coffee, a stack of rye bread, sausages, and at least half a dozen boiled eggs. We hear his inner thoughts – marking one of the most fondly aped lines in Canadian documentary film: 'Coffee ... black coffee ... some eggs in the morning!' He deserves every one of them. He has just come off his all-night shift in the heart of Winnipeg, Manitoba, near Portage Avenue and Main, long known as the windiest intersection in Canada.[1]

Thus ends *Paul Tomkowicz: Street-railway Switchman* (1954) directed by Roman Kroitor, a documentary prototype that emerged from the National Film Board's Unit B and became the best known of the *Faces of Canada* series. Still in active distribution, it is regarded as a classic of the Film Board's 'Golden Years,'[2] in which the Unit, led by producer Tom Daly, also created such ground-breaking documentaries as *Corral* (1954), *City of Gold* (1957), and *Lonely Boy* (1961).

Despite the film's success, very little has been written about it, except to recognize its importance in the development of NFB documentaries and to briefly articulate its existential tone.[3] A few pages here and there cite Lorne Batchelor's evocative 35 mm black-and-white camerawork and Roman Kroitor's seat-of-the-pants directing.[4] There is the story of how Kroitor came to record Tomkowicz's narration as told by D.B. Jones: 'To get Tomkowicz to open up about his life, Kroitor had hidden the microphone. During the recording Tomkowicz had walked around ... The tapes were unusable.' After going through several narrators,

Stanley Jackson (who co-wrote the scenario with Kroitor) suggested trying a friend, Tom Tweed, a Canadian radio actor who had worked on a Slavic construction gang in Manitoba, and could do Polish accents. Jones continues: 'Tweed used the exact words Tomkowicz had spoken. The tapes sounded exactly alike – except the new one was technically perfect.'[5]

Jones's version of the story is not completely accurate (the tapes weren't identical and the microphone wasn't hidden), but that's only fitting because it's a legendary tale about a film which, after all, is mythical – both in the imaginative sense, owing to the archetypal figure of Tomkowicz himself, and because of the film's status within the documentary canon. It deserves a larger study – one that goes beyond the usual account of its place in the evolution of documentary form. In this essay I will explore ways in which various temporal and spatial vectors converge and intersect in the film's Winnipeg location to form *coordinates of identity* that help map the film's significance as a myth of nation.

Placing Canadian Space

In the post-Cartesian universe it is virtually essential to have 'coordinates' for establishing identity in cyberspace; otherwise one risks becoming a kind of digitally 'displaced person.' In the pre-digital era, after fighting for the kaiser in World War I, Paul Tomkowicz was himself a displaced person. He had grown up in Poland, but then lived in Germany, Austria, Italy, and France before finally settling in Canada in 1927, during one of the last periods in which Winnipeg was a major destination for immigrants.[6] That he happened to choose the geographic centre of North America[7] is not without significance: there, maintaining the choreography of switches, Tomkowicz occupies the axial point of a geographic turnstile, his wintry dance with broom and salt pail facilitating what passes back and forth not only across space, but through time and history. Cyberspace notwithstanding, in this film, the coordinates of identity that lead to a deeper understanding are to be found in the physical location of Winnipeg – its *place* as a nexus of North American history and geography, of Manifest Destiny and western development. On the other hand, with the NFB's 'versioned' release in French, *Paul Tomkowicz: Nettoyeur d'aiguillages*, it is the choice to expunge all references to Winnipeg that is significant, as we shall see.

In 1953, during the production and versioning of *Paul Tomkowicz*, the Board was still located in Ottawa, where it had been since its inception

Paul Tomkowicz: *Street-railway Switchman* (1954), directed by Roman Kroitor. Courtesy of the National Film Board of Canada.

in 1939. Amid controversy, the whole operation moved to Montreal in the mid-1950s. The debate around where to situate the country's government-sponsored film studio underlined the fact that place, in the discourse of Canadian nationhood, was essentially space politicized, and in this case mattered to the extent it could be configured to beckon Canadian subjects in search of their famously elusive identities. Whether it was located in Ottawa or Montreal, the NFB was destined to remain a site of struggle over the cultural hegemony of the two so-called founding nations – English and French.

What is the philosophical relationship between space and place that lends itself to the convergence in Canada of geography, history, and documentary film? How does the culture produced by this mix take those received notions and reinscribe them in the national imagination? These are the kinds of questions a close study of *Paul Tomkowicz* raises. The switchman stands at the historic intersection of Portage and Main, where the fur-runners' trail coming down the Assiniboine crossed the trail running along the Red River. This site signals not only converging vectors of Canadian history and political economy but the whole Cartesian-Newtonian concept of space and time that underpinned North America's 'Manifest Destiny.'

Paul Tomkowicz represents a certain thinking about place as principally a derivative of space – as an extension of the process of naming and laying claim to the wilderness. This abstraction of place to provide identity for spatial coordinates – as positions to drop anchor in the void – is indebted to the rationalist philosophy behind the conquest and settlement of the New World. Descartes believed that 'place' and 'space' did not signify anything different from what occupied them; these were terms merely referring to size, shape, and relative position. Jeff Malpas argues that this notion of place as containment, to be subsumed within the idea of space as extension, resulted in the loss of place as a location with a character of its own. He notes: 'Places become interchangeable positions differentiated only by the objects that are located within them.'[8] One can see this in the Canadian film industry, where, for example, places often serve as American locations by the changing of flags, licence plates, and dialogue references. According to this thinking, even the neutral 'Let's go to the city' would be better for American audiences, say, than the confusing, 'Let's go to Moose Jaw' (even if that city offers a giant, concrete moose out by the Trans-Canada bypass).[9]

Place in Canada is not only appropriated by American films; Canadians do it to themselves. The French-language version of *Paul Tomkowicz*, besides eliminating all references to Winnipeg, strangely sets the documentary in Ottawa – much to the surprise of director Roman Kroitor. (Kroitor learned of this change only forty-six years later when this writer had the dubious privilege of informing him during an interview.) After his initial shock, he recalled that versioning activity at the Film Board, then under Jacques Bobet, was 'very jealously guarded.'[10] If the Board's mandate was making films designed to 'help Canadians in all parts of Canada understand Canadians in other parts,'[11] why were French speakers kept from learning where Tomkowicz really lived? To answer these and other questions, it will be necessary first to trace the history of the film, and examine the significance and identity of the city where it 'takes' place.

Freedom Speaks with a Canadian Face

Faces of Canada (1952–4) was a low-budget series of short black-and-white films, intended for theatrical release and conceived by NFB Commissioner Arthur Irwin. The documentary portraits were usually directed by younger, less-experienced filmmakers (both English and French), and fourteen in all were produced, although Kroitor's was the only one that remained in distribution. The series in French had the title *Silhouettes canadiennes*, and included original productions like *Le bedeau* (*The Sexton*), as well as films versioned in French, like *Paul Tomkowicz: Nettoyeur d'aiguillages*. Since portable lip-synch cameras hadn't yet arrived to revolutionize documentary, expository commentaries were contrived or, in the case of *Paul Tomkowicz* (at least the English version), transcribed and edited based on interviews with the subject. Raymond Garceau's *Le bedeau*, released in 1952, serves as a useful comparison with the Kroitor film because it is also about an older man who keeps things running behind the scenes – in this case he is the sexton of a parish church in rural Quebec. However, rather than radiating wisdom and strength – of character as well as body – like the switchman, the sexton comes across as a doddering, comic working man.

In *Movies and Memoranda*, D.B. Jones claims that *Faces of Canada*, besides fulfilling the mandate of interpreting Canada to Canadians, was designed to 'get young filmmakers to search out and find the "Canadian character" in their home towns. Each filmmaker was to find a person who was typically Canadian and yet an individual in his own right.'[12] Jones provides no source for this information, but he does acknowledge that 'Tom Daly was always available to talk, and he meticulously read a draft of every chapter and called attention to errors.'[13] When Kroitor was asked about a purpose for the series, he claimed he never heard of one. 'There were no instructions,' he insisted. 'There was a series and you came along and said what about a film on so-and-so, and they said yes or no.' Seen from the comfort of his streetcar window, the image of the lone switchman working in the cold night air had been, in Kroitor's words, 'burned into my brain,' and he decided to propose the idea for the film.

Summarizing *Faces of Canada*, Peter Morris observes that the approach was 'more intimate than traditional documentary, and avoids large social themes in favour of individual character study.'[14] This individual focus is expanded in Gary Evans's reading of *Tomkowicz* as a 'representative classic film':

> [It] portrayed the night street as an arena of near fantasy, thinly disguised by the veneer of inconsequential routine ... [The] mundane job of maintaining Winnipeg streetcar switches in the dead of night becomes a gorgeous study of contrasts in black and white, washed in an audioscape of authentic street sounds. The voice-over technique underscores the wordlessness of the on-screen people and Tomkowicz's alienation in the midst of a bustling urban winter vista. The multiple images of him as an outsider emphasize the isolation of so many of the deracinated who come to Canada, a place whose climate makes extreme physical demands while leaving a spiritual soul to meander where it will.[15]

Audiences inclined to existential film appreciation are not exactly what the NFB had in mind once Kroitor completed his 'gorgeous study.' The Board wasn't prepared for *Tomkowicz's* more cosmopolitan audiences when they penned the 1954 Information Sheet suggesting the film would be 'useful to groups interested in citizenship, immigration, or the experiences of new Canadians.' The sheet had already described the switchman as 'one who accepts his lot without complaint, considering himself fortunate that it is not worse. Paul Tomkowicz' need [*sic*] are simple, his wants are few.' Meanwhile the French Information Sheet half-heartedly beckoned, 'Pour tous les auditoires,' immigration being of little interest to the government of Quebec at the time. They had actually been banning NFB films since 1948, not just to reduce the federal presence, but because Premier Maurice Duplessis was convinced the Board was a 'Communist' institution.[16]

It is ironic that the idea for a film like *Paul Tomkowicz* can be traced back before *Faces of Canada* to a proposed *anti*-Communist series, *Freedom Speaks*. The idea was to show the benefits of democracy in Canada, where the state supposedly works for the individual, and not the other way around. Initiated by Irwin in 1950, the program of thirteen shorts never really got off the ground, although, as Evans has noted, many of the ideas eventually became Film Board productions. The proposed stories of individual Canadians, which included 'types' like Maritime Coal Miner, Montreal French Businessman, Ottawa Civil Servant, and Chalk River Atomic Scientist, also listed another one, referred to simply as 'New Canadian (Winnipeg).'[17] It is interesting to speculate how

Kroitor happened upon an idea that was already percolating at higher levels. For this we will have to turn to his co-writer.

Stanley Jackson wrote commentaries and narrated numerous NFB films. While not lending his vocal talents to the soundtrack of *Paul Tomkowicz*, Jackson was nevertheless involved from the start. Like Kroitor, he had grown up in Winnipeg, and the two were friends, though Jackson was twelve years Kroitor's senior. When Kroitor got the idea for the film, Jackson said he knew the manager of the Winnipeg Electric Company, and arranged for Kroitor to meet one of its switchmen. That he happened to be a 'New Canadian' may not be so surprising when one considers Jackson had been working at the Board for over ten years and may have had an inside take on strategies behind programs like *Freedom Speaks* – indeed, may have been the one to suggest 'New Canadian (Winnipeg)' in the first place.

Typifying Narratives and Aesthetic Excellence
Zöe Druick would probably consider Jackson's efforts as a contribution to the tactics of 'governmentality' (after Foucault) by which the NFB has moulded Canada as an imaginary community made up of identifiable, stable population groups, tactics by which individuals are produced as subjects. Druick argues that government funding of NFB films was not based on an interest in making innovative documentaries, but in regulating the conduct of citizens at the everyday level 'within discursive regimes and practices.'[18] She claims that NFB historians have ignored the governmental function of the Board and its hundreds of 'unremembered films' about citizenship, preferring instead to focus on the 'aesthetic excellence' of 'rare "great" works.'[19]

While Druick may be correct about the attention focused on some of the great films of the NFB, not one piece devoted to *Paul Tomkowicz* has ever been published. Ironically she adds to the film's reputed attention by citing the substitution of 'an uncredited actor' for Tomkowicz on the soundtrack.[20] She concludes that this tactic is 'symbolic of the representation of immigrants in so many NFB films: the films tend to craft a particular type of story that is largely independent of the actual people being shown.'[21] Accordingly, this results in a 'typifying narrative' that helps identify and stabilize immigrant groups. With this in mind, it is revealing to study the transcription of the original interview Kroitor conducted with Tomkowicz in a Winnipeg radio station in 1953 in order to compare it with the final narration Kroitor wrote for the film.

Running twenty-five pages, the interview – in which we discover

Tomkowicz eats sometimes thirteen eggs (only if they're small) – hand-ily eclipses the page-and-a-half actually given Tom Tweed to read. It suggests the motive behind the writing of the narration and substitu-tion of an actor may have had less to do with hidden ideological agendas, and more with salvaging something intelligible yet as close to Tomkowicz as possible, given the film's scant nine-minute length. Obviously, much editing had to be done. Writing the narration was, for Kroitor, a communications challenge, not just because of the poor quality of the recorded interview but also because of the long and convoluted speech of his subject. Witness the following (appearing here exactly as it does in the original interview transcript):

> I like this country – it's the besta country – why, that's good country, sure – I got mine job – XXXXXXXXXXXXXXXX – can't be better ... sure I feel happy – I'm satisfied mit Canada – sure. No trouble – nobody take you to jail XXXX if you make no trouble you know. I can go nighttime – daytime – between police – nobody says nothing (Transcript, 16. Multiple Xs mean unintelligible).

Just before this, Tomkowicz had noted, in reference to his sister's letter from Poland: 'The Russians on top – is danger – ah no – you can't go no more there. Go there – you no more come back. No, no. Ah – I have forget about that' (Transcript, 15). One would think, if Druick is correct about *Paul Tomkowicz* being symbolic of the Film Board's citizenship agenda, that Kroitor would have been pressed to exploit this ideologi-cal goldmine instead of just touch on it. But all Kroitor carries over to Tomkowicz's final narration is this: 'Winnipeg's alright. In Winnipeg you can go in the street – daytime – nighttime – nobody bother you.'

It seems the filmmaker principally sought aesthetic solutions for conveying his subject's character, and not rhetorical strategies for craft-ing a story independent of him. While 'governmentality' did seem implicated at the outset, the project moved further away from typifying narratives as it progressed in the editing room, and the film's working title, *The Switchman*, was dropped in favour of the switchman's actual name.

Pas plus compliqué que ça: Imagined Partitions
For something 'largely independent of the person being shown,' it is actually the French version that rises to the occasion. The commentary was written by Jacques Bobet, who was in charge of French versioning

at the time, and went on to play a key role in the formation of the French Production Unit at the Film Board. Despite erasing Winnipeg as the film's location, Bobet apparently thought geography was nevertheless critical. While Tomkowicz is seen from inside a shop window, out in the cold salting switches, the French narrator states:

> Et un tramway qui doit tourner à gauche ne doit pas tourner à droite. À gauche, c'est Ottawa; l'Ontario; la langue anglaise. À droite, ce sont les ponts; la ville de Hull; la province de Québec. On va à droite, ou on va à gauche. Lui, ça lui est égal: il est Polonais. [And a tram line that must turn to the left must not turn to the right. To the left is Ottawa, Ontario, the English language. To the right are the bridges, the city of Hull, the province of Quebec. One goes to the right, or one goes to the left. It's all the same to him: he is Polish.][22]

While the cultural identity of the 'person being shown' is maintained, the rest of his profile is largely independent, there only to outline partitions between Canada's two dominant charter groups. But it goes beyond that: not only need this business be of no concern to immigrants but they should concentrate on work and leave nationalist pursuits to legitimate stakeholders. In a slightly earlier draft of the commentary, the following line appears right after 'il est Polonais' (someone has crossed the line out, but it is still readable): 'Son travail, c'est l'entretien des aiguillages; pas les destinées d'un peuple.' [His job is maintaining the switches; not the fate of a people.][23] It is ironic, though Bobet may not have known, that Tomkowicz was a well-travelled man who had acquired a working knowledge of six languages – among them French.

The coordinate 'à droite' indicated more than just 'right' in the eastward direction of Hull and the province of Quebec. The destiny of Quebec as a 'people' was in the hands of the right-wing nationalist Duplessis government, whose attitude toward the working man could be summed up in the French version's refrain about Paul Tomkowicz's job: 'Un coup de balai; une poignée de sel. Pas plus compliqué que ça. Mais il faut que ce soit fait, et bien fait.' [A stroke of the broom, a handful of salt. Nothing more complicated than that. But it must be done, and done well.] This good-natured reminder finally ends the largely typifying French narrative after being repeated three times.

Paul Tomkowicz: Nettoyeur d'aiguillages could have been chosen for the huge retrospective of Canadian cinema at the Georges Pompidou Centre in Paris in 1993, but it was the English version that was screened instead – with simultaneous French translation. The film was accompanied by an exhibition catalogue placing it squarely in Winnipeg. Apparently, what was intended for French domestic consumption (i.e., Quebec) was not considered good enough for France.

Quebec's sovereigntist leaders have often engaged in a certain amount of doublespeak – for example, promoting Montreal's bilingualism to international investors while insisting back home that citizens consider it a unilingual French city. But this is to be expected in a country where the coordinates of space and place are so politically interwoven. Benedict Anderson points out that while centres defined sovereignty in the past, and borders tended to be indistinct, the modern conception operates evenly 'over each square centimetre of a legally demarcated territory.'[24] Within this territory, he describes how the nation is imagined as a community by members who conceive a 'deep, horizontal comradeship' despite never getting to know, or even hear of, most of their fellow members. In the case of Quebec, were it eventually to succeed in separating from Canada, sovereigntists have insisted current boundaries be respected, despite large pockets of loyal federalists equally adamant about staying in Canada. Ironically labelled 'partitionists' within Quebec, many of these people live in areas bordering the Ottawa River – precisely the divisional point stressed in the French version of *Paul Tomkowicz.*

One wonders what kind of identity coordinates the original Winnipeg location represented that provoked such a geographic switch – a switch that overlooked the largest French-speaking community west of Quebec, Saint Boniface. Like Hull, it stands on the east bank of a river splitting predominantly French and English communities. The river is the Red River, and the community on the other side, Winnipeg.

For most Canadians, the nation is not imagined in Ottawa, or in Toronto, though it may be controlled there, but in those outlying communities that established the extent of Canada's sovereign territory – places like Winnipeg, long known as Canada's 'Gateway to the West.' Winnipeg represents the divisional point between Eastern and Western Canada, but rather than separating the country, it links it, through the space-binding technology of the railroad – the same technology Paul Tomkowicz represents as a switchman. The films of the NFB are themselves instances of space-binding technology, perpetuating the nation as an imagined community from coast to coast.

Maurice Charland argues that Canada 'imagined itself into existence' and now depends upon the rearticulation of a rhetoric of space-binding technology which he calls 'technological nationalism.' While not mentioning the NFB, he cites the Canadian Broadcasting Corporation's production of *The National Dream* – Pierre Berton's history of the Canadian Pacific Railway – as an example of the 'dominant discourse of the official ideology of nation-building through state-supported broadcasting.' Charland claims this technological rhetoric is the 'dominant discourse of Canadian nationalism in anglophone Canada.'[25] Winnipeg is a key coordinate of this discourse. By omission, the French version of *Paul Tomkowicz* recognized this fact, and reassigned the street-railway switchman to the role of *uncoupling* at a divisional point – the Ottawa River border of Quebec and Ontario – rather than letting him continue *connecting* the rest of Canada at its western 'gateway.'

Identifying Coordinates
It was the threat of being connected southward – American annexation – complicated by the Red River Rebellion of French-speaking Métis, led by Louis Riel, that motivated Manitoba to join the Canadian Confederation in 1870. From a tiny population at the time, Winnipeg grew to 3,700 by 1874, many of the newcomers being free traders and volunteers from Ontario who had come to put down Riel.[26] To help the North-West Mounted Police in suppressing the rebellion, Ottawa was soon able to send out troops on the transcontinental railway, which had been completed to Winnipeg. A trip that used to take three months via the Dawson Route and Lake of the Woods could now be done in a matter of days. Now Ottawa could extend its political power by using the railroad to foster immigration, and thousands of settlers headed west by train, many to stay in Winnipeg and others to fan out over the vast Western plains, effectively discouraging Minnesotans from moving north.[27] Winnipeg had become the third-largest city in Canada by 1911, controlling the grain trade and manufacturing of the entire west, and prompting William E. Curtis to write that year in the *Chicago Record Herald*:

All roads lead to Winnipeg. It is the focal point of three transcontinental lines of Canada, and nobody ... can pass from one part of Canada to another without going through Winnipeg. It is a gateway through which all the commerce of the east and west, and the north and the south must flow.[28]

Still, the city's location was not ideal. Alan Artibise refers to the 'early and continuing necessity to concentrate ... capital and energy on counterbalancing the effects of Winnipeg's poor geographic location.'[29] *Paul Tomkowicz* was filmed only a few years after the deluge of 1950, when the flood-prone Red River overflowed its banks – an event repeated in 1997, but kept from catastrophic results to Winnipeg by the efforts of thousands of volunteers. As a myth of nationhood, this heroic struggle against the environment could be shared by Canadians as an imagined community on *The National* – the nightly television news broadcast of the state-owned CBC. *Paul Tomkowicz* is but an early instance of this mythic pattern – indeed, given the film's status as a documentary prototype, it helped establish this pattern in the first place.

As the big bang that was Confederation in 1867 contracts into the centripetal rhetoric of technological nationalism, it leaves among the planetary debris of outmoded technologies new symbols – like Winnipeg's tallest building. Aptly named the Toronto-Dominion Centre, it rises thirty-three stories at the very intersection where Paul Tomkowicz braved the elements – Portage and Main. The *Michelin Green Guide* sketches the scene: 'This corner, long known as the windiest in Canada, is dominated by tall buildings, all connected underground by an attractive shopping area – Winnipeg Square.'[30] The great east–west vector of Canadian history and economic development – quite literally Anderson's 'horizontal comradeship' – finds itself bisected by a new, vertical axis, nourished by the root systems of underground shopping malls, up through the high-rise trunks of communication towers, and out via the invisible branches of digital networks to join the global economy. The old street-railway switches Tomkowicz once tended have long since disappeared. Warren Buffet noted that a similar site in Omaha, Nebraska, where two streetcar lines crossed, had once been prime real estate: 'People said, "who would ever tear up the streetcar lines?" ... Now, with the Internet, the streetcar lines get torn up everyday.'[31]

On the Internet, a remarkable image from the *Canadian Geographic* website shows Winnipeg, marked in red, not simply at the centre of North America, but in the middle of the *world* – with the Earth's great cities in circular orbits. Titled, 'A Winnipeg's-Eye View of the World,' it asks:

How many Canadians know that from Winnipeg, the east/west centre of the country, China is closer than Greece? That the shortest air route to

Rome is over Greenland? ... On this map a straight line from Winnipeg to any other point on the globe shows the most direct route.[32]

While all roads once led to Winnipeg, flight paths, it seems, lead away.

Coordinating Identity: Myths at the Core

Despite Winnipeg's displacement by Vancouver as Canada's western gateway, its mythological gatekeeper, Paul Tomkowicz, lives on – at least in the imaginations of those familiar with the canon of Canadian film. As a classical piece of mythic nation-building, and as a prototype from the NFB's 'Golden Years,' *Paul Tomkowicz* has achieved near-mythic status. But there is more to the mythological aspects of this film than its reputation. In his introduction to *Movies and Mythologies: Towards a National Cinema*, Peter Harcourt says that while mythology can be viewed as a 'distortion of history,' on the other hand, 'some form of mythology seems to be necessary to achieve the feeling of a national identity.'[33] *Paul Tomkowicz* achieves this by leading beyond the pro-filmic, but it does so by leading us beyond the film to the deeper level of archetypes and myths. These set the heroic figure of Tomkowicz, with his sagacity and Paul Bunyanesque constitution, in a larger imaginative context, establishing a cultural grid on which coordinates of identity can be re-mythologized nationally.

This mythological aspect somehow resonated with French speakers at the NFB, because as much as *Paul Tomkowicz: Nettoyeur d'aiguillages* erred (purposely) about the film's local geography, it was remarkably on track when it came to the switchman's possible connection to other realms:

> Cet homme bâti comme un Hercule, transporte un fanal comme Diogène, et un balai comme les sorcières. Ce sont aussi les attributs du nettoyeur d'aiguillages. [This man, built like Hercules, carries a lantern like Diogenes and a broom like the witches. These are the attributes of a street-railway switchman.][34]

Diogenes, founder of the Cynics, reputedly walked through Athens in broad daylight with a lantern in hand, claiming he was looking for an honest man. In the film, Tomkowicz also carries a lantern (though at night, of course) not only to see the switches better but to provide a warning beacon for protection from oncoming traffic.

While the NFB may have sought simply to portray certain Canadian 'types,' they involuntarily revealed an archetype even more appropriate than Diogenes: The Hermit, Major Arcana number nine of the Tarot. The card shows an old man who has travelled far, tramping through snow with a lantern in his right hand seeking wisdom and truth. He carries a staff in his left to fend off that which deters. A snake moving alongside him represents his spiritual self, which is 'the conduit to that wisdom which will help him surmount the obstacles ahead.'[35] Just like the Hermit, Tomkowicz moves over the snow carrying a lantern in his right hand, has a staff (his broom) in his left, and – if one looks carefully – what appears to be a snakelike cord running beside him. It turns out that Batchelor had modified Tomkowicz' weak kerosene lamp with a photo bulb, and was trying to keep the electrical cord hidden with snow.

With the elements swirling about him, Tomkowicz is portrayed as a force of frontier-like stoicism and stability, a point of stasis at the centre of an urban dynamic of passing motorists and pedestrians too busy to notice him facilitating their own traffic. Here again the Hermit applies. According to one Tarot source, 'in times of action and high energy, he stands for the still center that must be created for balance.'[36] Balance and compromise are a reputed part of the Canadian identity that *Paul Tomkowicz* represents. As a modern myth in filmic form, it takes its place with other myths as a fixed point from which the world – in this case, Canada – has taken and takes shape.[37] This relationship between identity and fixity is crucial to any understanding of home in the conventional sense. However foreboding the environment, to be at home has traditionally meant to 'situate the world around oneself at the unmoving center.'[38] The rootedness with which Paul Tomkowicz is depicted, despite his cold-induced reveries of elsewhere, creates a stability in which the immigrant is shown content and at home – literally in the middle of Canada.[39]

In contrast to the stabilizing coordinates of this and other institutional Canadian films reflecting citizenship, the postmodern reflex of independent films that emerged from the Winnipeg Film Group, starting with John Paizs's work in the early 1980s and Guy Maddin's soon after, actually destabilizes it. In fact, films like Paizs's *Springtime in Greenland* (a.k.a. Winnipeg) (1981) so trouble the relation between geography and identity that they effectively *dislocate* their characters.[40] Nevertheless, the strangely mute character played by Paizs himself in *Springtime* (and most of his other Winnipeg-based films) shares something in common with his street-railway precursor, who also appears silent on screen.[41]

While Paul Tomkowicz facilitates the movements of others, he displays fortitude, practical wisdom, and a quiet calm at what poet T.S. Eliot, in 'Burnt Norton,' called 'the still point of the turning world.' Here the switchman manifests his immigrant hermit archetype as a spiritual myth of nation. Ethel Cornwell described Eliot's meta-religious 'still point' concept in terms one could apply, in a Canadian context, to *Paul Tomkowicz*: 'Here, in its final form, the "still point" becomes the source of all energy, pattern, and movement, the spiritual center where all opposites are reconciled, the complete vision perceived.'[42]

Postscript

Saturday morning, 18 November, the year 2000. As I eat my one egg for breakfast and contemplate the approach of winter, I open the Toronto *Globe and Mail* to the 'Saturday' section. 'Baby, It's Cold Outside,' sings the huge headline. There, in full colour, taking up half a page, is an artist's rendition of a man *up to his neck* in snow. He stands under a prominent street sign: it is the corner of Portage and Main.[43] Upon opening the section, I note that CBC television will be broadcasting a Guess Who concert taped in the summer. The famous rock group has resurrected itself for a cross-Canada tour ending in Winnipeg, their home town. Later, as I watch the telecast, an electrical storm attacks the outdoor audience with such intensity that the musicians have to flee to the wings. Great bolts of lightning illuminate the city skyline and its towering TD Centre. When the storm finally abates, the soaked audience is miraculously still there. Not surprised, lead singer Burton Cummings triumphantly observes, 'Only in *Winnipeg* would the crowd stay!' Then, in a patriotic gesture, he dedicates the final song, 'Share the Land,' to his home town, 'smack dab in the middle of the greatest country on Earth.' Somehow this only suggests *Paul Tomkowicz: Streetrailway Switchman* couldn't have been about anywhere else.

Notes

I would like to thank NFB Archivist Bernard Lutz for his invaluable help with this project, and Roman Kroitor for allowing me to interview him and for giving me access to his personal production files.

1 See, for example, *Michelin Green Guide to Canada* (1999 edition), 121.

2 Two chapters in Evans, *In the National Interest,* use this phrase in their titles.
3 Morris, *The Film Companion,* 233.
4 See Evans, *In the National Interest,* and Jones, *Movies and Memoranda.*
5 Jones, *Movies and Memoranda,* 62–3.
6 Tomkowicz, interview with Kroitor, 1953 (exact date unknown); original transcript courtesy of the filmmaker.
7 The distance calculator in the 1998 *World Book* encyclopedia (Macintosh Edition) shows the city to be about 2590 kilometres from the border of Alaska, 2540 from Labrador, 2420 from Florida, and 2521 from San Diego, in the southwestern United States.
8 Malpas, 'Finding Place,' 31.
9 In 1993 I entered my experimental documentary film, *Moose Jaw: There's a Future in Our Past,* in the Indiana Film Society's 5th Annual Festival of Canadian Cinema, only to have it rejected for having 'so many Canadian references.'
10 Kroitor, interview with the author, 12 February 2000. Upon being told the text of the French commentary, Kroitor several times called the changes 'hilarious.' All quotations by Kroitor are taken from this interview, unless otherwise stated. There is still in the French production file an exact English-to-French translation (22 October 1953); however, a completely different commentary, written by Jacques Bobet, was added, and on 18 December 1953, it was recorded with Jean Duceppe as narrator.
11 Canada, An Act to Create a National Film Board, in Statutes of Canada, 3 George VI, Ch. 20 (Ottawa: Joseph Oscar Patenaude 1939). In 1950, the Film Act was expanded to include 'films designed to interpret Canada to Canadians and to other nations.'
12 Jones, *Movies and Memoranda,* 61–2.
13 Ibid., 'Acknowledgements.'
14 Morris, *The Film Companion,* 105.
15 Evans, *In the National Interest,* 75.
16 Ibid., 16, 19. Also see Bidd, *The NFB Film Guide,* xxxvi.
17 Evans, *In the National Interest,* 20–1, 342.
18 Druick, 'Documenting Government,' 56–7.
19 Ibid., 56, 76. Druick has perhaps overlooked Ed Mathews's attempt to analyse these films in 'Immigrants and the NFB.'
20 Ibid., 71. True enough, Tom Tweed gets no mention on the screen (nor was he even paid, since he was doing the work as a favour, according to Kroitor). He was, however, credited on the NFB's Information Sheet.
21 Ibid., 71.
22 Bobet, 'Commentaire,' *PAUL TOMKOWICZ nettoyeur d'aiguillages*

(18 December 1953), *Paul Tomkowicz* French Production File, NFB archives, Montreal.

23 Bobet, draft commentary, *L'AIGUILLEUR* (15 December 1953), *Paul Tomkowicz* French Production File.

24 Anderson, *Imagined Communities*, 19.

25 Charland, 'Technological Nationalism,' 196–7.

26 Artibise, *Winnipeg*, 16.

27 Charland, 'Technological Nationalism,' 199.

28 Quoted in Artibise, *Winnipeg*, 23.

29 Artibise, *Winnipeg*, 22.

30 *Michelin Green Guide to Canada*, 121.

31 Miller, 'Buffet Scoffs at Tech Share Prices.'

32 'Geomaps,' *Canadian Geographic Online* (accessed 5 November 2000): <www.canadiangeographic.ca/geomaps.htm>. The mapping technique illustrated – azimuthal equidistant projection – allows pilots to determine the shortest distance between two locations.

33 Harcourt, *Movies and Mythologies*, 2.

34 Bobet, 'Commentaire.'

35 'The Internet Tarot by Michael Bromley, Celtic Shaman' (accessed 29 September 2000): <www.tarot-reading.com/the-hermit/index.html>.

36 See 'The Hermit,' in Joan Bunning, 'Learn the Tarot – An On-Line Course' (accessed 10 March 2002): <www.learntarot.com/maj09.html>.

37 Rapport and Dawson, 'Home and Movement,' 22. The authors are making a reference to Claude Lévi-Strauss's discussion of myth in *The Raw and the Cooked*.

38 Ibid., 21. Rapport and Dawson point to a reconceptualization of home which now takes into account mass movements of people around the globe who appear at home in movement, and for whom 'movement can be one's very home.'

39 Stability had not been something that Winnipeg could claim in its early dealings with immigrant populations, particularly the largest groups – Slavs and Jews – who were openly discriminated against by the British majority at least until the end of the Second World War (as they were in other parts of Canada). These 'aliens' and their supposed Communist connections were blamed for the Winnipeg General Strike in 1919, which was violently suppressed with tragic consequences. See Artibise, *Winnipeg*, 132.

40 See Gilles Hébert, 'Dislocations,' introduction to Winnipeg Film Group, eds., *Dislocations*, catalogue of an exhibition held at the Dunlop Art Gallery, Regina, Saskatchewan, 22–4 October 1994.

41 And in Paizs's preceding film, *The Obsession of Billy Botski* (1980), also
    starring a silent Paizs, someone else's voice is used for the narration, as in
    Paul Tomkowicz.
42 Cornwell, *The 'Still Point,'* 4.
43 MacDonald, 'Baby It's Cold Outside.'

The Days before Christmas and the Days before That

SETH FELDMAN

Cinema's evolution, like biological evolution, seems in retrospect not so much a steady progression as a series of relatively sudden and extreme responses to dramatic disruptions of the status quo. No sooner does moving photography evolve its own mode of narrative expression amid the visual and performing arts than it is challenged by the coming of sound. Sound too creates a cinema previously undescribed and perhaps indescribable. The same happens with colour, widescreen, video, and digital. These challenges not only come in the production of new work but are also manifested in the consideration of what came before. Silent film only becomes 'silent film' – with all the historical and aesthetic connotations of that phrase – after the advent of the talkies. Colour calls attention to the aesthetics of black and white, just as widescreen makes screen ratio an issue for both directors and audiences. Television causes us to consider cinema as simply one platform for the diffusion of the moving image. Digital has awakened a perception of cinema's mechanical (or, worse, analog) nature and redefined it as a retro medium within the ever-shrinking circumference of nondigital expression.

Another such abrupt jolt in the evolution of cinema was the advent, in the mid-1950s, of technology that enabled nonfiction shooting on location with synchronous sound. In most historical narratives, the beginnings of this sort of nonfiction film are seen as contentious in that the technology appeared to dictate two vastly differing and somewhat contradictory responses. One was 'cinéma vérité,' a term coined by the film historian Georges Sadoul in reference to Jean Rouch and Edgar Morin's 1960 film, *Chronique d'un été*. That film is characterized by an on-screen filmmaker using the new equipment to conduct interviews and record conversations and then using it again to interview subjects about their appearance on-screen and to discuss the success or failure of the film itself. This practice has little to do with the American use of the same equipment seen for the first time that same year in the Drew Associates film, *Primary*. Here the filmmakers are, to use a later phrase, 'flies on the wall.' They are invisible not only to the viewer but, we are asked to assume, to the subjects they are filming. Drew and Richard Leacock coined the term 'direct cinema,' to describe their approach. The two schools confronted each other at a 1963 conference in Lyons, forever cementing their fundamental differences.[1]

Or so the story goes. As it turns out, neither cinéma vérité nor direct cinema is indicative of the earliest, most comprehensive, and perhaps most coherent adaptation of the new technology: 'candid eye' filmmaking. Literally speaking, *The Candid Eye* was the title given to the series of seven half-hour films produced by the National Film Board's Unit B for screening by the CBC in the fall of 1958 and another seven films in the fall of 1959 (when they were also referred to as 'Documentary '60'). In a broader sense, though, candid eye filmmaking was an aesthetic in its own right, one that owed little to American or Continental antecedents. It was a product almost exclusively of the NFB. As we shall see, candid eye filmmaking was 'candid' in both senses of the term.[2] It asserted the camera's right to be surreptitious, ubiquitous – though in a way far more sophisticated and thoughtful than the Americans' 'fly on the wall.' And the candid eye was 'candid' in the sense of being forthcoming. Without indulging in Rouch's angst, it acknowledged the role of the filmmaker in the production and deliberately asked the viewer's complicity.

The first film shot in *The Candid Eye* series was *The Days before Christmas* (1958, jointly directed by Terence Macartney-Filgate, Stanley Jackson, and Wolf Koenig).[3] Seen today, the film has an aura approximating that of early cinema. It may be seen as nothing but a set of sequences in which the ordinary people of a now quaint era go about their business in the foul weather of a Montreal December. They shop, sing in choirs, crowd into bars, go to office parties, and stand in long queues at the railway station. Brinks guards collect the loot from Christmas sales and a cabbie discourses on his fares' holiday behaviour. A lucky few fly south while a less fortunate man telephones his mother in far-off Scotland to tell her he won't be home again this year.

The filmmakers go out of their way to document familiar iconography in much the same manner that an itinerant Lumière cameraman would try to provide audiences with his preconception of what he was shooting. As they would be with early films, the audience is left to be startled not by what they see but by how they see it. The Christmas choirs are in synch – even as their directors are correcting them. So is the department store Santa Claus and the frustrated traveller whose train has not pulled into the railroad station. In 1958, audiences may not have been sent screaming from the screen, but they might well have been excused for wondering how the camera was able to hear actuality with the same acuity with which it was seen.

The Days before Christmas, in its television half-hour, provided a sampler of what could be done with the new equipment – location interviews, spontaneously captured emotion, highly mobile camerawork, and, what would be especially important in this early use of the new apparatus, a judicious editing of these elements. But the film was more than just a test reel. It was a coherent statement in its own right, a work whose makers adapt a remarkable amount of the thematic focus they have established in previous work. It is our work here to suggest that even from our own perspective today, *The Days before Christmas* is a film that challenges the way films before it can be read and films after it made.

Origins
Like everything else that happened during the golden age of the NFB, the influence of John Grierson lingered over the creation of *The Candid Eye*. Ostensibly, this was a negative influence as it seems that nothing could be further from Grierson's idea of documentary than candid eye filmmaking, cinéma vérité, or direct cinema. Grierson's writings made the sound and images of the individual documentary secondary to a preconceived point that the film would hammer home. The British documentaries he directed, produced, or otherwise inspired, poetic as they may have been, were made to illustrate specific points. The films Grierson supervised at the wartime NFB were, if anything, even more didactic. The Board's two most widely distributed newsreel series, *World in Action* (1942–5) and *Canada Carries On* (1940–59), were generally composed of found footage cut to bombastic music and Lorne Greene's voice-of-doom narration. Their function was to reduce the proto-cinematic world to metaphor, and then pile metaphor upon metaphor, until the film defined precisely one element of Grierson's (and, from time to time, the Canadian government's) geopolitics.

And yet there were elements of Grierson's style that did lend themselves to what would become candid eye filmmaking. There was, for instance, the practice of dealing with large amounts of footage to make the compilation films. It was, to be sure, found footage. But if one was to make high shooting ratio films of any kind, then there would have to be both an institutional experience with, and a tolerance for, digging the finished product out of a voluminous amount of exposed reels. Second, Grierson's insistence on organizing his films around ideas, often quite abstract ideas, set something of a precedent. It would have been all too easy to maintain a government film department simply to satisfy the immediate, pragmatic goals of agencies sponsoring the films. In fact, this was the Board's bread and butter. But it was Grierson who insisted upon making at least some films not tailored too tightly to immediate needs.

In 1948, not too long after Grierson's departure, that practice would lead to the Film Board's creation of Unit B, whose mandate it was to pursue just this kind of conceptual film. Three years later, Tom Daly was appointed Unit B's executive producer. Daly would be to Unit B what Grierson had been to the wartime Film Board, taking a hands-on interest in most of its productions and in the people who made them. This was the way Grierson had trained him and the way he was determined to train others. Daly recruited Koenig, Roman Kroitor, and Colin Low (and later, Macartney-Filgate) into what would become a decade-long workshop on the evolution of nonfiction film. As Koenig recalls: 'The 50s, for all of us was a time of exploring limitations – of our own, of the medium, of the organization. With Tom Daly's patient help, we discovered what the medium could do: using image, sound and editing to tell a story (even though the material may not have had much of a story to begin with).'[4]

Daly's own training would also have a practical influence on the development of The Candid Eye. After he was hired in 1940 as one of Grierson's first Canadian appointments, Daly's initial assignment was as a research assistant to Grierson's lieutenant, Stuart Legg, producer of Canada Carries On. His job on Canada Carries On was to locate and later edit the source material. He established the Film Board's stock shot library. This in itself would prove valuable. Kroitor notes that Daly defended the high shooting ratios of the Candid Eye productions by citing the compilation film work as a precedent.[5]

Daly's initial experience at the wartime Board also directed him toward the collection and use of location sound – even in what were largely voice-over documentaries. As he recalled to D.B. Jones:

> the principles of matching, mixing, synching and enhancing the sounds were identical whatever the quality and I took to the challenge with great pleasure. On my own, I began to assemble a library of sound effects, mostly derived from the excellent and advanced sound recordings on captured German material. These sounds were almost always *not* covered by commentary, because the Germans intended that the accompanying text be worked out locally, in the language of each country they had overrun. It was fun to use their sounds right back at them.[6]

There was, in other words, an appreciation in Daly's own work of the intrinsic value of synchronized sound or, at very least, the approximation of synch through the use of accurate sound effects.

Daly's interest in location sound would certainly be shared with the Unit B filmmakers as their work progressed through the fifties. But these technical experiments took place within the very different intellectual context of the postwar period. The postwar aesthetic was based on a rejection of the certainties underlying war propaganda and the less convincing revival of that didacticism brought about by the Cold War. During the golden age of Unit B, Daly oversaw the idea of moving away from fixed ideas. Peter Harcourt ably describes the Unit's work in his classic article 'The Innocent Eye':

> There is in all these films a quality of suspended judgment, of something left open in the end, of something undecided ... there is also something academic about the way the Canadian films have been conceived. There is something rather detached from the immediate pressures of existence, something rather apart.[7]

The heroes of the Unit B films were the miners in *City of Gold* (1957), who fight their way into the Yukon and then never get around to prospecting, or the astronomer in *Universe* (1960), whose huge, phallic telescope serves only to reveal his own insignificance in the cosmic order. The tone of the Unit B films is set by the absence of narration in the film *Corral* (1954). What are we to think of the cowboy rounding up the herd and then 'breaking' a single horse? Is he mastering the animals or working with them? Is this relationship between man and beast meant to have some metaphorical meaning? It likely would have in the wartime newsreels; Lorne Greene, the omniscient voice of doom, would have told us just what to think. But in lieu of commentary – in lieu of the long heritage of voice-over documentary commentary – all we see is what happened before the camera. The action is entirely existential, only itself.

The use of a silent narrator in *Corral* seems, in retrospect, to be symptomatic of Unit B's eclectic approach to documentary tools, an 'open-endedness' not only in thematic concerns but in the use of the medium's technology. Unit B incorporated the Film Board's animators, and, from the beginning, there was no apparent hesitation in crossing generic boundaries. *The Romance of Transportation in Canada* (1952), directed by Low and animated by Koenig, was a straightforward animation whose ironic distance from the subject at hand was in keeping with the Unit's postwar ethos. (Norman McLaren's *Neighbours*, made the same year, presents a far more graphic, 'documentary' reality.) Low and Koenig co-directed *City of Gold*, a film that made use not simply of stills but of stills animated both through camera movement and Daly's editing. Kroitor and Low's *Universe* is a documentary dependent almost entirely on studio-generated special effects.

The Candid Eye
Unit B's familiarity with unconventional forms of documentary made the move to candid eye filmmaking a natural progression. For these filmmakers, the improvements in synch sound recording, lighter cameras, and high-speed film were, like animation and special effects, another alternative technology for the production of documentary. As Gary Evans charts it, this technology began arriving at the NFB in 1951–2 in the form of the lightweight Arriflex 16 mm camera. This was followed in succeeding years by yet-lighter cameras and tape recorders.[8] NFB technicians themselves played no small role in the invention of these new tools, most notably Chester Beachell for his work on perfecting sprocket tape and Eric Miller for his development of improved cameras. Peter Morris, in an unpublished paper, finds that all the new filmmaking tools were created outside the purview of Unit B. He quotes a number of authors, asserting that the technology of cinéma vérité arose 'in straightforward response to the aesthetic demands of filmmakers' and concludes:

> The technology that was developed during the fifties arose from quite different demands. These were primarily economic ones (associated closely with television). But they were also allied very immediately with military

research. Only later, in the late fifties and early sixties, did aesthetic demands mesh with technological developments. And, even then, it might
be argued, they only did so because of fundamental changes in socio-
cultural life.[9]

As Morris points out, the Auricon camera (a television news camera
that recorded synchronized sound onto a magnetic strip on the film)
was first used at the NFB not for documentaries but for Bernard Devlin's
series of television interviews entitled *On the Spot* beginning in 1953.
Between 1955 and 1958, sprocket tape and the newly developed lightweight cameras were used in *Perspective*, a series of short dramatic
films.

While this technology developed elsewhere at the Board, the Unit B
filmmakers were responding to the first manifestations of a more spontaneous, location-oriented filmmaking. Macartney-Filgate recalls particularly the influence of the British Free Cinema, most notably Karel
Reisz and Tony Richardson's 1955 film *Momma Don't Allow*:

> This was a revelation not in its style or technique, which was nothing new,
> but perhaps the approach to the subject. It was shot *in situ*, it was lit, when
> they had some lighting. There was some direction, they'd directed their
> people but they [sic] were an attempt to take people *in situ* as they were
> rather than forming them into a story.[10]

A second, often discussed, influence on the generation of the candid
eye filmmakers is the work of the French photographer Henri Cartier-
Bresson. As Koenig recalls:

> The real inspiration for our work came from a stills photographer: Henri
> Cartier-Bresson. I had received a book from a colleague (Herb Taylor) as a
> Christmas present: *The Decisive Moment* – photographs by Henri Cartier-
> Bresson. I was blown away by the pictures. We passed the book around
> among ourselves and we began to discuss the possibility of doing in film
> what Cartier-Bresson was doing with stills. I doubt that we ever suc-
> ceeded in equaling Cartier-Bresson's artistry, but his work defined for us
> what we should aim for. Without his example, I doubt that we would have
> done much more than the standard type of documentary.[11]

What Koenig and his colleagues found alluring in Cartier-Bresson's
1952 collection, *The Decisive Moment*, were both the photographs them-

selves and the photographer's introduction to them. In that introduction, Cartier-Bresson defines his aesthetic of spontaneity:

> The photographer's eye is perpetually evaluating. A photographer can bring coincidence of line simply by moving his head a fraction of a millimeter. He can modify perspectives by a slight bending of the knees. By placing the camera closer to or further from the subject he draws a detail – and it can be subordinated, or he can be tyrannized by it. But he composes a picture in very nearly the same amount of time it takes to click the shutter, at the speed of reflex action.[12]

In his book, *Image and Identity: Reflections on Canadian Film and Culture*, Bruce Elder argues that Koenig and the other Unit B filmmakers misinterpreted Cartier-Bresson. Elder asserts that the photographer was less interested in random spontaneity than he was in conceiving of his spontaneously composed images as part of a larger statement about the 'sameness' of humanity. And while earlier Canadian thinkers may have been comfortable with this notion, its rejection by Unit B is, to Elder, indicative of an affiliation with an American-style empiricism.[13] If we accept Elder's thesis, it is possible to suggest that Unit B's existential predilections made their interpretation of Cartier-Bresson inevitable. To adapt the new technology to any higher calling – the 'sameness' of humanity – would be a return to Grierson's use of the image as metaphor and, worse, to a hiding of that process beneath a façade of objectivity made possible by the new technology. On the other hand, to believe, or at least to act as if, film image and now sound could dictate their own composition would be another step in rescuing the proto-cinematic world from its subordination to metaphor.

The Days before Christmas

By 1957, when they had become aware of some of the new technology, the Unit B filmmakers had some idea of what they wanted to do with it. They would set out to define themselves – to borrow from Elder's evaluation of them – as 'empiricists' going about their business. Part of that empiricism would be an examination not only of their subject but of the means of recording that subject. This, in turn, led to a proposal for a set of television films designed to highlight the potential of the new technology. In the face of some resistance, Daly secured approval for a prototype film for the series. The film's $17,403 budget was submitted by Unit B only on 11 December 1957 and approved by the Film

Commissioner on 18 December. This meant that time would become a factor in the shooting of the film. The filmmakers decided to use the equipment available at the moment rather than wait for new cameras and recorders that were already being developed. As Macartney-Filgate recalls, this resulted in the non-synch footage being shot on the Film Board's old Arriflexes using 100-foot rolls. Synchronous sound shooting was done with the old 20 kilogram Auricons. The original negative had to be put on a specially constructed dubber so that the sound could be transferred onto a 16 mm tape for conventional editing. Film stock was rated at 350 or 400 ASA and was occasionally pre-flashed to increase its speed. Available light was used in all locations except for the nightclub, where some gels were put over the club's lights.[14]

It was also this timing that suggested the subject matter for *The Days before Christmas*. The holiday season provided a topic that would allow for a variety of situations in which the new technology could be tested. Koenig, Macartney-Filgate, Jackson, Kroitor, Daly, and their several collaborators (Michel Brault and Georges Dufaux on camera, Jack Locke, George Croll, and Kathleen Shannon on sound) began selecting locations they thought would work for them and for the new equipment. As Koenig remembers it:

> It was relatively easy to decide what to shoot. Everyone involved tossed ideas into the hat. Stanley Jackson suggested a choir practice; John Feeney wanted to do a piece about shop window decorations; Terry Filgate had the notion to film in a night club; and so on. Everyone had their own particular optique of the season and so we fanned out across Montreal and got to work. Finally, it was a collective creation.[15]

There was in all these 'optiques' a tremendous sensitivity not only to what would work well with the new equipment but what could be seen by the viewer as working. The shooting style was defined first as a kind of declaration of independence, a demonstration of the newly arrived free and ubiquitous nature of the camera. Most emblematic of this is Koenig's shot following the Brinks guard's gun from inside the bank to out on the street (where he takes the gun from his holster) to the Brinks truck. It is not only a long take done remarkably well (in the days before Steadicam) but it is both brazenly voyeuristic and somewhat iconoclastic. The gun is an intrusion upon the Christmas spirit, an object we should ignore both for this reason and because of the more primal aversion inspired by its potential violence. Yet Koenig follows it, unafraid, insists on following it, insists further upon breaking the taboo against calling attention to these solemn men going about what could be their deadly business. He follows them right into their truck and, from inside that truck, candidly (in both senses) photographs first the Brinks guards then the Christmas crowds going about their (now spied upon) lives.

The variety of shots to be produced by the ubiquitous camera was essential for the film's thematic concerns. It was important to establish within the shooting not just the various contradictions of Christmas (underlined, in the finished film by Stanley Jackson's brief voice-overs) but the implication that there were as many different kinds of Christmases as there were people living through them. Christmas was not just some kind of dialectic (between, say, commercialism and the sacred) but was made to appear, in the end, as an irreconcilable variety of experience. In keeping with this, the film's subjects reveal their subjectivity to us not only in synch (the cab driver, for example) but also in the tiny spontaneous acts that distinguish them from the clichés of the festive season. The department store Santa Claus fights off his boredom in both official languages. A policeman appears to be explaining some offence to an elderly woman. An ambulance arrives in the midst of the bustling shoppers. The woman buying Christmas dinner mutters about the price. A man in the francophone choir is caught looking at his watch. And indeed the choirs may be read – if I dare use the word – as a metaphor for the entire film, the sacred collective breaking up into its very human, individual components.

Underlying much of this approach to the shooting are the implications of whether or not the subject is aware of the camera. Planning sheets for the film have marginal notations of which sequences were conceived of as being 'candid.' In this instance, the term 'candid' appears to refer only to hidden camera shots. And *The Days before Christmas* does indeed make use of hidden camera in, for instance, the shots of the woman buying meat at the market and of the man at the train station ticket window. It also uses candid photography that seems to call attention to the fact that the camera is hidden: shots taken inside the bar and shots spying on the office party framed in a distant window. But, as Kroitor remembers it, even in the planning sessions, the most frequent use of hidden camera was intended to be instances in which the camera was to be made invisible by the subject's being too busy to notice it.[16] This is the most common use of candid camera in the film, its uses including: the children in their Christmas pageants, the choirs in rehearsal, and the department store Santa Claus.

The Days before Christmas is also 'candid' in the sense of being forth-coming. In both the mise-en-scène and montage of this first use of the new equipment, there is a remarkable maturity and lack of self-consciousness, an assertion that there is no particular need to either hide or expose the filmmaking. The viewer is invited to become a co-conspirator, an outside observer. When the cameraman hides in order to film his subject, we often hide with him. When subjects are too busy to acknowledge the camera, we are cognizant of the setup that distracts them. The sequence of the young Scot, Michael Devine, calling home, for instance, may be read as the elaborate setup it indeed was: two cameras shooting, one in close up, one in mid-shot, in order to allow the single take to be edited.[17] We are not told to read the sequence as a means of recording the intimate conversation – in the way, say, that the voice-over introduction to *Primary* promises us a new sort of intimacy via direct-cinema techniques. Nor are we encouraged to agonize over it, the way Rouch and Morin worry about the authenticity of their film at the conclusion of *Chronique d'un été*. But we lose nothing of the se-quence's impact or credibility by understanding the circumstances in which it was made.

Our complicity is more actively elicited in Macartney-Filgate's taxi driver sequence. The taxi driver talks directly to the unseen and un-heard cameraman, acting both as an acknowledgment of the camera-man's presence and as an on-screen narrator. This is likely the first instance of what would become a cliché of direct cinema, the one-sided interview shot in a moving car (for example, Hubert Humphrey in *Primary*).[18] In *The Days before Christmas* another aspect of this setup – one that would recur in later *Candid Eye* films – is that the taxi driver is not identified by name, differentiating the shot from a conventional interview. The connotation is that we are with him not because he is an authority or any other kind of privileged figure. He is one of the faces in the crowd, a further connotation being that any of the other anony-mous faces may also turn around and speak to us. This itself has a certain structural utility in that it implies the potential for a far greater amount of synchronized sound than was actually used in the film.

Kroitor and Daly's editing of *The Days before Christmas* underlines this theme. Not only do we see the elements of this new sort of filmmaking, but we are invited to watch them being put together. At the beginning of the film, for instance, we are introduced to an anglophone choir rehearsing. We watch them struggle with their music and then, just as they seem to be getting it right, the editors use the choral music over images of people going about their Christmas busi-

The Days before Christmas (1958), directed by Terence Macartney-Filgate, Stanley Jackson, and Wolf Koenig. Courtesy of the National Film Board of Canada.

ness on the Montreal streets. The sound at this point becomes post-diegetic – that is, we listen to the off-screen music with a specific awareness of its origins. Later in the film, we hear choir music over shots of the Brinks guards making their rounds. We cut to a francophone choir rehearsing, struggling with the music. When they seem to be making progress, the editors place their singing over more shots of people in the street. In this instance, we are introduced to pre-diegetic sound, its diegetic origins, and, again, its post-diegetic application. We are being invited to participate in an ever more elaborate editing structure.

Another way of saying this is that we are candidly invited to see the editing as editing. This is especially apparent in one of the film's more poignant sequences. Toward the end of *The Days before Christmas*, we see a children's Christmas pageant. At first, this seems poorly placed. We are well past the part of the film dealing with children and Christmas; we haven't seen any children in some time. But then there is a series of shots of mothers watching the pageant with its subtle implication that this is not so much about the children as it is about their parents. We cut back to the children, and one of them says, 'Is there anything I can do or get for you that will make you happier in heaven?' During that line, we cut to a single man sitting alone. It takes an instant to realize that he is not a parent looking at the children; he is alone at a bar staring into nothing. We cut then to chairs being stacked in a bar and the floor of the now-empty train station being mopped by a maintenance crew. At once we realize that the cutting of the film has not simply been between the contradictions of Christmas but has, in fact, worked its way toward a greater intensity of those contradictions. Now we are at the most profound of those contradictions: that between the innocent joy and the intense sorrow of the holiday season, 'the promise of rebirth,' and the more immediate reality of 'the darkest days of the year.'

This is exactly what we were told to expect by Stanley Jackson's narration. That narration is not a vestige of earlier, voice-over documentary. There is no attempt to focus the images on a single meaning. On the contrary, the narration begins with an invitation to distance ourselves from the footage by allowing us to choose from a number of possible meanings. Over shots of a crowded department store, Jackson tells us:

> For most people, Christmas will mean a joyous celebration of a promise fulfilled, and for all people it will mean a celebration of another promise, the promise that in the due cycle of nature, the season's warmth and brightness will return out of the winter's cold. And for some people it will mean sore feet, frayed nerves and an upset stomach.

We are invited to find both the sacred and the profane. Later, we are invited to do more. Immediately after the cut to the lonely man at the bar and the Christmas cleanup, Jackson introduces his recital of the second verse of the eighteenth-century carol, 'The Praise of Christmas.' Under the recital are the images of the surreptitiously filmed office party. A man at the party kisses a woman on her cheek to Jackson's reciting of the line: 'If wrath be to seek, do not lend her your cheek.' At this juxtaposition, the viewer is left with the options of: reading the image as undermining the narration; reading the narration as lifting the image to a more spiritual plane; or simply realizing, in the ironic mode of the film as a whole, that the sacred and profane aspects of Christmas are coexistent if not interdependent.

It is, of course, this last reading that would be most in keeping with the melding of the hidden or ubiquitous camera in candid eye filmmaking with the products of that camera presented to us in the most forthright means possible. There is no ultimate direction here, no single metaphor for what the camera has found and the editor has assembled. *The Days before Christmas* shows us that Christmas means nothing other than all the things we can see and hear at that time of year and all the ways we can see and hear them. The more we edit them, the more disparate they become. The suggestion is that filmmaking, like the horse-breaking in *Corral*, is itself an existential act, being only what it is. The incorporation of a new technology is the revelation of that technology – not revelation itself.

Legacy
In the years that followed *The Days before Christmas* this message seems lost in what can only be called the confusion of styles that attended the new filmmaking technology. That confusion expresses itself first in the two contending styles of cinéma vérité and direct cinema. The ur-films for both styles have the advantage of the Canadians' expertise: Brault worked on *Chronique d'un été*; Macartney-Filgate shot footage for *Primary*. Yet neither film allows itself the poignant detachment of either the *Candid Eye* films or the remarkable work of the NFB's French Unit. Instead, the candid eye filmmakers worked their way toward their masterpiece, *Lonely Boy*, in which Kroitor and Koenig all but exhausted the vocabulary of the new technology. Meanwhile, for the NFB's French Unit, the candid eye aesthetic gave rise to an extraordinary set of films including: *Les Raquetteurs* (1958), *La Lutte* (1961), and *À Saint-Henri le cinq septembre* (1962). These films and the work of Pierre Perrault – beginning with his 1963 film *Pour la suite du monde* – were, in their ostensibly disengaged manner, the first, and arguably the most, politically effective products of the new technology: quiet films inspiring the Quiet Revolution.[19]

Another aspect of the stylistic confusion was the adoption of handheld location camerawork in fiction filmmaking. The potential for doing this in a direct, self-conscious manner is periodically rediscovered in films like Peter Watkins's *The War Game* (1966), McBride and Carson's *David Holzman's Diary* (1967), Rob Reiner's *This Is Spinal Tap* (1984), the pretensions of Dogme 95, and our own moment's post-ethical production, *The Blair Witch Project* (1999). This transition also owes something to Canadian work of the period. Like the French New Wave filmmakers, Canadians proved themselves adept at harnessing the new tools to feature film production. Jutra did it first in his 1963 film *À tout prendre*. He was followed the next year by the two 'accidental' first features growing out of documentary projects: Gilles Groulx' *Le Chat dans le sac* and Don Owen's *Nobody Waved Good-bye*. It was these films and the later low-budget features like them that would make the case for finally establishing an ongoing Canadian feature film industry, an event signalled by the creation of the Canadian Film Development Corporation in 1967.

What remains for us today from *The Days before Christmas* and *The Candid Eye* is the milestone they erected between the new technology and previous documentary practice. The Unit B filmmakers helped reduce what had been documentary – or at least the Griersonian school of documentary – to simply one set of options for the creative treatment of actuality. They set the stage for the eclecticism of most contemporary documentary practice – films that seamlessly combine voice-over and music with synch and non-synch location footage. It may be worth noting that contemporary documentary filmmakers do not draw the same sort of rigid line between Griersonian didacticism and the ideology of a disengaged observer. Just as we no longer take seriously the voice-of-doom narrator, the existential bent seen in the films of Unit B and *The Candid Eye* is less common today. But then so is existentialism. Contemporary documentary filmmakers choose their level of engagement just as they choose their subject matter and equipment. That we take these choices for granted in both making and viewing documentary films is perhaps the most significant legacy of Unit B, *The Candid Eye*, and *The Days before Christmas*.

Notes

1 See Marcorelles, *Living Cinema*, 30–7. Marcorelles himself helps confuse the issue with the title of his book. To confuse matters further, cinéma vérité is often regarded as the umbrella term for both the French and U.S. practices. For example, Peter Wintonick's 1999 film entitled *Cinéma Verité: Defining the Moment* covers the French and U.S. work as well as the candid eye. A third term, '*cinéma direct*,' was coined by Quebec filmmakers of the early 1960s to describe their use of the same equipment. The current state of

confusion is briefly noted in the Wintonick film when Michel Brault and Jean Rouch make the point that the style has come to be called *cinéma direct* in francophone countries and cinéma vérité in the English speaking world, almost a complete reversal of the original distinction. (I am indebted to Gillian Helfield, whose as-yet-unpublished dissertation discusses in some detail the roots of this contradictory nomenclature.)

2 None of the sources I consulted were able to pinpoint who coined the phrase *The Candid Eye*, although the most frequent guess is Tom Daly. The most obvious precedent would seem to be Allen Funt's U.S. television program *Candid Camera*, broadcast on its own or as segments of other programs since 1948.

3 Although the film was the first shot in *The Candid Eye* series, it was actually shown as the last film of the 1958 season on 7 December of that year at 5:30 P.M. (Notes in the production file indicate that the film was shown at a later date on some CBC affiliates and on Christmas Day on the BBC.) According to Koenig, shooting on *The Days before Christmas* continued until Christmas Eve, 1957. Kroitor and Daly's editing of the film took place, on and off, for a full eleven months, Daly signing the 'Notice of Test Print Approval and Completion of Film' only on 24 November 1958. During production, the film had working titles that included 'Christmas Film' and 'Christmas Comes to Montreal.' The final title was chosen during or before August, when the credit sequence was ordered from the lab.

4 Electronic mail correspondence with the author, 25 October 1999.

5 Conversation with the author, 1 November 1999.

6 Jones, *The Best Butler in the Business*, 20–1; emphasis in original.

7 Harcourt, 'The Innocent Eye,' 72.

8 Evans, *In the National Interest*, 70–2.

9 Morris, 'The Origins of Direct Cinema: Technology, Economics, Aesthetics,' 2.

10 Jennings, 'An Interview with Terence Macartney-Filgate,' 1–2.

11 Electronic mail correspondence with the author, 25 October 1999.

12 Cartier-Bresson, 'The Decisive Moment,' 385.

13 Elder, *Image and Identity*, 103–18.

14 Interview with the author, 8 October 1999. It was this ability to shoot in available light, Macartney-Filgate recalls, that caused the most excitement among European filmmakers who saw *The Days before Christmas* in the late 1950s.

15 Electronic mail correspondence with the author, 25 October 1999. Notes in the production file also indicate a number of sequences that do not appear in the finished film, including: 'guy trying to find burnt out bulb in Christ-

mas tree'; 'liquor commission'; 'Madame Audette's'; 'Christmas in jail'; 'Salvation army – jovial bums' (perhaps pointing to *The Candid Eye*'s next subject); 'animals in zoo'; 'sleighs on Mt Royal.'

16 Conversation with the author, 1 November 1999.

17 Koenig's setup was, according to Macartney-Filgate, even more elaborate. The sequence was made on a hastily constructed set at the NFB in order to be able to record both ends of the conversation. Mike Devine was an NFB employee, and, for the information of documentary ethicists, the NFB paid for what was then a very expensive telephone call. Interview with the author, 8 October 1999.

18 By the time of the 1959 *Candid Eye* film *Glenn Gould: On the Record*, the Canadians were already looking for variations on the shot. Gould, talking inside a taxi in Manhattan, is shot from a camera placed in front of the windshield.

19 The impact of this work on the Quiet Revolution is the focus of the Helfield dissertation noted above. For our purposes, it is enough to say that the event itself was a complex interaction of cultural and political changes generally dated from Jean Lesage's election as provincial premier in June 1960. The net result was to move Quebec from an authoritarian, conservative society dominated by anglophone business interests and the Catholic church to a more secular, socially progressive, and increasingly independence-minded francophone state.

From Obscurity in Ottawa to Fame in Freedomland: *Lonely Boy* and the Cultural Meaning of Paul Anka

BARRY KEITH GRANT

In this essay I want to explore the cultural meaning of Canadian pop singer Paul Anka, and examine Anka in terms of what Richard Dyer, in his discussion of the phenomenon of stardom, calls 'a complex configuration of visual, verbal and aural signs,' and how that meaning is expressed by Wolf Koenig and Roman Kroitor in their short documentary film, *Lonely Boy*.[1] Made in 1961 by members of Tom Daly's Unit B of the National Film Board, *Lonely Boy* is recognized as 'one of the most famous of all the Unit B films,' and a major contribution to documentary filmmaking in Canada.[2] The film has been firmly canonized in Canadian film history and is generally regarded as one of the greatest achievements of the NFB at a time when some of its filmmakers, along with a few others in France and the United States, were revolutionizing documentary film practice with the use of new, lightweight 16 mm cameras and portable synch-sound equipment.

Unit B moved away from the Griersonian certainties that had informed the NFB's documentary style since its inception in 1939. Instead, its 'candid eye' approach tended, as David Clandfield notes, to be that of 'a detached, ironic observer' who 'registers surface impressions of a myth-laden aspect of Canadian life, in order to de-mythicize and de-dramatize it but without analysis or critique.'[3] However, I want to suggest that *Lonely Boy* is not only an ironic demythification of the cultural icon that is 'Paul Anka'; and not only is it about, as the first words of the voice-over narrator plainly tell us, the more general 'astonishing transformation of an entertainer into an idol'; it is also an incisive examination of the phenomenon of pop 'idoldom' itself. In fact, *Lonely Boy* anticipates in its brief twenty-seven minutes much of what subsequent critical discourse will identify as the material economy involved in popular culture's construction of desire and sexuality.

Surprisingly, despite its significant place in Canadian film history, there has been almost no sustained discussion of *Lonely Boy* in the published critical material on Canadian cinema. In his history of the NFB, for example, D.B. Jones acknowledges that the film is 'tightly structured,' but then rather disappointingly goes on merely to describe some of *Lonely Boy*'s more memorable shots and to dismiss Anka's worship by fans as the curious behaviour of 'hordes of silly young girls.'[4] Critics have been unanimous in their praise of the film's richness of observational detail and its importance within the nation's film history, but none has really grappled with its textual specifics, particularly how the film functions simultaneously as observation and essay.

At first glance, *Lonely Boy* seems a straightforward Canadian success story: a celebration of Anka's commercial success in the United States, the feel-good story of a local Canadian boy who has broken through in the big-time American entertainment industry. The film shows Anka being praised by fans of all ages and successfully performing in a variety of venues in the United States, from theme parks to swanky night clubs. He even speaks to us about his artistic inspiration as if he were a true Romantic poet, subject to divine inspiration. Yet a close reading of *Lonely Boy* reveals that the film expresses a more cynical view of Anka's cultural meaning. Koenig and Kroitor deftly manipulate their observational footage so as to examine and question, rather than simply document and celebrate, Paul Anka's 'success.'

Anka as Icon

Anka is the ideal subject for Unit B's questioning cameras. Depending upon one's point of view, his success in the American entertainment industry represents a resistance or capitulation to cultural colonization by the United States. On the one hand, Anka embodied a sense of national pride for Canadians. After all, he was the first Canadian rock-and-roller to break into the American pop charts singing his own material rather than covering black American rhythm and blues songs.[5] Anka was a singer-songwriter, and his biggest hits were tunes that he had written himself. Anka's success thus demonstrated to Canadians that popular culture could also move in a southerly direction, from Canada to the United States, reversing its usual northerly flow. As a result, Anka opened the door for numerous other Canadian artists in the various forms of popular culture to succeed in the larger and more lucrative American market.

On the other hand, Anka can be read as a Canadian who abandoned his cultural roots for greater fame and fortune in the United States. Growing up in what *Lonely Boy*'s narrator seemingly without irony refers to as 'the obscurity of Ottawa,' the fourteen-year-old Anka gamely went to New York City in 1956 looking for a contract with a record company, and through sheer persistence finally obtained one from Don Costa at ABC/Paramount, a major record label. Anka was known mostly for the dogged tenacity with which he pursued his career, and the liner notes for his LPs and other promotional material during his years of teenage fame dwelled on his unswerving efforts to 'make it.' The fact that he did perhaps invokes the American Horatio Alger myth of 'the road to success' more than it does anything particularly Canadian. 'Anka's early life,' write Geoff Pevere and Greig Dymond in their book *Mondo Canuck: A Canadian Pop Culture Odyssey*, 'abounds with stories of a most un-Canadian chutzpah.'[6]

If, as I have argued elsewhere, early Canadian rock music can be seen as articulating either an imitation or inflection of American rock music genres and forms, Anka clearly exemplifies the paradigm of imitation.[7] Anka initially modelled himself on a particular generic type, the teen idol, and rode the crest of a wave of teen idols that inundated American popular music from approximately 1959 to 1963. This was the age of the Frankies and Tommies and Johnnies and Bobbys – including Canada's own homegrown Bobby Curtola. The teen idols carried on the process, begun with pop covers of r & b, of changing the image of male youth, in Richard Staehling's terms, from wild to mild, by providing a cleaner, more wholesome image of masculinity than that of the previous era's rebellious rockabilly heroes like Eddie Cochran and Gene Vincent.[8] Yes, Anka did write his own songs, but even if we are not inclined toward one critic's judgment that Anka's 'songs were unbelievably mechanical, and lyrically they were pure doggerel,'[9] there is no question that Anka submerged himself within the codes of this established American pop genre.

Paramount had some genuine r & b artists on its roster, including Lloyd Price and Fats Domino and later Ray Charles, but it emphasized Anka's status as a teen idol rather than a rock-and-roller. In 1957, his first single for the label, 'Diana,' supposedly written for his 'babysitter' Diana Ayoub, on whom Anka had a crush, went to number one on the American and British charts, selling over ten million copies worldwide and abruptly making the fifteen-year-old singer an international star. In the next few years Anka released on the label a series of schmaltzy top-ten hits all on the theme of romantic teen angst, including 'You Are My Destiny' (1958); 'Put Your Head on My Shoulder' and 'It's Time to Cry' (both 1959); 'Puppy Love' (1960), about his infatuation with Mousketeer Annette Funicello; and, of course, 'Lonely Boy' (1959), the song from which the film gets its name.

Anka's popularity waned significantly in the mid-1960s with the coming of psychedelic rock and the British Invasion. As pop stars let their hair grow, Anka displayed a noticeably receding hairline. But he did manage one more big hit in 1974 – much to the chagrin of feminists – the neoconservative ballad 'Having My Baby.' Anka understood that his teen idol image would fade as quickly as it had flared, and so he turned his attention both to transforming himself into a nightclub performer and to writing hit songs for numerous other artists, including 'She's a Lady' for Tom Jones; 'My Way' for Frank Sinatra, commissioned by the Chairman of the Board as a song to sum up his career; and the ubiquitous *Tonight Show* theme song.[10] As a singer-songwriter Anka had the opportunity to emerge as an important auteur in the 1970s, for it was the period in which such artists as Paul Simon, Joni Mitchell, and Carole King dominated popular music; but instead, Anka's 'personality,' seemingly so charismatic and commented on by everyone in *Lonely Boy* from Trenton teenagers to the owner of New York's exclusive Copacabana nightclub, virtually disappeared.

Teen Idolatry

Lonely Boy was made at the height of the teen idol craze, when Anka was nineteen, four years after his initial success and at that point in his career when he was consciously seeking to change his image to a more adult one. The film begins by looking at Anka's phenomenal popularity with adolescent girls, goes on to show his successful engagement at the Copacabana nightclub, and then returns to Anka as a teen idol in a New York amusement park. Anka seems something of a chameleon who can adapt to his circumstances (as he instructs the Freedomland band, 'after I feel the audience ... I might take something out'), an entertainer who can slip with seeming ease from a teen idol to a lounge lizard.

Rock historians and cultural critics uniformly dismiss the teen idol as a corporate product, an inauthentic pseudo-artist manufactured by record companies to cash in on a trend.[11] Steve Chapple and Reebee Garofalo, in their history of the popular music industry, *Rock 'n' Roll Is*

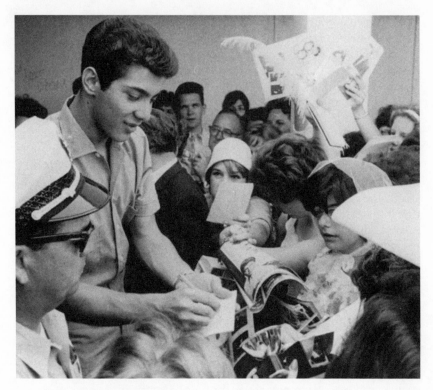

Lonely Boy (1961), directed by Wolf Koenig and Roman Kroitor. Courtesy of the National Film Board of Canada.

Here to Pay, bluntly describe the music of the teen idols as 'schlock rock: the death of rock n' roll.'[12] Often, teen idols were groomed (the very word Anka's manager Irvin Feld uses in the film to describe his preparation of Anka for appearing in New York's elegant supper clubs) and promoted because of their looks rather than for any innate talent (the example of Fabian leaps to mind). Most teen idols did not write their own material, but had formula tunes pumped out for them by slick pop songwriters from New York.

An essential component in the marketing of teen idols was an emphasis on memorabilia, fetishistic objects fans might purchase and collect. *Lonely Boy* emphasizes this aspect of Anka's popularity when early on we see his fans collecting and displaying Anka buttons, postcards, and other items. One of his fans boasts that she has all his records as well as '555 pictures of Paul all over my room, and I have a Paul Anka sweater.' Such memorabilia are central to 'the apparatus of fetishism, a network of fantasy' that interpellates adolescent girls as consumers of the teen idol image of male sexuality.[13] This dynamic is nicely suggested in *Lonely Boy* in the shot of one teenage girl gazing longingly at the singing Anka through a haze of cigarette smoke, spellbound by his teen idol image, a perfect incarnation of what Simon Frith and Angela McRobbie describe as 'an unformed sensuality, something sulky and unfinished in the mouth and jaw ... a dreamy fantasy fulfillment.'[14]

Perhaps the most important aspect of the teen idol image is its construction of sexuality, both masculine and feminine. Male teen idols do not express an aggressive phallic sexuality; rather, they offer themselves to girls as heterosexual objects of desire without being overtly masculine or sexually threatening – 'big fluffy candy-colored images of male niceness on which to focus their pubescent dreams,' in the words of one critic.[15] In *Lonely Boy*, Anka's fans describe him as 'cute' and 'sweet.' His music, like that of teen idols generally, falls squarely within that category of rock music Frith and McRobbie call 'teenybop.' In opposition to the aggressive, boastful sexuality of 'cockrock,' teenybop rock presents an image of 'the young boy next door: sad, thoughtful, pretty and puppylike.' The lyrics of teen idol songs tend to be 'about being let down and stood up, about loneliness and frustration.'[16] The teen idol, accordingly, is 'soft, vulnerable, and caring' – exactly the persona constructed by Anka in his songs: Anka is soft because he knows when it's time to cry; he is vulnerable in his loneliness, a lonely boy lonely and blue; and we know he cares because he supportively invites us to put our heads on his shoulder.[17] For Frith and McRobbie, 'the teenybop fan should feel that her idol is addressing himself solely to her; her experience should be as his partner.'[18] Anka does exactly this with his 'special material' at the Freedomland concert when he pulls one lucky girl from the audience onto the stage and sings 'Put Your Head on My Shoulder' to her as he gently coaxes her head to rest on his arm.

The film shows nothing less than the construction and regulation of adolescent desire by the culture industry. In the film Anka concedes that sex is the primary element of pop music success, but, consistent with his teen idol image, he dances around the word before finally saying it ('a word which we all know and which I'm not in accord to using but it's the only word which can sum up what I have to say which is sex') with a noticeable gulp of discomfort. At the Freedomland concert there is a montage of female faces all gripped in paroxysms of desire; several shots of screaming girls fill the screen, and there are also a couple of shots of the muscular arms of male policemen firmly clutching nightsticks, literally attempting to contain this intense effusion of female fantasy. At one point the screaming girls surge forward and almost knock down a large, heavy-set man involved in controlling the crowd. Early in the film we see two female Anka fans dressed the same with the same hairstyle, equally breathless in the presence of Anka – the living proof of Theodor Adorno's condemnation of pop music as 'a system of response mechanisms wholly antagonistic to the ideal of individuality in a free, liberal society.'[19]

Central to its investigation of the pop idol phenomenon, the film consistently emphasizes Anka's constructed image. Anka first appears in the film as a name on a billboard. His name moves across an electronic marquee (its fleeting nature as it moves across the screen providing one of the film's comments on the ephemerality of pop fame), which is echoed subsequently in the graphic design of the title credit. Next we see a billboard image of Anka. When we finally do see Anka himself, he is in performance, singing the title tune (accompanied by female screams on the soundtrack), after which he exits the stage and returns for an encore, at which point the film's credits begin. By delaying the appearance of the credits in this manner, the film underscores its presentational aspect as well as that of its subject. Anka's theme song, played whenever he takes the stage, is 'Anka's Away' (a pun on the official song of the U.S. Navy, 'Anchors Aweigh'), the lyrics of which also address his fabricated career ('This do-it-yourself-type showman') and his changing image ('I'll be in my twenties with my hair turning grey').

As the film goes on, Anka becomes a multiplicity of images, like a hall of mirrors at the Atlantic City boardwalk on which he strolls. He appears on photo buttons worn by his adoring fans, on the many photos they carry and affix to their purses, on the covers of fanzines, and on concert programs. Dressing before a show, Anka is reflected in a mirror – an image of an image. The 'real' Anka seems impossible to locate behind his multiple images in the film. When a handwriting analyst extrapolates Anka's personality from a sample of his writing, we see an image of a blow-up monster, presumably at one of the boardwalk attractions, in the process of inflating. The implication is that Anka himself is a carnivalesque creature, an inhuman being, hyped and shaped by the media, that just might be empty inside.

Tellingly, the first of two interview sequences with Anka's manager concerns the singer's physical appearance rather than his talent. Feld praises the qualities of Anka's mouth and his eyes ('Paul's features are excellent') and talks about Anka's recent plastic surgery job on his nose. He boasts of the fact that Anka today looks nothing like his photographs of four years before. Anka himself focuses on his image in the first of his two talking-head scenes. 'I realized with my looks you can only go so far,' he confides, and goes on to reveal that he worked out four hours a day for months to lose weight and that he battled with his hair for over a year and a half to retrain it ('this went down, this went up, and this came down'). He equates appeal with appearance, saying 'You've got to look like you're in show business.' Anka's complete physical makeover gives his playful request for help as he hurriedly dresses to go on stage at the Steel Pier concert ('shoes, scalpel, sponge') a somewhat ironic edge. From a contemporary perspective, Anka's radical transformation anticipates such postmodern pop performers as David Bowie and Michael Jackson in that he composed not only his music but his body as well.[20]

The Art of the Real

The film's most pointed critique of Anka as constructed image comes in the two scenes with Copacabana owner Jules Podell. In the first, Podell explains how he came to hire Anka. While Anka relates to the camera by pretending to be unaware of its presence ('forget they're even there,' Paul says while dressing backstage), Podell openly acknowledges the filmmakers and engages them in lighthearted banter, asking if it is alright to light his cigar. The scene begins with Podell, apparently in response to a request from the filmmakers to have the waiters move around in the background in order to give the picture more kinetic appeal, passing on this instruction to his head waiter. Four times during the rest of the scene, waiters traverse the frame from one side to the other behind Podell, and we cannot help but wonder whether they are genuinely working or merely performing for their employer and the camera – the same question we keep asking about Anka.

Thus the film acknowledges its own constructedness, admits that it is, like its subject, a series of images, a text to be read. So throughout the film we see cameras, the apparatus of image making, or we are made aware of their unseen presence. When Anka enters his dressing room, pretending the camera is not there, he nevertheless quickly but noticeably glances at it as he passes by. As he then dresses for his performance, the film camera and camera operator are reflected in Anka's mirror. Elsewhere, photographers snap photos of Anka while he dresses and rehearses, and of course fans at each concert have cameras.

In the second scene with Podell, at the conclusion of his two-week engagement at the Copacabana, Anka presents the club owner with two gifts, one of which is his own image – that is to say, a photographic portrait, similar to the film *Lonely Boy* itself. An upscale instance of teen memorabilia, it is displayed not for Podell's point of view, but for that of the camera and spectator. As Anka unwraps it for Podell, he says, 'It's a picture of me,' and again darts a glance at the camera. Podell seems duly appreciative, and Anka and 'Uncle Julie' kiss. The moment is doubly manipulated, first by Anka and his manager, and then by the filmmakers, as from behind the camera comes a voice asking them to 'do the kiss again, please' and explaining that the camera moved (which it did, but only slightly, not enough to ruin the shot). Anka laughs loudly and uncomfortably, his excessive reaction betraying the insincerity behind the gesture. His kiss, finally, is no more – or less! – genuine than those we see him earlier giving to the anonymous girls who parade by to receive autographs.

The still photographer in Anka's dressing room cannot get his flash to operate, while Koenig and Kroitor film away, suggesting the superiority of the film medium for revealing the 'true' Paul Anka. The photographers take publicity photos, teen idol images; but our intrepid filmmakers, in the animating spirit of direct cinema, will penetrate the persona and show us the man behind the myth, as the narrator promises at the beginning of the film. However, apart from the beefcake shot of Anka in his underwear, little is really revealed. This, ironically, is the film's big revelation. There are moments of 'truth' in the film to be sure, but there is nothing in *Lonely Boy* comparable to, say, the breakdown of Jason in Shirley Clarke's *Portrait of Jason* (1967) or Paul Brennan's growing self-doubt in the Maysles brothers' *Salesman* (1969). These films begin by showing us their subjects' socially constructed personas, and then proceed to break them down by capturing intimate moments of personal crisis on camera.

Lonely Boy reveals the performing persona of 'Paul Anka' but does not get beneath it. In this film there is no 'privileged moment,' that flash of insight so coveted by observational filmmakers. In the context of direct cinema, *Lonely Boy* thus reveals a gaping but meaningful absence at its centre. The closest it comes is in the final shot, a close-up of Anka's seemingly tired face as we hear a refrain of 'Lonely Boy' on the soundtrack. Yet the shot is ultimately ambiguous: for is this really the weary lonely boy emerging behind the impossibly upbeat performer we see now, or is it the same droopy-eyed idol ('something sulky and unfinished') we saw in the film's opening, on the billboard and then in a matched close-up of Anka on stage?

We do not see the 'real' Anka because, as a condition of pop stardom, Anka is always in performance. Anka is a lonely boy precisely because he is *never* alone. In fact, nowhere in the film do we see Paul Anka by himself. Instead, Anka is constantly 'on stage,' whether literally or not. Even in his talking-head scenes, he is in the presence of the unseen filmmakers and their equipment (he begins by acknowledging one of their questions). Backstage at the Copacabana, he emerges dynamically through the door of his dressing room as he dons his tuxedo jacket, his masquerade complete. (Is it mere coincidence, then, that after he meets Podell, Anka strikes a match to light the club owner's cigar exactly on the note that launches into his theme tune, 'Anka's Away'? This music may well not actually have occurred simultaneously with the action in the shot, since its source is off-screen, and may have been added later by sound editor Kathleen Shannon.)

Since Anka's identity seems unstable – unanchored, so to speak – he is shown in *Lonely Boy* as adrift in space, located in a limbo between two worlds: private and public, person and persona, obscurity in Ottawa and fame in Freedomland. When the handwriting analyst says Anka 'thinks in a straight line,' we are shown images of the singer spinning in circles on bumper cars. In some shots in performance, Anka seems engulfed in blackness, like the doomed protagonists of film noir. According to the liner notes on Anka's 1962 RCA Victor LP *Paul Anka: Young, Alive and in Love*, 'As an entertainer ... Paul was "at home" anywhere and everywhere' – meaning, of course, that he was truly at home nowhere.[21] The second song we hear Anka sing is, rather ironically, 'My Home Town' (1960), and as he sings the film cuts to an exterior long shot looking across the water at the Steel Pier pavilion as Anka's voice fades on the soundtrack as if dwindling in the distance. The last shot of the film holds on Anka, sitting wearily in a car shuttling from one gig to another as we hear a refrain from 'Lonely Boy' on the soundtrack.

His Destiny
At Freedomland, Anka towers over the crowd and camera, which shoots him from an extreme low angle, showing him as both individual and

icon. Feld explains to us that because he believes Anka has a gift greater than anyone in the last 500 years, Paul 'doesn't belong to himself anymore.' Talking of Anka's plastic surgery, Feld says 'We had a nose job' (emphasis added). The film then cuts to girls armed with memorabilia chanting, 'We want Paul.' A few shots of screaming female fans, lit from below, make them look ghastly, their screaming mouths hungry to consume Anka as if in a zombie movie. At one point the music is eerily absent on the soundtrack, the strange silence emphasizing their ghoulishness. As one of the policemen at the Freedomland concert says, 'It's Paul Anka that has to be afraid. They're not after me.'

Anka was so successful in his quest for American stardom that he is described in no less an authoritative tome than *The Rolling Stone Rock Almanac* as a 'Philadelphia teen idol.'[22] Anka had his name up in lights and found a place within the American entertainment industry – right along with the movies, the high-diving horse, the General Motors exhibit, and live television shows advertised on the Atlantic City billboard we see in the film. But the teen idol, as Anka himself recognized, was a fad, as ephemeral as the cresting waves in one of the establishing shots of Atlantic City at the beginning of *Lonely Boy*. At the end of the film Anka is already passé, in the act of being passed by two young women who seem to glance at him with little more than curiosity (do they recognize him or not?) from a car going faster than his own. As we hear the refrain of 'Lonely Boy' we see a metaphoric shot of the setting sun. The inevitably fleeting nature of fame in a media-saturated society, a world Canadian media critic Marshall McLuhan called 'the global village,' is presumably what Kroitor was referring to when he said that in *Lonely Boy* he wanted to present Anka as a 'tragic figure.'[23]

It is telling that in the book *Rock Dreams*, featuring drawings that offer a visual impression of the musical 'world' of major rock musicians and groups, artist Guy Peellaert provides for Paul Anka a series of cartoon panels parodying the full-page advertisements for the do-it-yourself Charles Atlas bodybuilding programs that commonly appeared in American comic books in the 1950s. Peellaert's imagery for Anka is strikingly anomalous in the book because it is about Anka's body, his physical appearance as image, not his music. The fragmentation of Anka's page into panels also suggests an instability in the singer's identity due to his drive for success that *Lonely Boy* explored a decade earlier.[24] Indeed, the film was prescient in its cultural critique, using Anka to take a broader view and examine the 'star-making machinery' of popular culture.

Notes

1 Dyer, *Stars*, 38.
2 Morris, *The Film Companion*, 182.
3 Clandfield, *Canadian Film*, 26.
4 Jones, *Movies and Memoranda*, 68. (Un)surprisingly, the closest reading of *Lonely Boy* is by an American critic who focuses her analysis on the representation of adolescent female desire and is not at all concerned with the film's implications for Canadian identity or culture; Gaines, '*Lonely Boy* and the *Vérité* of Sex.'
5 In the mid-1950s, the major record labels engaged in the practice of 'covering' – having white artists redo in a smoother style – black rhythm and blues songs originally recorded for small, independent companies. The independent labels did not have the ability to distribute their records beyond a regional basis, and the radio stations that had strong signals for wide broadcast would not play black music. Black radio stations had limited range, and many white listeners therefore were not able to hear the original recordings. Pat Boone, for example, established his career covering songs by the likes of Little Richard, Fats Domino, and The Flamingos. The two examples of Canadian recording artists to make it on the American rock charts before Anka, The Crew Cuts and The Diamonds, were both white vocal harmony groups from Toronto who specialized in covering r & b songs recorded first by black American groups. Both groups recorded for Mercury Records in Chicago, the most thorough of all the major labels in covering black r & b. The Crew Cuts, who had once been known as the Canadaires, had their first big hit in 1954, 'Sh-Boom,' which was originally recorded by the Chords for the independent Cat label earlier the same year. The group had no less than seven major chart successes in the next three years, most of them r & b covers. The Diamonds had a hit in 1956 with a cover of Frankie Lyman's 'Why Do Fools Fall in Love,' and they steadfastly continued in the same groove, recording many covers of doo-wop classics by such groups as The Willows, The Rays, The Cleftones, and The Heartbeats. The group's biggest hit, 'Little Darlin'' (1957), had been a regional hit for The Gladiolas from South Carolina. According to Dave Laing and Phil Hardy in their book *Encyclopedia of Rock: The Age of Rock 'n' Roll*, the Diamonds were one of the villainous 'prime perpetrators' of rock's dilution as a result of white covers of black rhythm and blues; quoted in Melhuish, *Heart of Gold*, 12–13.
6 Pevere and Dymond, *Mondo Canuck*, 8.
7 Grant, '"Across the Great Divide."'

8 Staehling, 'From *Rock around the Clock* to *The Trip.*'
9 Shaw, 'The Teen Idols,' 98.
10 Melhuish, *Heart of Gold*, 19.
11 On the importance of the ideology of authenticity in rock music, see, for example, Shuker, *Understanding Popular Music*, 36, 38.
12 Chapple and Garofalo, *Rock 'n' Roll Is Here to Pay*, 246.
13 Sweeney, 'The Face on the Lunch Box,' 52–3.
14 Frith and McRobbie, 'Rock and Sexuality,' 378.
15 Sweeney, 'Face on the Lunch Box,' 51; Shaw, 'The Teen Idols,' 97.
16 Frith and McRobbie, 'Rock and Sexuality,' 375.
17 Sweeney, 'Face on the Lunch Box,' 51.
18 Frith and McRobbie, 'Rock and Sexuality,' 375.
19 Adorno, 'On Popular Music,' 305.
20 A similar theme is taken up in Canadian cyberpunk author William Gibson's novel *Idoru* (1996), in which rock stars of the near future are sophisticated holograms.
21 RCA Victor LSP/LPM 2502 (1962). Pevere and Dymond note that Anka was booed off the stage in his first Ottawa concert after 'Diana,' his first big hit, and didn't perform there again until 1974; *Mondo Canuck*, 8.
22 *The Rolling Stone Rock Almanac*, 40. Philadelphia is the American city where many of the teen idols were created and given early exposure by Dick Clark on his popular *American Bandstand* TV show.
23 Kroitor, quoted in Morris, *The Film Companion*, 182.
24 Peellaert and Cohn, *Rock Dreams*, unpaginated.

Images and Information: The Dialogic Structure of *Bûcherons de la Manouane* by Arthur Lamothe

PETER HARCOURT

The best way to lie is to use cinéma vérité.
Arthur Lamothe (1976)[1]

Like a mechanical monster from outer space, a bulldozer moves left across a black screen, its twin spotlights like extraterrestrial eyes lighting up the darkness of the night. The engine of a truck turns over as we hear the crunch on the snow of men marching towards it. They climb in and exchange glances (a few with the camera), talking about the cold. Leaving their camp in the early morning, they are going to work – to cut wood nine miles away.

Now in its own truck, the camera travels in front of them, the snow cast up by the truck with the camera caught in the headlights of the truck with the men. As the opening credits appear, natural sounds give way to fiddles playing a traditional Québécois gigue. The sky grows lighter as the men continue on their way, revealing snowy landscapes largely deprived of their trees. An aerial shot surveys the territory below.

So begins Arthur Lamothe's *Bûcherons de la Manouane* (*Manouane River Lumberjacks*, 1962), his first *court métrage* (28 minutes) and one of the few films he made for the National Film Board.

Background
Born in 1928 in the south of France to a family of farmers, Arthur Lamothe initially studied agriculture. He was involved with rural unions and was secretary of a co-operative at Saint-Mont, his home town.

In 1953, he emigrated to Canada, where, for a time, he was a student at the School of Agriculture in Saint-Hilaire. He then worked as a taxi driver, refrigerator salesman, house painter, and lumberjack in the Abitibi region.

Eventually, he studied political economy at the University of Montreal and, in 1957, joined the news department at Radio-Canada.[2] Meanwhile, he had become interested in cinema, helping to found the film journal *Images* in 1955. He also wrote for *Cité libre*, *Liberté*, and for the film society of Radio-Canada.

In 1961, he joined the NFB as a researcher, working on *Manger* (1961), *Dimanche d'Amérique* (1961), and *Pour quelques arpents de neige* (1962), during which time he directed his first short, *Bûcherons de la Manouane*.[3] The film was part of *Temps présent*, a half-hour television series that also included *Québec USA* (1962), *Golden Gloves* (1961), *Les Enfants du silence* (1963), *La Lutte* (1961), and which was 'a true melting pot for Quebec cinema.'[4]

Like other films made at that time, for example Clément Perron's *Jour après jour* (1962), the film was too accusatory for the NFB. Lamothe couldn't name the lumber company, nor could he mention the fact that the bosses were all anglophones who made enormous profits and that there were no appropriate schools for the Native children.[5] Lamothe felt, however, that, even with the prohibitions, enough came through to allow the film to proceed.[6]

Although Lamothe went on to found his own production companies, for whom he made fiction features as well as documentaries, including *Chronique des Indiens du Nord-Est du Québec (1973–83)*, his ethnographic study of the lives of the Montagnais, *Bûcherons de la Manouane*, established his political priorities.[7]

Structure

The opening moments declare the film's dialogic structure.[8] There is a dialogue between technology and nature, between the severity of cold and the warmth required for the men. The harsh reality of the lives of the lumberjacks is contrasted with the mythological image, suggested by the music, of life in the woods – of the romanticized endurance of *coupeurs de bois*. As we fly over the vast terrain seven times the size of France and the commentary begins, another set of relationships establishes itself – between the individuality of men and statistics that reduce them to ciphers within the imperial requirements of the pulp and paper industry.

Back at camp, as the camera tracks along the empty bunks where the men sleep, the commentary intones:

Two by two and four by four,
The Bretons – Le Gouin, Keruzoré, Hénouf –
Over from the old country, from Morbiand and Finistère;
And Émile, the cook, with his assistant, Lucien, known as Smiley

While the commentary continues its recitation of names, the camera tracks along the empty tables set for the midday meal:

Henri Frénette, Jean-Charles Charron, Guy Charron,
Flavien Charron, Normand Lafontaine, Henri-Paul Labonté:
They're all from the old parishes of Quebec
Where the soil is poor and unyielding,
From the Laurentians to the Gaspé,
From Beauce County to Lac St-Jean,
And they've come here to work as they've never worked before.

This strategy of naming the men in their absence further depersonalizes the lives they lead.

While we see images of men at work, slicing through logs with their chainsaws, we hear information about the economics of lumber. Working in groups of two, a cutter and a stacker, the lumberjacks share six dollars a cord, which is a pile of wood four feet wide, eight feet long, and four feet high. Similarly, the workers who drive the wood to the rivers are paid sixty cents a cord, also to be shared between two men. Each year, thirty-five trucks dump their logs into the freezing rivers – 52,000 cords of wood, 'enough to supply newsprint,' the commentary explains, 'for the *Montreal Star* for fifteen months or the *New York Times* for two.'

As we see trees being felled, carted by trucks, and then dumped into the river, this recitation becomes a celebration of place names in Quebec:

Down the Manouane they'll float; then down the St Maurice to mingle with 2,000,000 trees felled by 8,000 lumberjacks and cut into 125,000,000 four-foot logs which every year are carried down stream to La Tuque, Grand-Mère, Shawinigan, and Trois-Rivières to produce as much paper as is exported by the whole of Scandinavia.[9]

Theory

Most critics would agree with Peter Morris that throughout his career Lamothe 'has explored specific social issues with a precise focus on the dispossessed.'[10] As Yvan Patry suggested when writing about *Bûcherons*: 'To enter the life of the lumberjack is to become aware of the extent of his disinheritance.'[11] At heart, Lamothe is a researcher and social activist, and the information contained in *Bûcherons de la Manouane*, plus its deliberate political focus, saves the film from the 'lie' that, according to Lamothe, is cinéma vérité.[12]

Although I do not wish here to trace the differences that exist between the various schools of direct-cinema practice with their various claims to truth,[13] David Clandfield has established a useful theoretical distinction. The less mediated a work might be, he suggests, as in the Leacock–Pennebaker films of the early 1960s or in the *Candid Eye* films at the NFB, the more it must

> rely on a rhetoric of empirical objectivity as its guarantee of authenticity. On the other hand, a vision of reality which foregrounded its mediating function by emphasizing formal elements inherent in the process would have to rely on a rhetoric of sincerity to guarantee its authenticity. The filmmaker's commitment to his documentary material must be demonstrated not by his effacement before the formal imperatives of the profilmic event ... but by his honesty about his own role in the filmmaking process.[14]

Although in much of his work Lamothe has utilized the techniques of cinematic capture associated with direct cinema – less a script than a shopping list, a hand-held camera, available light, and location sound – the construction of his films transformed them into the poetic polemics that most of them are. This twin stylistic provides yet another level of dialogue in his films. *Le Mépris n'aurait qu'un temps* (1970), his detailed study of the lives of construction workers, is the most authoritative of his social investigations; but through its 'rhetoric of sincerity' (as Clandfield has defined it) and the comprehensiveness of the economic investigation, *Bûcherons de la Manouane* set the tone for all the films that followed.[15]

Style

As the film continues, it acquires a dreamlike quality, largely through the sound. Similar to the score he prepared for *Jour après jour*, Maurice

Blackburn has devised a *musique concrète* that gives the film a surreal quality.[16] Although we still see chainsaws cutting through logs, we now hear the sound of axes chopping away at trees, as they must have done for hundreds of years in the past. While these vestigial sounds alternate with the increasing roar of logs being dumped into the river, a dialogue is now established between the past and the present.

The woods seem haunted by the echoes of labour that has been exploited there since the French settlers, arriving on the North American continent in the seventeenth century, first began to harvest trees to service the ship-building needs of the mother country across the seas. This was the time as well when the dispossessed lumberjacks served further to dispossess the Native people, who, until the white invasion, had lived at home in the woods. The commentary explains:

> Thirty-five trucks, sixty-five horses,
> eight caterpillar tractors,
> 165 men for nine months,
> 22 Indians for fifteen days
> and eight years of labour
> to dump into the river forty square miles of forest.

The Indians are assigned the job, lasting for only two weeks, of clearing away logs too small to interest the white men. After a scene of their midday dinner – a meal that lasts for only ten minutes – we see an encampment of the Attikamek tribe, the wives and children having moved their tents to be with their men.[17] The women are standing in the snow in weather that is −50° Fahrenheit (−45°C) – in cotton dresses without coats, without access to schools or other amenities.

I know of no sequence in all of cinema that conveys such a sense of intolerable cold, a sense compounded when the camera closes in on a shivering dog. In this scene we observe the bottom rungs of the economic ladder of the lumber industry, with an additional sense, derived largely from the sound, that this exploitation has been going on for ages.

After the scene with the Indians, the film moves into its most *vérité* moments, with shots of the wood being hauled, stacked, and measured. There are fewer statistics in the commentary, fewer sounds from the past. Lambert, one of the lumberjacks, has had enough. He is going home tomorrow, like some men from other camps, 'who pack up one night on an impulse – for the company of a woman, for the comfort of a house, to relax in a tavern, to sleep between sheets.'

Bûcherons de la Manouane (1962), directed by Arthur Lamothe. Courtesy of the National Film Board of Canada.

Sitting about in the railway station at Sanmaur, the men share their griefs and their dreams. They all either have come from a better life or hope for a better life – like buying a farm – but the odds are not in their favour. As a song sermonizes during the penultimate scene in the film, 'even when you've earned your money, you go on a binge in Quebec City and in a couple of weeks you'll be broke once again.'

The film ends with Guy Charron from Rivière-du-Loup, another lumberjack, taking out his horses in the frozen morning air, getting them ready for work. As they disappear into the distance in weather that is still −50° Fahrenheit, the final song continues and the closing credits roll.

Culture

If the films of the French Unit had a greater political thrust than those of the English units, it is because they were part of a then-flourishing collective movement. As Jean Pierre Lefebvre explained at that time: 'French Canada puts itself the question of its existence and of its survival, while English Canada puts itself no question.'[18] Moreover, there was a flourishing of intellectual periodicals – from the early days of *Cité libre* (1950–66) through *Liberté* (1959+) to *Parti pris* (1963–8), not to mention film magazines such as *Séquences* (1955+), *Images* (1955–6), *Objectif* (1960–7), and *Cinéma Québec* (1971–8).[19] There were no equivalent film periodicals in English Canada until the original *Take One* (1966–79) and *Cinema Canada* (1972–89), and even then they scarcely served to mobilize the nation.

In an interview with Michel Euvrard, Lamothe has acknowledged the role that these periodicals played in the development of his ideas. *Bûcherons de la Manouane* was part of an impassioned cultural movement that began with *Cité libre* (1950), passed into film with *Les Raquetteurs* (1958), and continued throughout the province at least until the election of the Parti Québécois in 1976.[20]

Conclusion

Alternating naturalistic scenes with moments of lyrical suggestiveness, scenes of information with those of reflection, of explanation with illustration, of talk with songs, the overall form of *Bûcherons de la Manouane* confirms its dialogic structure. It is also, in this way, a cinematic roundelay. Furthermore, the insistence on economic information plus the general detachment of names from the faces of the men gives the film a classic Marxist dimension. The lumberjacks cut wood but not in circumstances chosen by themselves.[21]

At the same time, these very qualities entail a hint of patronization – a hint that is more intrusive in the English version. During the scenes of their meal and at the railroad station, the dialogue of the men is voiced-over by the English commentary, erasing the authenticity of their speech. The same practice is inflicted on the songs.[22] However, through the authority of the commentary, this dimension of condescension is also present in the French original. The film fondly but deliberately presents these men as peasants.

At the beginning of the film, the French commentary explains: 'Dallaire is a French Canadian who speaks no English. Of Cuba and the common market he knows nothing. Nor does he know what's going on in the Congo and Algeria. He cuts wood for six dollars a cord, nine miles from camp.' While the facts are undoubtedly true, the tone is unfortunate – certainly to contemporary ears. Like Luchino Visconti in *La terra trema* (1948) but unlike Gilles Groulx in *Golden Gloves* (1961) or *Un Jeu si simple* (1965), Lamothe cares about his workers but is not one of them. And yet the distance established between filmmaker and filmic subjects gives to *Bûcherons* its authority and its restraint.[23] Lamothe would agree. As a Frenchman, he cannot be one of them (as he has often admitted). The distance is crucial for him to avoid the 'lie' of cinéma vérité. In this way, *Bûcherons de la Manouane* stands apart from the films made at the Board at that time that concern 'the rituals of the urban masses,' as Clandfield has described them.[24] However, these same characteristics bestow upon this admirable film both its seminal promise and its enduring authority. Without *Bûcherons de la Manouane*, Québécois documentary would be decidedly less accomplished.

Notes

I would like to thank Nicole Périat of the National Film Board Archives for providing me with scripts, in both French and English, for the commentary of this film. In my own transcriptions, I have sometimes blended the two versions. All translations from the French have been freely rendered by myself.

1 Lamothe, quoted in Bonneville, ed., *Le Cinéma québécois par ceux qui le font*, 510.
2 Gilles Groulx was also working in news at Radio-Canada at the time.
3 Biographical details are from Coulombe and Jean, eds., *Le Dictionnaire du cinéma québécois*, 265. See also a study guide to the film, source not available, at the Film Reference Library of the Toronto International Film Festival Group.
4 Euvrard and Véronneau, 'Direct Cinema,' 81.
5 Lamothe, quoted in Lafrance, ed., *Cinéma d'ici*, 89.
6 There seem to have been further 'euphemisms' imposed on the English version of the film for its release in 1963. In English, we are told that the company denied the men beer and liquor at the camp but sold soft drinks. In French, it sells Coca-Cola. In the English print, the commentary states that 'Indians have never changed.' In French we are told that 'On les appelle encore sauvages' ('They are still called savages').

7 He first founded the Société général cinémathographique and later the Ateliers audiovisuels du Québec. Following *Le Train du Labrador* (1967), the film during which he first made contact with the Montagnais, and working now with anthropologist Remi Savard, Lamothe designed his extended aboriginal Chronicle to consist of two series of films – *Carcajou et le péril blanc* (eight films) and *La Terre de l'homme* (five films). More recently, he has written and directed *Le Silence des fusils* (1996), a fictionalized account of the struggle of the Native Innu in northern Quebec to reclaim their right to fish for salmon in the river along which they have lived for centuries.

8 If in language all dialogue is 'formed in the process of social interaction,' as Mikhail Mikhailovich Bakhtin and his Circle have argued, leading to 'the interaction of different social values,' in film dialogue works in less interactive ways. Images and information within a fixed structure cannot influence one another in the way that speech can within a social situation. They must be content to register a tension between their different values, leaving viewers to imagine how the tensions might be resolved; see 'The Bakhtin Circle,' by Craig Brandist, *The Internet Encyclopedia of Philosophy* <http://styluspub.com/books/book5553.html> (accessed 26 October 2001).

9 The recitation of place names is a recurring characteristic of Québécois films of this period, affirming the vastness and particularities of the land. For example, see the map sequence in Jacques Leduc's *Tendresse ordinaire* (1973).

10 Morris, *The Film Companion*, 172

11 Patry, 'Arthur Lamothe: Réalisateur,' 117.

12 Reality is not out there, waiting to be grabbed: it has to be constructed according to one's own values. One has to declare where one stands. Indeed, in one of his accounts of the film, Yvan Patry has suggested that Lamothe was the first to make cinéma vérité films in the first person (ibid., 117). In another context, Lamothe has stated that he prefers the term *cinéma réel* to cinéma vérité (Patry, *Arthur Lamothe*, 15).

13 For the differences between American and English-Canadian practice, see Elder, 'On the Candid Eye Movement,' and for a distinction between direct cinema and cinéma vérité, see Barnouw, *Documentary*, 254–5.

14 Clandfield, 'From the Picturesque to the Familiar,' 116.

15 For an extended analysis of *Le Mépris*, see Patry, *Arthur Lamothe*, 6–11.

16 In spite of apparent contradictions, Lamothe has acknowledged his debt to surrealism; see Bonneville, ed., *Le Cinéma québécois par ceux qui le font*, 510.

17 Called 'Tête-de-Boules' in the film, these members of the Algonquian linguistic group in 1972 reclaimed Attikamek (White Fish) as their authen-

tic indigenous name: <http://www.nativetrail.com/en/first_peoples/index.html> (accessed 24 September 1999).

18 Cited in Leach, 'Second Images,' 102. I would suggest, however, that in Tom Daly's Unit B at the NFB – in films such as *City of Gold* (1957), *Universe* (1960), and *The Living Machine* (1962) – questions *were* asked but they were more philosophical than political, more ontological than sociological.

19 For an extended discussion of the role these magazines played within the French Unit at the NFB, see Véronneau, *Résistance et affirmation*, 109–17.

20 Euvrard, 'Interview with Arthur Lamothe,' 14.

21 'Men make their own history, but ... they do not make it in circumstances chosen by themselves'; Marx, *The Eighteenth Brumaire of Louis Bonaparte* in Bender, ed., *Karl Marx: The Essential Writings*, 227–8n.

22 An entire essay could be written about the imperial implications of the 'Englishing' of Québécois films at the NFB, from the execrably mutilated *Moontrap* (1964, 84 minutes) – the abbreviated version of Pierre Perrault's *Pour la suite du monde* (1963, 105 minutes) – to the much more successfully voiced *Un Pays sans bon sens* (1970). To save a bit of money and in the hope of television sales, the Board has been reluctant to use subtitles, although a new subtitled version of *Pour la suite du monde* is now available; see the essay by David Clandfield in this volume.

23 Even the reference to the Indians as 'sauvages,' mentioned in note 6, might represent a further condescension in relation to Quebec's Native people.

24 Clandfield, 'From the Picturesque to the Familiar,' 115.

Linking Community Renewal to National Identity: The Filmmakers' Role in *Pour la suite du monde*

DAVID CLANDFIELD

One of the most faithful adherents to the principles of the so-called *cinéma direct* documentary, the late Pierre Perrault (1927–1999) made twelve feature-length films, three *moyens métrages*, and two short films, without counting the series of thirteen shorts on which he had earlier collaborated with René Bonnière. This stands in addition to seven collections of poetry and one collection of found poems, seven highly annotated film transcripts, four collections of essays, one play, one book-length interview, almost a hundred articles, and almost 700 radio documentaries averaging thirty minutes in length. The scholarship on the work of Perrault is equally impressive. There are books about his films by sociologists, film scholars, another filmmaker, and even one by a poet who was a central focus of two of Perrault's films. Over seventy articles are cited in a recent select bibliography, and doctoral theses have been devoted to his work in Montreal, Ottawa, and Paris.

Michel Brault (b. 1928) had already worked as the cinematographer on more than fifty short films (both theatrical and for television) and was already recognized as one of the great cameramen of the world when he joined Pierre Perrault as cinematographer and co-director of *Pour la suite du monde*. His work had included collaborations with most of the National Film Board directors working in the French Unit and some of those in the English-language Unit B, as well as such central figures in the cinéma vérité movement in France as Jean Rouch and Mario Ruspoli.

Pour la suite du monde
Of all the work of these two filmmakers, the one that has risen to the top of the film canons of both Canada and Quebec, selected for top ten

lists, garlanded with awards, used in university film courses, cited and written about by almost every critic and scholar of films made in Canada is *Pour la suite du monde*.[1] What is left to say about this film? The challenge is indeed formidable. In addition to the reviews that accompanied its release, detailed analyses have already appeared, most notably by Michel Brûlé, and in 1992 Perrault finally published his own heavily annotated transcript of the film, complete with both *Préambule* and *Postface*.[2] With Perrault's death (23 June 1999), his work now stands complete as his monument and legacy. In the one hundredth edition of the Québécois film journal *24 Images*, ten critics were each asked to name their 'landmark' Québécois film of all time. Yves Rousseau picked *Pour la suite du monde*.[3] And at least one obituary writer would select from Perrault's extensive oeuvre the same film as the turning point not only in his career but in the evolution of filmmaking in Quebec generally.[4] However, very little analysis of the film has ever appeared in English. The essay that follows attempts to position the film within the context of my own earlier work on Perrault in general and will consequently make little reference to this abundant French-language criticism.

My point of departure is a protracted analysis of the remarkable first four shots, which anticipate, even epitomize, the subsequent film. These shots are a written title, a segment of speech over a black screen, a silent moving image, and a short title sequence that combines written text, sound, and image together.

The written title (twenty-two seconds) summarizes the project of the film by way of exposition: 'Jusqu'en 1924, les habitants de l'Île aux Coudres tendaient une pêche aux marsouins sur le fleuve Saint-Laurent. À l'instigation des cinéastes, les gens de l'île ont "relevé la pêche" en 1962 pour en perpétuer la mémoire.'[5] The time, place, and content of the film's action are indicated clearly and precisely. But so too is the filmic process. The events are not spontaneous, but have been instigated by 'the filmmakers.' The film will be a documentary, then, but one in which the filmmakers participate as catalysts of a collective performance and are willing to acknowledge that participation.[6] And, we are told, the meaning of the film lies in the affirmation of a continuing link with the past. Such links are the stuff of identity formation, and the filmmakers are in solidarity with that effort.

Now, the screen goes black (for four seconds). We hear an elderly male voice. We at once reinterpret the black as darkness. From this darkness the voice is telling us that its owner is in no condition to dance but is ready to begin singing.[7] The accent is clearly regional, and instead of using the generic verb *chanter*, he says he is ready to *turluter*, to perform the nonverbal tongue-singing that accompanies old-time fiddle and step dance in Quebec. We are entering a traditional, popular, rural culture. The voice, as we shall later learn, is that of island farmer Louis Harvey (Grand-Louis), a 67-year-old village *raconteur*.

This snatch of conversation has been uprooted and recontextualized, thus acquiring another function. It draws our attention to self-conscious performance. The darkness takes on a theatrical connotation: the moment the lights go down, the moment of anticipation.

The third shot is even shorter (three seconds). Soundless, it shows an elderly man in glasses, lighting his pipe. It is the gesture of the pause, the relaxation, the prelude to reflection and recital. This, we shall later learn, is Alexis Tremblay, father of Léopold, who will lead the revival of the beluga trap. Alexis is the community patriarch, principal authority on the history of the island and its origins. His readiness to recite will be confirmed following Grand-Louis' *turlute* in the next shot, when we hear his voice introducing a reading of Jacques Cartier's *Le Brief Récit*. The act of striking the match coincides with the cut. Light seems to spring from the apparent darkness that preceded this shot.

Writing, speech, and image are thus presented sequentially as the preamble to the film. Much has been said of Perrault's status as a '*cinéaste de la parole*,'[8] and many have remarked on the significance of Brault's camerawork in finding images worthy of the spoken word in this film.[9] Written text is far less important in the film, but it does have a role to play, one that has perhaps not received enough attention. All three will eventually work together to affirm the genius of the community, its identity and its continuity. The sequence also recapitulates the trajectory of Pierre Perrault, the man of the written word, a trained lawyer, poet, and essayist, who discovered his avocation in radio documentary before gaining the sense that the recorded image was a necessary addition to complete the record of the performance.

The synthesis of the three modes of communication comes with the title sequence. The printed announcement of producers, title, and filmmakers is accompanied by Grand-Louis' *turlute* and overlays a remarkably evocative shot that carries much of the film within it.

This shot is composed of two architectural elements seen against a grey wooded hillside whose deciduous trees show no leaves. As later shots confirm, it is late fall. On the right is the upper half of the white steeple of Saint-Joseph-de-la-Rive on the Île aux Coudres,[10] while on the left we see what appears to be a watchtower from which a man's head is protruding, looking right and left. At one moment, a seagull flies across the picture. We are beside the river, and we shall soon realize that the watchtower is on the afterdeck of one of the island's schooners.

The shot works as a metonymy for the community's identity: its religion on the one hand and its economy on the other, the spiritual and the material. These two island institutions are governed by the cycles of the moon, the maritime economy by the tides,[11] and the Church's liturgical year by the moon cycles that govern its movable feasts, Lent and Easter,[12] whose ritual celebration is highlighted in the film. The moon is later thematized in the film.[13] A lively exchange among islanders about the moon's influence punctuates the auction sale for departed souls early on, and the moon returns visually and in conversation in the final sequence.

This title shot is a 'found image.' Its poetry springs from the capture of a 'Decisive Moment,' to use photographer Henri Cartier-Bresson's memorable phrase, the fortuitous discovery of an instant when visual elements combine in a recordable way connotatively or figuratively. At the same time, there are elements of performance that prefigure themes in the film: the improvised singing of Grand-Louis and the watchful head movements of the returning seafarer. Performing and watching characterize much of the film's action. Moreover, the highly connotative value of the image springs from the part played by the cinematographer (Brault), who finds and seizes this moment (using a telephoto lens that flattens perspective and gives watchtower and church equal space within the image), and the director/editor (Perrault), who has constructed this opening minute of the film and who has combined oral performance and a performative gaze within one shot. The filmmakers privilege the enactment of meaningful gestures caught in their familiar surroundings. And in relaying this enactment, they are themselves drawing attention to that performance by the evident choices of composition and lens.

Finally, it needs to be said how extraordinarily evocative these four opening moments are. If on the one hand they are expository (setting the scene) and self-referential (drawing attention to aspects of film language), on the other they can claim mythical power. The sequence moves from the word to darkness to the coming of light and finally to a finished universe with its signifiers of the world of work (the sweat of the brow) and the promise of spiritual redemption (the church). If

Perrault is conscious of creating a new cinema, he has certainly chosen a mighty metaphor to represent that creation.[14]

From this little *mise en abyme* of Perrault's poetic method, we may now embark upon an analysis of the whole film. We shall recall that Perrault, the poet, has always insisted that his films are the result of his immersion in lived reality and are not the product of a fictionalizing or dramatizing ambition that he controls. At the same time he presents here a tightly constructed sequence of moments that tell the story of the moontrap, punctuated with incidents in the life of the community that add valuable thematic material to that story.[15]

The Structure of the Film

The film's transcript uses titles that name the sequences of the film. They are as follows, in free translation. The italicized sequences do not advance the story of the revival of the beluga trap (these numbers will be used henceforth to refer to shots within the film):

1. *The Raising of the Buoys (the coming of winter)*
2. *Auction for Departed Souls and the Formidable Moon (community rituals and beliefs)*
3. The Three Negotiations (Léopold consults the community elders)
   3a. Léopold and his brother Marcelin agree to consult their father Alexis
   3b. First Negotiation: Alexis Tremblay in his kitchen
   3c. Léopold and his brother Marcel talk about the first negotiation
   3d. The Negotiation in the Hulk: Père Abel
   3e. The Negotiation in the Sawmill: Grand-Louis
4. The Two Churches (proclaiming the intent)
5. The Meeting of the 33 Shareholders, not to mention the onlookers (securing community support)
6. The Traces and the Ancestors' Genius (preparing the trap site – first spring low tide)
7. *Mid-Lent – masks (community rituals and beliefs)*
8. Planting the Poles (constructing the trap – second spring low tide)
9. *Blessing the Palms (community rituals and beliefs)*
10. Planting the Poles (continued) (constructing the trap – second spring low tide)
11. *The Rudders (of the toy boats) (children's lore and ritual)*
12. The Beluga's Instincts (completing the trap)

13. *Easter Water and the Mysteries of God (community rituals and beliefs)*
14. The 'Indian' patrol (monitoring the trap)
15. *Easter Water and the Traces that Remain (community rituals and beliefs)*
16. *The Rooster that Mates throughout the Year (agricultural analogy)*
17. *Grand-Louis Earthing in his Potatoes with his horse Carlot-Marabout (agricultural analogy)*
18. The Man Who Has a Habit of Dropping in While Passing (anticipating the catch)
19. The Forge and the Man in an Argumentative Mood (preparing tools for the catch)
20. The Blessing of the Trap (institutional endorsement of the trap)
21. *The Children among the Dandelions (children's lore and ritual)*
22. The 'Indian' patrol (monitoring the trap)
23. *The Souls in Purgatory among the Flowering Daisies (community rituals and beliefs)*
24. The Capture of the Beluga (success of the trap)
25. The Patriarchs Congratulate the Trapmaster and the Souls (aftermath)
26. An Invitation to the Best of All Journeys (preparations for sale and delivery)
27. The Best Journey of My Life (sale and delivery)
28. *The Bright Moon and the Supreme Being (community rituals and beliefs)*

The structure of the film is broadly chronological but alternates sequences that advance the central 'plotline' (the revival of the hunt) and sequences that show the community's rituals and beliefs being enacted physically or verbally in other ways, ones that often emphasize the cycle of the year. To be sure, each aspect (plotline or ritual/recital) is usually present in both kinds of sequence, but in any one sequence either the propulsion of the action predominates over the reflective, demonstrative mode or vice versa.[16]

Essentially this structure consists of two living cycles, those that shaped the experience of the community and filmmakers. Most evident is the cycle of the seasons of one year. The shifts in prevailing weather and natural growth are coupled with the liturgical round of the Catholic Church and produce the following sequence of events:

raising the buoys for winter – the deep snows of winter – spring tides of April – Mid-Lent Carnival – Palm Sunday and Easter – the farmer's ploughing and animal husbandry – the arrival of the *capelin* (smelts) – the flowering fields of high summer – the peat-harvesting – all culminating in the returning ice-floes and the onset of another winter.

The other cycle constitutes the first year of a revived beluga-trapping enterprise in the St Lawrence River off the Île aux Coudres:

first planning and publicity – the meeting that relaunches the co-operative – cutting the sapling poles (mentioned, not shown) – rediscovery of the old trap-line in the river – planting the 3,000 saplings for the new trap – surveillance of the trap – first catch – first sale and delivery of a live beluga to a New York aquarium.

The use of a cyclical structure recalls the Griersonian films of the interwar period in Britain that powerfully influenced the development of documentary at the NFB.[17] The British 'social' documentary, however, directed attention at economic activity in order to raise awareness of its place within a liberal democracy. Its exemplars stood as evidence that the 'system' could work effectively to provide and distribute goods and services. The cycles were naturally repeatable.

Perrault, on the other hand, has chosen a work cycle at the time of its first revival and transformation. The island folk use the revival as an attempt to reconstruct the sense of identity that can link generation to generation. But things have changed. The beluga no longer serves as the basis for their own local production of oil (as in the past) but is now a live resource wanted to build tourist attractions in distant cities.[18] So the reaffirmation of collective identity is occurring within a changing world that puts the whole enterprise at risk. The exemplar is rooted in a traditional society in decline. How can it serve as an example of identity formation within modern society, and how can the film make use of the new documentary aesthetic and technique to realize this end?

The Participatory Gaze
In an earlier article on the *cinéma direct* in Quebec, I suggested that, unlike their English-Canadian counterparts, the Québécois filmmakers of the late 50s and early 60s sought strategies to express their solidarity with a community engaged in expressing itself.[19] Prominent among

those strategies was the inclusion of shots showing members of the community engaged in watching its collective rituals. In this way the filmmakers aligned themselves with a watching community – as co-celebrants, one might say.

Examples of this abound in *Pour la suite du monde*: the public attending the auction sale for the souls (2), the islanders seated in their homes watching the mummers step dancing in the Mid-Lent Carnival sequence (7), the congregation in the Palm Sunday service (9). The practice of looking and watching is embedded within the construction and management of the beluga trap itself: the seeking out of the old pole stumps on the sandbar to find the trapline (6), the sightlines necessary to establish the right design of the trap (10), the silent patrols to see if a beluga has been caught (14 and 22), and the intercut shots of excited islanders spotting the first beluga out in the trap (24). There are also moments of contemplative watching, when the camera picks up one of the islanders standing alone looking out at a scene: Rémy Harvey looking out from his watchtower in the title sequence; Grand-Louis, carrying his pail of Easter water at dawn, stopping to look out over the river; and Père Abel, looking out over the river from his solitary station among the poles of the trap.

There are three modes of watching here: celebratory watching (of ritual enactments), instrumental watching (involving the trap), and contemplative watching (of nature). Each one of the three is reflected in Brault's participatory camerawork: getting up close to the step dancers in wide angle (2, 6, 7),[20] watching the trap construction by jumping into the water, and wading alongside the islanders or crouching down on the sandbars,[21] and long shots such as the slow pan over the immensity of the beluga trap from a distant shore (22).

Performance and Solidarity

The renewal of a sense of collective identity through ritual entails performance. The various forms of oral performance among the inhabitants of Île aux Coudres were what attracted the poet Perrault in the first place. These performances, which are the everyday currency of an oral culture, became Perrault's 'found poetry' for which he first used a tape recorder to bring them to a wider Québécois audience on the radio.[22] What Perrault sought from his cinematographer Brault was the equivalent in visual moments: found poetry in gesture, movement, and artefact. Unlike the empirical documentary, in which the presence of the camera is expected to have no influence on the action, the Québécois

Pour la suite du monde (1963), directed by Pierre Perrault and Michel Brault. Courtesy of the National Film Board of Canada.

cinéma direct magnifies performance by its presence, as does the presence of watchers generally. Grand-Louis is the arch-performer. The sequence in which Léopold consults Grand-Louis at the sawmill (3e) cannot disguise Grand-Louis' propensity for 'hamming it up.' Performing for the camera he may be, but we have already witnessed his animated gestures in the debate over the moon at the auction sale (2) and will later see his exaggerated gestures and facial expressions with the children in his farmyard (15) or in the daisy field with Edgar Bouchard (23). It is clearly sufficient for Grand-Louis to have an audience to put on a performance. He is energized by watchers, be they community members or a camera crew.

The sense of performance and the incorporation of the filmmakers into the watching community are emphasized when islanders acknowledge the presence of the watching camera. In one scene documented by Gilles Marsolais, Léopold Tremblay gestures to Père Thomas to sit in the boat so that the camera can have an unobstructed view of Alexis, who is talking (22).[23] When Alexis later joins Père Abel to congratulate him on the success of the trap (25), he assumes a position that is designed to offer the clearest view for the camera. Such evidence of almost theatrical blocking is reinforced by evidence of other posed moments: Alexis perched on his stool in the forge, leafing through Cartier's book (19), and similarly posed in the peat bog sequence (26), not to mention the contemplative watching shots of Grand-Louis and Père Abel mentioned above. Certain entrances have a staged quality, most particularly the first appearances of Alexis and Marie Tremblay, who each make separate entrances into their living room down the stairs (3b). Léopold's dramatic arrivals by truck in two scenes are also clearly staged (18, 24, 25), as is his coming across Alexis in the peat bog (26). These moments are interspersed with set pieces that are performed specifically for an audience that the camera observes and joins: the church services, the dances, Alexis' readings of Cartier (1), and Léopold's address to the meeting (5).

There are moments too when the islanders directly acknowledge the presence of the filmmakers themselves. After reacting to the trap project when it is first broached by Léopold (3b), Alexis ends his remarks by looking quickly into the camera and saying: 'C'est tout!'[24] Grand-Louis' evening of *turlute* and step dancing during the Mid-Lent Carnival (7) ends as he says forlornly: 'Chus-t-au coton, Perrault! Chus-t-au coton!'[25] At the moment of the first capture of the beluga (24), Léopold forgets himself and excitedly cries out: 'On n'a pas manqué notre coup, Pierre!'[26] The film's transcript reveals that on one occasion the voice we hear proclaiming the genius of the islanders (6) is that of Marcel Carrière, the sound engineer.[27] Perrault does not suppress these moments, preferring to maintain such evidence of his integration into the action.

Once more it is worth emphasizing that this sense of self-conscious enactment, performance, staging, and participation is not a challenge to the tenets of the *cinéma direct*. Such behaviour is the norm within community rituals, and the opening up of the community to its visitors in this way softens the sense of intrusion and guarantees its authenticity.

Until now, we have discussed the profilmic events and their recording on camera. The filmic process, which Perrault called a reading of the real, performs its own mysterious wonders. The selection and sequencing of shots reveal the filmmakers' desire to reproduce the rhetorical exploits and devices that characterize the performances of the islanders. Their complicity in modes of watching (see above) is only a part of that effort to bind themselves to their subjects by analogy. The convoluted gestures of Grand-Louis, the expansive gestures of Père

Abel, find their echo in the acrobatics of Brault, whose efforts to capture the intimate are legendary. The handheld Arriflex is tilted in extreme low angle in scenes on the sandbar or on the trip to New York, once even whipped through a daisy field in a fast forward tracking shot just inches above the ground (23). The visual equivalent for the vivid story-telling of Grand-Louis, always alert to the revealing small element, can be found in Brault's capture of background detail: the migrating geese found by the camera during the raising of the buoys as another symbol of the changing season (1); the 'milkmaid' caught in the background of Grand-Louis' ploughing shot as he obliviously sings his gallant love song to himself (as though it is for her he sings); the notice board tucked in behind the mummers (7) publicizing a bowling alley and restaurant down the road (a reminder that the self-made world of the mummers is threatened by more commercial fare).

The film is most celebrated for the many dreamlike shots of the sapling poles, with the rippling reflections and the silent movements of the boatmen. In scenes with children, Brault exhibits the playfulness that characterized much of his work with the French Unit directors in Montreal. The sequence in which Léopold shows the youngsters how to make little sailboats from shingles (11) begins in the empty stock-room as a large tire rolls silently and incongruously across the floor and develops into a scene of children's play as Brault himself moves with the camera around the boy rotating inside another tire. Another sequence, this one indicating the passing of the seasons, shows a group of children blowing dandelion seeds around each other (21) as Brault gets down to their height and films them against the light to produce the effect of a sparkling snowstorm.

The montage devices also show a similarly playful quality, emphasizing the organizing presence of the filmmaker while allowing poetic resonances to occur. Sound–image links and visually matched cuts are not infrequent, especially between sequences. Grand-Louis' reference to *la porte des deux églises* links to the mass where the priest is announcing the forthcoming beluga hunt (3e–4). The priest's exhortation to moderation in the Mid-Lent Carnival, especially with the young women, links to an outdoor shot of a teenage girl in a swing bridging to the sequence where the town crier announces the shareholders' meeting (4).

Visual matches include the use of Grand-Louis in his brimmed hat, smoking, as the focal point shared between the last shot of the town crier's sequence and the first of the shareholders' meeting (4–5) and

even more noticeably the movement of the step-dancing Noëlla jumping off the upturned boat on the sandbar, which links to the young girl
jumping from a tree into the dandelion meadow (20–1). More powerful
are the thematic, visual matches as when the scene of a boat by the trap
links to a shot of youngsters playing with toy boats and bridges to the
church behind to ease the transition to the Palm Sunday service inside
(8–9). The reverse effect occurs at the end of the second Easter-water
sequence, when a sequence of young boys playing with toy boats yields
a cut from a model schooner on a rivulet to a full-sized schooner
emerging from behind a harbour wall (end of 15). As Perrault's transcript poetically remarks: 'La mer des hommes reproduit la mare des
enfants.'[28]

Transitions are also eased by intercutting and overlapping sound and
music on several occasions in the film, but more noticeable is the use of
asynchronous sound–image editing. Perrault's *cinéma direct* thus asserts itself most clearly against the conventional use of authoritative
voice-over to interpret the image. The spoken segments include the
mythes fondateurs and the 'found poems' that Perrault's transcript de-
marcates from transactional speech by using short-lined verses centred
horizontally and printed in italics.[29] Over the raising of the buoys (1),
Alexis reads the text from Cartier's *Brief Récit* that describes the explor-
er's discovery and naming of Île aux Coudres. Alexis' reading of Cartier's
awestruck description of the first sightings of beluga whales runs over
the images of the first of them entering the new trap (24).

Over the first efforts to find the old trapline, Alexis' own words are
heard from his kitchen describing the Native origins of the trap and
how the old lines were found (6). The poles are planted over Alexis'
description of the technique (8), and the trap is finished as Alexis
describes the behaviour of the beluga and the workings of the trap (12).
Skipper Joachim Harvey tells a story of his boyhood experiences of the
carnival over the images of the mummers (7). Grand-Louis' account of
the tradition of collecting water from a running stream before Easter
dawn accompanies images of his early morning trip to do so (13).
Whenever a description or explanation is needed, Perrault uses the
voice of one of the island personalities, who performs the necessary
recital. By mingling the improvised descriptions of his storytellers with
the measured tones of Alexis reading the great *mythe fondateur* of the
island, Perrault makes the junction with a community identity that
gains its strength and authority from its power to endure.

There may be no one form of the *mythe fondateur* that commands consensus. Whether the hunt originated with the Native peoples before Cartier or with the French who brought the tradition with them is hotly disputed twice in the film (6 and 19), a classic debate about exogenous or indigenous cultural origins. In Perrault's film, the point is not to settle that question but to demonstrate how closely tied up with the sense of a collective past is the beluga trap. This realization holds the key to the transition from particular to general.

To endure, a collective identity requires belief in a heritage passed from generation to generation, a heritage played out in ritualistic behaviours, a heritage surviving through the tales that commemorate it and the efforts made to reenact it. The close ties of these behaviours with religious observance and belief are underscored time and again in the film, most noticeably through the scriptural reverence with which Alexis treats Cartier's written account. The animistic association of the souls and the moon with the outcome of unpredictable events (such as the beluga hunt) is also contested, but in ways that involve community members in visions of their collective future.

In the end, the question that arises is whether the community can survive in recognizable form the changes that threaten its identity. Perrault's film is about this rather than a pleasant account of a quaint tradition that we can enjoy as tourists. The answer proposed by Perrault's film is that identity can be reaffirmed by reviving and adapting the skills, knowledge, and culture of community ancestors. This is the way to retain a shining distinctness, the sense of belonging to an unbroken line that will form the defence against assimilation into a dominant culture at the expense of one's own. That defence is not secure, as the debates within the film make clear. But the loss of connection with a sense of a shared past, it is suggested, leads to a loss of distinct identity. And that distinct identity is the key to the creation and maintenance of a national spirit every bit as much as of a community spirit.

How does the *cinéma direct* help? The answer is that it provides the method by which the encounter between one culture and another can be resolved. A modern urban culture based on recorded communication (whether in print or on film) is potentially at odds with a traditional rural culture based on oral communication and the constant reenactment of rituals of identity formation. Indeed, I have argued elsewhere that the recording and projection of these performances through the medium of film constitutes a radical break with the spontaneous, variable expressions experienced in the community itself. The recording of such celebrations of identity is a way for the modern, urban society of Quebec to find its connection with its rural past, not through the rejection and denial of change but through the accommodation of ancient ways to modern contexts. With *Pour la suite du monde*, Perrault has recapitulated the Romantic dream of modelling the general in the particular, of blurring the distinction between subject and object, of finding community through common celebration. For this to occur, according to Perrault, the film can only be considered to come alive again through the collective of its audience. 'Le vrai film est dans la salle,' he would say.

One recalls Victor Hugo's preface to *Les Contemplations*:

Ma vie est la vôtre, votre vie est la mienne, vous vivez ce que je vis; la destinée est une. Prenez donc ce miroir, et regardez-vous-y. On se plaint quelquefois des écrivains qui disent moi. Parlez-nous de nous, leur crie-t-on. Hélas! Quand je vous parle de moi, je vous parle de vous. Comment ne le sentez-vous pas? Ah! Insensé, qui crois que je ne suis pas toi![30]

It is enough to replace the first person of the Romantic poet with the experience that united filmmakers and community in *Pour la suite du monde* to understand how rural Quebec was expected to speak to urban Quebec. And the *cinéma direct* furnished the tools to carry out the project.

Notes

1 Canadian Film of the Year (1964) and Canada's first official entry in the Cannes Film Festival in 1963. First prizes at festivals at Evreux (1963), Bilbao (1963), and Columbus, Ohio (1966), and a diploma of merit in Melbourne (1966). Information from Abel et al., eds., *Le Cinéma québécois à l'heure internationale*, 313, and Larouche, ed., *L'Aventure du cinéma québécois en France*, 239.

2 Brûlé, *Pierre Perrault ou un cinéma national*, 17–42; Perrault, *Pour la suite du monde*, hereafter shortened to *Suite*.

3 Rousseau, 'Contre la fuite du monde,' 31.

4 Marie-Claude Petit, quoted in Côté, *Québec 2000*, 245.

5 'Until 1924, the people of the Île aux Coudres used to set a trap for beluga whales on the River Saint Lawrence. Prompted by the filmmakers, the islanders revived the trap in 1962 in order to keep its memory alive.' Text is quoted from a video copy of the French version of the film released by

the NFB in 1999. This version periodically uses French subtitles. These titles are not quoted since they are edited transcriptions of a fuller spoken text. The authority for the spoken text is Perrault, *Suite*. The translations are those of this author.

6 Ironically, insofar as Perrault's original project for the film had stated: 'Ce film ne sera pas un documentaire en ce sens que nous nous proposons de provoquer fictivement la reprise des pêches aux marsouins' [This film will not be a documentary inasmuch as we are proposing to revive the beluga trap by provoking it artificially]. *Suite*, 13. Needless to say, Perrault consistently rejected this account after making the film.

7 'Ben, j'ai dit: comme ça ... moé, je pourrai pas danser. Me v'la encore ammanchée pour turluter.' *Suite*, 19.

8 This is indeed the title of a book of transcribed conversations between Paul Warren and Perrault, published by L'Hexagone in 1996. Perrault's own words are: 'Si je suis cinéaste, je suis cinéaste de la parole vécue.' Perrault, *Cinéaste de la parole*, 59.

9 Not least of whom was Perrault himself in a postface to the film transcript called 'L'Image du verbe.' *Suite*, 286–9.

10 We know this from the transcript, not from our viewing of the film. *Suite*, 20.

11 The extra-low spring tides will be particularly important for the discovery of the old trapline and the planting of the new poles for the beluga trap.

12 Easter falls on the Sunday following the first full moon after the vernal equinox.

13 We should not forget that the title of the first English voice-over version of the film was *Moontrap*. In 1999, the NFB finally replaced this older abbreviated and reedited version with a subtitled video edition with the less memorable title, *Of Whales, the Moon and Men*.

14 *Suite*, 277, 285–6.

15 It is worth recalling Perrault's book of found poetry: *Discours sur la condition sauvage et québécoise*. It is composed of fragments of the spoken word that Perrault collected over the years of making radio broadcasts and films until 1977. These are accompanied by stills taken from his films or during their production. Perrault's contribution lies in the work of selection and sequencing, and indeed the layout of the words upon the page. These constitute the part played by the poet's consciousness. This speech is found, privileged, and organized by another, an 'other,' whose voice is not present in the transcribed text or among the faces shown in the selected photographs. But this 'other' is present nevertheless as an assembling consciousness.

16 In Roland Barthes' taxonomy, we might say that the film alternately privileges the proairetic and hermeneutic codes; see Barthes, *S/Z*.

17 For example, *Drifters* (John Grierson, 1929) and *Night Mail* (Harry Watt and Basil Wright, 1936). This is referred to in Clandfield, *Canadian Film*, 19–21.

18 A similar link from rural Quebec to New York occurs in Arthur Lamothe's *Bûcherons de la Manouane* (1962), as the voice-over tells us how many logs are needed from this remote logging operation to publish an edition of the *New York Times*; see Peter Harcourt's essay in this volume.

19 Clandfield, 'From the Picturesque to the Familiar,' especially 121–2.

20 For Brault's notion of the wide-angle style and its application to *cinéma direct* techniques, see Clandfield, 'From the Picturesque to the Familiar,' 118. Perrault himself describes *Les Raquetteurs* as 'the film that dances along with the dancer ... walks along with the walker ... runs along with the runner ... but does not speak with the speaker.' *Suite*, 279.

21 See production stills in *Suite*, 278 and 288.

22 See Clandfield, 'Ritual and Recital,' especially 143–4.

23 Marsolais, *L'Aventure du cinéma direct revisitée*, 107. Marsolais incorrectly identifies Thomas as Abel Harvey (Père Abel).

24 'That's all!!' *Suite*, 55.

25 'I'm bushed, Perrault! I'm bushed!' *Suite*, 126.

26 'We didn't miss out, Pierre!' *Suite*, 225.

27 *Suite*, 103.

28 'The grown-ups' river reproduces the children's rivulet.' *Suite*, 171. These two matched cuts carry the flavour of the ending stanzas of Rimbaud's *Bateau ivre* (*Drunken Boat*), in which a similar juxtaposition occurs.

29 I discuss this hierarchization of speech more fully in 'Ritual and Recital.'

30 'My life is your life, your life is mine, you live what I live; our destiny is one. Grasp this mirror then and gaze upon yourself. People sometimes complain about writers who say "I." Tell us about ourselves, they cry. Alas! When I speak to you of myself, I am speaking to you of yourselves. How can you not feel that? Ah, how foolish to think that I am not you!' Hugo, *Les Contemplations*, 6.

Dark Satanic Mills: Denys Arcand's
On est au coton

JIM LEACH

The Film Board makes thousands of films to say that all goes well in Canada, that the western wheat fields are very beautiful, that Glenn Gould plays the piano well and that Paul Anka is an extraordinary star. So I think it is just normal that there should now and then be a film which says that everything is rotten and that we live in a country that is corrupt from top to bottom.

Denys Arcand[1]

One of the most awkward questions raised by the documentary traditions associated with the National Film Board and its founder John Grierson is how to tell the difference between public service and public relations. Although Grierson saw documentary as a force for social change, the NFB has constantly had to find ways to make innovative and challenging documentaries without alienating the government bodies on whom it depends for its funding. Most of the films produced at the NFB are functional works of information often commissioned by government departments and used in educational contexts. In this way, the NFB provides a service, but its reputation depends on a smaller number of films that engage with aspects of contemporary reality and often expose the need for social change.

Inevitably, there are times when this tension within the NFB runs up against social or political circumstances that reveal the fragile basis of its policies and practices. One such time was October 1970, when the federal government imposed the War Measures Act in response to the kidnapping of two hostages by the Front de Libération du Québec (FLQ). While the police raided houses and imprisoned many citizens, the administration at NFB headquarters in Montreal was trying to decide what to do with an almost three-hour-long documentary on the textile industry.

In the circumstances, it was not surprising that many people saw the decision to ban Denys Arcand's *On est au coton* (1970) as an act of censorship directed against the Quebec separatist movement, and supporters of that movement certainly regarded it in this way. Illicit video copies were circulated and widely screened, with the result that, according to a 'conservative estimate,' at least 20,000 spectators saw the film before the NFB lifted the ban in 1976.[2] However, the initial pressure to ban the film was not directly related to the political situation in Quebec but came from the Canadian Textile Institute, which objected to its unflattering depiction of the industry. The NFB came under attack for using public money to support separatist or Marxist propaganda or both.

On est au coton has been dismissed as 'a painfully long, cinematically clumsy piece,' but it has also been praised as 'one of Quebec's greatest political films.'[3] In this essay, I will explore the challenge that the film poses to the forms of documentary as well as to the prevailing modes of political and cultural analysis. It is a frankly 'negative' film, as signified by its title, a pun on a colloquial phrase (meaning 'we're fed up' or 'we're in a mess') that conveys the sense of frustration felt not just by the workers depicted in the film but also by the filmmakers, who were appalled by what they discovered in making it.[4]

The film established Arcand's reputation for cultural pessimism, and I will argue that it is best seen as an extension and modification of the Frankfurt School analysis of 'mass culture.' It raises major questions of cinematic and cultural theory and practice that are rooted in its historical context but have certainly not lost their relevance or their urgency in the intervening years.

Two Paradoxes

In his introduction to a dossier on Arcand published in 1971, Réal La Rochelle suggested that two paradoxical contexts had to be taken into account in dealing with his films. The first of these was the role of the NFB as 'producer and castrator,' a reference, of course, to the banning of *On est au coton* but also to the uncertain fate of Arcand's second feature-length documentary, eventually released as *Québec: Duplessis et après ...* (1972).[5] Yet, as Arcand acknowledged, these films could not have been made without the NFB's support. He pointed out that *On est au coton* was a 'colossal enterprise,' at least in the context of Canadian cinema, employing six men for two years and costing about $100,000: 'That was possible only at the NFB. That is the dilemma.'[6]

Arcand had joined the NFB in 1963 and soon expressed his discontent with the working conditions there, especially in the so-called 'French Unit.' In April 1964 he joined with several of his more experienced colleagues, who contributed essays critical of the NFB to the left-wing journal *Parti pris*. In his essay, Arcand referred to the 'candid eye' films of the French Unit that had to reflect the opinion of the Canadian government on whatever topic they dealt with.[7] His use of a term usually applied to the films of Unit B, from which *The Candid Eye* television series originated, implied that the political constraints also involved a demand for films using the supposedly observational and impersonal approach to documentary form associated with the English-Canadian filmmakers at the NFB.[8]

As a recent history graduate, Arcand had been hired by the NFB to do historical research but was soon pressed into service as a director. He made several short documentaries, mainly on historical topics, that failed to satisfy him but also frequently dissatisfied the government departments that had commissioned them. After leaving the Board for a while, he submitted a proposal for a film that eventually became *On est au coton*, his 'first personal film.'[9] It was this film, then, that fully brought into play the second of La Rochelle's paradoxes: 'the personality of Arcand the filmmaker, simultaneously objective and subjective in his vision of the socio-political history of Québec.'[10]

Although the opening credits list the filmmakers involved in alphabetical order, suggesting that its production was a group effort, Arcand initiated the project, and the film clearly reflects his training as a historian. It is also the first full expression of the 'pessimism' that became a consistent feature in all his major films and has led to attacks on his work from conservative, liberal, and left-wing critics. Often interpreted as cynicism, this quality is better seen as a resistance to what theorists of the Frankfurt School called the 'affirmative' character of mass culture.[11]

This view was most fully developed in the work of Theodor Adorno, who, like most of his colleagues, left Germany for the United States before the Second World War. His critical perspective on the cultural conditions he encountered in North America had a dual focus. On the one hand, there was a 'culture industry' producing escapist fantasies that distracted attention from social contradictions and injustices; on the other hand, a 'positivist' science sought to explain reality on the basis of empirical facts uncontaminated by subjective bias or theoretical speculation. In the cinematic context, the result was an insistence on the separation of entertainment and documentary films, the former devoted to fantasy and illusion, the latter to objective reports on actuality. According to Adorno, both approaches work against a critical perspective and encourage a conformist acceptance of the way things are.[12]

When most of the Frankfurt theorists returned to Germany after the war, Herbert Marcuse stayed in the United States, and his ideas had a major impact on the new social movements that emerged in the 1960s. His highly critical account of 'advanced industrial society' in *One-Dimensional Man*, first published in 1964, depicted a 'one-dimensional universe in which man is trained ... to translate the negative into the positive so that he can continue to function, reduced but fit and reasonably well.'[13] As we shall see, *On est au coton* includes quotations from this book, and the film reverses the approach that Marcuse attributes to mass culture. Arcand explained: 'We are saying, exaggerating our pessimism a little: nothing is going to happen, don't expect anything.'[14] The tactics of negation and exaggeration discourage ready-made responses that provide comfort by ignoring the full complexity of the situation.

The Frankfurt School critique also contributes to the blurring of the distinction between objective and subjective vision that La Rochelle attributes to Arcand's personality, unsettling traditional notions of documentary form and political argument. While the NFB could justify banning the film by consulting 'impartial experts' who concluded that it was both inaccurate and politically motivated, *On est au coton* called into question the positivist assumptions that supported the NFB's standards of 'impartiality.'[15] The result was a film that clearly presented itself as a political intervention but resisted the political categories into which critics tried to place it. From La Rochelle's perspective in 1971, the effect was unfortunate because the film's ambiguity made it unsuitable for use as 'a tool for political action.'[16]

An Intellectual Experiment

By the 1990s, La Rochelle had changed his mind about *On est au coton*. In an essay on the use of sound in Arcand's films, he argues that both the NFB and the Left had misinterpreted the film by viewing it as political propaganda, whether successful or otherwise. Instead, La Rochelle now found the film 'much more compelling as a lyrical poem than as a documentary or objective report,' and supports his argument by quoting from an interview in which Arcand insists that the film is 'the subjective vision of my own discovery of the world of labour.' Although La Rochelle denies that the film is 'a working-class documentary/manifesto akin to Vertov's *Kino-Eye*,' his claim that it is 'an industrial symphony' evokes Dziga Vertov's innovative use of sound in *Enthusiasm* (1930), also known as *The Symphony of the Don Basin*.[17]

As in Vertov's film, the formal play with 'audiovisual counterpoint' in *On est au coton* may seem to distract attention from its social and political concerns, but the full meaning depends on the uneasy interaction of its lyrical and didactic impulses. Sequences in which the camera tracks through the textile mills, accompanied by the deafening noise of the machines, punctuate interview sequences in which workers discuss their plight and historical accounts of earlier attempts by workers to assert their rights.[18]

The filmmakers decided to focus on two basic questions: 'what could be done with a dying industry' and how people could accept such 'painful' working conditions.[19] *On est au coton* thus explores the problem of reconciling the lyrical with the didactic, the subjective with the objective, while investigating the uncomfortable tension between exposing the dreadful working conditions in the industry and having empathy with the workers' fears of losing their jobs.

This dual focus is quickly established at the beginning of the film. The sense of personal intervention and discovery by the filmmakers emerges in the shots that precede and follow the credits. A politician responds rather uneasily to the (off-screen) presence of an NFB film crew in his office, and then a door opens through which the filmmakers (and we) enter a mill. Arcand then intercuts between shots of workers operating machines and an interview with the politician, now identified as the deputy mayor of Coaticook, who explains that the civic authorities could do nothing to prevent the closure of the mill because the company claimed it was losing money. The camera tracks past rows of machines, whose noise dominates the soundtrack, until there is a sudden cut to the same space, empty and silent, in what amounts to a flashforward showing that the mill has indeed been closed.

The issues surrounding the closure of this particular mill function as a springboard from which the film takes off to incorporate a wide range of materials that extend its analysis to the broader industrial and political contexts. As the film develops, it continues to juxtapose shots filmed in different places and at different times. It shows other factories with

On est au coton (1970), directed by Denys Arcand. Courtesy of the National Film Board of Canada.

similar problems, observes meetings of workers and owners, and includes interviews with individual workers. A historical context is provided by interviews with Madeleine Parent, a former activist, who describes earlier strikes and protests, illustrated by photographs and documents. The original version also included interviews with Edward King, the president of Dominion Textiles, the company that owned many of the mills, including the one in Coaticook. However, Arcand was forced to remove all the material dealing with King, including a section that compared the lives of the anglophone executive and one of his francophone workers. In protest, Arcand inserted two passages in which the screen remains black while he explains what has been omitted.

For some critics, this layered structure was determined by a political argument imposed on the material and designed to manipulate the spectator into accepting its terms. D.B. Jones likened *On est au coton*, and the other censored French-language films, to the NFB's wartime documentaries because they 'avoided a true "creative" struggle with "actuality,"' starting from 'a received premise' and collecting material 'to tack on to an unoriginal and rather hackneyed message.'[20] Arcand himself rejects this view of the film and insists that he 'started with an attitude that was neither politically militant nor determined in advance' and that the production process was an 'intellectual experiment,' in which the necessary research was done while shooting and which changed directions on several occasions. The experience convinced him of the need to be 'open to the unexpected and to the richness of the real.'[21]

The experiment began with an initial hypothesis that proved to be false. Having never been in a factory before making the film, Arcand expected to find workers actively opposed to the system that oppressed them but was surprised to find little evidence of rebellion. As a result, the film developed its 'negative' dimension, and *On est au coton* became 'a film on resignation.'[22] This discovery led to the filming of a long interview with Carmen Bertrand, a young worker whose quiet desperation contributes to what La Rochelle calls the 'lyrico-tragical flow' of the last part of the film.[23] A character based on this woman appears in *Gina* (1975), Arcand's fiction film about a stripper working in the Eastern Townships at the same time that a film crew is preparing a documentary on the textile industry. In both films, the female worker is simultaneously a 'cultural dope,' illustrating the power of the dominant ideology, and a quietly dignified figure

Although La Rochelle initially felt that the 'tragic' tonality detracted from the film's political argument, he later stressed the way in which Arcand orchestrates the noise of the machines. This is not just a formal exercise. As La Rochelle points out, the 'timbres and rhythms [of the machines] are resonant with ideological and political overtones.'[24] The sequences showing the machines have a kind of nightmare beauty and function simultaneously as affect and as evidence. In the opening sequence, the sudden cut from the noise of the machines to the silence of the abandoned mill heightens awareness of the deafening noise, as does a later sequence in which the soundtrack cuts out completely several times. When a retired worker describes the symptoms of the lung disease he contracted on the job, the impact of his words is reinforced by the coughing fits that punctuate them and by insert shots of small pieces of fibre that have settled on the machines.

The combination of argument, affectivity, and evidence in *On est au coton* proved unsettling for some of its critics, and even the filmmakers were not in complete agreement about the final effects of the film. According to Gérard Godin, who collaborated with Arcand on the film and would later become well known as a Parti Québécois politician, its primary purpose was didactic and educational, to teach people 'how they are exploited, by whom, and under what conditions.' On the other hand, Arcand defended his refusal to adopt a didactic mode of address as a refusal to imply that the filmmakers knew more than the people they were addressing. He acknowledged that he did not know more than the workers and felt that all he could provide, as a filmmaker, was a more detached perspective on their situation.[25]

The limitations of a didactic approach are demonstrated in the film itself in a sequence in which Claude Lemelin, an economist, explains the structure of a multinational corporation to Bertrand Saint-Onge, a worker whose curiosity has been sparked by his participation in the film. Lemelin lectures in a classroom with the aid of a large chart and, although he demonstrates that Saint-Onge is a small cog in a vast corporate machine, the academic explanation seems very remote from the worker's personal experience.

Unlike the NFB's wartime documentaries, to which Jones compared *On est au coton*, there is no voice-of-God commentator to provide the information necessary for the argument, and this is virtually the only occasion on which Arcand resorts to an expert witness to serve this purpose. The elimination or downplaying of the commentator had been a common feature of NFB documentaries since the work of Unit B in the 1950s and the early films of the 'French Unit.' There is still considerable debate about the purposes and effects of the new forms of 'direct cinema' but, from their apparently very different perspectives, both Godin and Sidney Newman, the NFB commissioner, would have been happier if there had been a commentary in *On est au coton*.

For Godin, the film's didactic effect was lessened because it does not provide sufficient explanations for the situations it depicts, and he suggested that there should have been 'a narrator who could have explained the situation.'[26] Newman also regretted that 'too many things have not been explained, or badly explained in the film.' In defending his decision to ban the film, Newman pointed out that Arcand and the

NFB told the textile industry that they were making 'an impartial film' and added that 'our reputation is based on our objectivity.'[27]

To protect this reputation, Newman called in 'impartial experts,' who reported that the film did not accurately represent 'the reality of the textile industry': a worker was apparently wrong when he asserted that Canadian workers were paid less than their U.S. counterparts; Lemelin's analysis of the role of international conglomerates did not acknowledge that 70 percent of the industry was Canadian-owned; one of the mills depicted had since installed 'silent' Japanese machines.[28] A voice-of-God commentator could have made things easier, either by drawing explicit political conclusions (as Godin wished) or by correcting the errors made by the film's informants and acknowledging the changes that had occurred since the filming. By not taking this option, Arcand challenged the distinction between subjective experience and objective analysis and acknowledged the difficulty of doing justice to the personal experience of the workers while drawing attention to the ideological context in which this experience is embedded.

The Challenge of Change

Arcand's project was approved by the NFB in 1969, when Jacques Godbout, a well-known novelist and filmmaker, was director of French Production. At that stage, 'it was called *Les informateurs*, a three-part story of technocrats who are the backbone of the modern state.'[29] The focus on the textile industry came about because Arcand wanted to test the idea that technology could solve social problems by confronting some technical experts with a particularly intractable problem. As Arcand almost certainly anticipated, it soon became clear that the methods of the technocrats could not provide a solution, and the filmmakers turned their attention to the plight of the textile workers.

Hugo McPherson, the NFB commissioner at the time, had just introduced an ambitious new program called Challenge for Change. Although the NFB had always identified itself as a force for social progress, the political movements of the 1960s questioned traditional forms of authority and viewed state-funded institutions like the NFB with suspicion. In response to these pressures, the NFB's new program was designed to put 'the means of communications into the hands of the people' and to help 'to prepare Canadians for social change.'[30] It began in 1967 but only received official government support in 1969, at which time it was expanded to include a French-language counterpart under the title 'Nouvelle société.'

In Quebec the call for social change was especially associated with the movement known as the Quiet Revolution. After years of government by the conservative Union Nationale, led by Maurice Duplessis and closely allied to the Catholic Church, Quebec belatedly became a modern industrial society in which technology was the agent for social change. Although the ideas that spurred these new developments had been gaining momentum since the Second World War, the election of the Liberal government of Jean Lesage in 1960 is usually seen as the beginning of a period of rapid social and cultural change. The 'liberal' ideas that came to the fore during this period included a confidence that technological progress would improve social conditions, and this optimism also provided the impetus for the Liberal triumph, under the leadership of Pierre Trudeau, in the 1968 federal election.

As a historian, Arcand thought that the Quiet Revolution was 'a relatively superficial phenomenon,' as did the group with which he was associated at *Parti pris*, a magazine founded in 1963 to counter the views developed by Trudeau and others in *Cité libre*.[31] The *Parti pris* writers insisted that without political change, technology would serve the interests of those in power, and they argued that social change could occur in Quebec only through a political movement that would overthrow the capitalist system and demand independence from Canada. By the time he finished *On est au coton*, Arcand no longer shared the political confidence associated with these demands, but the film still refuses to separate technology from the ideological frameworks that govern its use.

On est au coton was not part of the Challenge for Change program, and Arcand insisted that his film was 'light years away' from the philosophy behind the NFB's new initiative.[32] On the other hand, Marc Beaudet, the film's producer, argued against the ban by pointing out that *On est au coton* was 'doing precisely what Challenge for Change/ Société nouvelle was trying to do.' He thought that the decision to suppress it only confirmed an apparent double standard that allowed English Canadians to vent frustration but 'when French Canadians did the same, it seemed that the state was in jeopardy.'[33]

By the time the film was completed in 1970, Godbout had been replaced. After McPherson demanded some changes, Newman took over as commissioner and eventually decided to ban the film. The NFB's legal experts advised him that 'the film purported to incite violence and sedition charges were possible' and, as we have seen, the suppression of the film enabled separatists to claim it for their cause.[34]

Since the workers are all francophones (although there are references to immigrants who will work for less money) and most of the mill owners are English-speaking, the film does suggest that the workers are doubly victimized because of their class and their language.

However, it was the film's class politics that troubled the Canadian Textile Institute. The mill owners, who had cooperated with the production, no doubt assumed that an NFB documentary would project a positive image of the industry, and, as Arcand amusingly suggests in his fictional reconstruction of the events in *Gina*, the filmmakers encouraged them in this assumption. According to Arcand, the owners felt the finished film depicted 'a class struggle between Anglo-Saxon capitalist exploiters and exploited workers,' and some critics have agreed that it is 'an openly Marxist film.'[35]

Yet, just as Arcand claims that he does not know if he is 'for or against the independence of Quebec,' he also insists that he has never made a film to defend a cause. He suggests that the mill owners ignored the film's critical perspective on the unions, whose position differs little from that of the owners (a view expressed by Lemelin in the film).[36] Newman inadvertently corroborated Arcand's point when he justified his actions by pointing out that even the unions had complained about the film.[37] Apparently, this did not constitute evidence of impartiality.

Although the Challenge for Change program broke with many of the conventions of Griersonian documentary practice, it was essentially an extension of his goal of promoting a unified society by developing an informed public who would elect governments responsive to their needs. The key political task was to persuade people to accept the necessary technological changes as determined by the dispassionate advice of trained professionals. Objectivity was basic to the documentary aesthetic and to good government.

It was thus important that the NFB's decision to ban *On est au coton* not be seen as politically motivated. While Trudeau privately expressed his approval, the government officially respected the NFB's independence. According to Gary Evans, Newman briefed Gérard Pelletier on what was happening, but the secretary of state insisted that public institutions should be independent so that 'the specialists who direct them may base their actions on professional rather than political criteria.'[38]

It is hardly surprising that *On est au coton* fell victim to this kind of thinking since, according to Arcand's own assessment, it was his main target in making the film. He wanted to expose the effects of 'substituting the techniques of administration and planning for a dynamic and global vision of society.'[39] Initiatives like Challenge for Change sought to manage change by presenting it as a technical and administrative challenge rather than a political issue, but it was easier to expose this process than suggest alternative arrangements. Arcand felt that 'the old Marxist strategy is inoperative' in the new situation: 'We must find something else. But what?'[40]

Enter Marcuse

As John Harkness has suggested, 'Arcand's political documentaries ... are among the most powerfully pessimistic documentaries Canada has produced.'[41] Their negativity is not, however, cynical or despairing, and Arcand prefers to see them as documentaries on the slow progress of political thought.[42]

A clue to a more productive reading of *On est au coton* is found in one component of its complex texture that I have not yet mentioned. The film is periodically interrupted by brief messages, typed out to the accompaniment of typewriter noises that sound like gunshots (an effect first used to provide the opening credits). These were introduced during the editing process and were taken from Marcuse's *One-Dimensional Man*. There is no acknowledgment of the source in the film itself and, as La Rochelle pointed out, the quotations are fragmented and taken out of context (and they certainly do not act as a substitute for a commentary).[43] Nevertheless, their presence does suggest the context in which the film operates.

Arcand claims that he had not read Marcuse before starting the film, but, once he did, he must have recognized many of his own concerns. Whether it is a question of influence or affinity, the discovery of Marcuse must have assisted in the struggle to give the film its final shape. Arcand was especially impressed by Marcuse's emphasis on 'the extraordinary recuperative power of our system.'[44] According to Marcuse, the working class was being 'incorporated into the technological community of the administered population,' with the result that 'domination is transfigured into administration.'[45] It is precisely this alliance between technology and administration that Arcand saw in the new technocratic thought and in the attempt to manage change in such well-meaning efforts as the Challenge for Change program.

The key question in Marcuse's text, as in Arcand's film, is why the workers are willing to accept the situation. In accordance with Frankfurt School theory, Marcuse argued that the system works by constructing 'false needs,' especially through advertising: people have been 'indoctrinated and manipulated (down to their very instincts)' so that they cannot distinguish between true and false needs.[46] Arcand and Godin came to similar conclusions through their observation of the textile workers. While Arcand thought that the younger workers had been bought off with their colour television sets, Godin made the same point more theoretically when he said that the film was about 'the alienation of the Quebec working class and its capacity for integration into the system.'[47]

Yet this view of the workers is not notably apparent in the film. They are treated with respect, and most of those interviewed give thoughtful accounts of their circumstances. The interviews with Madeleine Parent may expose the lack of radical dissent in the present, but the contrast between past and present works less to discredit modern workers than to reinforce a sense of the complexity of the situation. Because 'administration' successfully disguises the causes and effects of 'domination,' it is difficult to envisage political solutions.

Perhaps the most important point of contact with Marcuse's argument is the insistence on the need for a political and theoretical analysis of the social effects of technology. Marcuse saw machines as 'the *potential* basis of a new freedom for man' but insisted that this potential cannot be realized without radical social change. Similarly, he argued that facts are 'not immediate data of observation, measurement, and interrogation.' They become data 'only in an analysis which is capable of identifying the structure that holds together the parts and processes of society and that determines their interrelation.' He acknowledged that his form of 'critical theory' may seem impotent because it reveals the obstacles to change, but he saw this as preferable to 'an empirical sociology which, freed from all theoretical guidance except a methodological one, succumbs to the fallacies of misplaced concreteness, thus performing an ideological service while proclaiming the elimination of value judgments.'[48]

For Arcand, the experience of making the film made him aware that 'the fundamental problem is a matter of ideology.'[49] Accordingly, the ending of the film shifts the focus to the political arena and includes interviews with several provincial and federal politicians. The final sequence depicts the ceremonies to mark the opening of a new session of the provincial legislature. Here band music replaces the noise of the machines and politics becomes a spectacle that has no bearing on the issues that the film has raised. This ending anticipates the failure of

Arcand's pursuit of a political solution in his next film on the 1970 Quebec election campaign: the experience of making *Québec: Duplessis et après ...* only convinced him that the workers' situation was not likely to change under a different government.[50]

As in the case of Marcuse's critical theory, this gloomy view of the future makes more pragmatic approaches seem very tempting. In *On est au coton*, Arcand created a film that resists this temptation and embodies both his belief that 'practice should give birth to a theory that must then be reverified in practice' and his recognition that 'what we lack now in our situation is the theory.'[51] There was, of course, no lack of theories that claimed to explain the situation in Quebec in 1970. Once the film was completed, its efforts to unify theory and practice were inevitably evaluated against both the technocratic values that it denounced and the nationalist analysis of Quebec's colonial status.

As we have seen, Arcand saw the value of the film in the detached perspective it provides on the workers' situation, but he also admitted experiencing 'a feeling of weakness analogous to that experienced by the workers faced with their situation.'[52] This tension brings together the two paradoxes discussed at the beginning of this essay, and it is playfully dramatized at the end of *Gina*, when the documentary filmmakers are seen, after their film is banned, making a commercial crime film, much as Arcand did in his first fiction film, *La Maudite Galette* (1972).

In his fiction films, Arcand often explores the temptation to 'sell out' in a society in which political change seems impossible. By using an extreme case to test the limits of technocratic and administrative thought in *On est au coton*, Arcand refused to sell out, but he ended up with a film that was itself an extreme case that tested the limits of similar patterns of thought at the NFB.

Notes

1 Arcand, quoted in Harkness, 'The Improbable Rise of Denys Arcand,' 235.
2 Perreault, '*On est au coton* refait surface.' Several other NFB French-language productions ran into trouble at this time; Jacques Leduc's *Cap d'espoir* (1969) and Gilles Groulx's *24 Heures ou plus ...* (1972) were also banned.
3 Evans, *In the National Interest*, 183; Véronneau, 'Alone and with Others,' 16.

4 An English-subtitled version was released by the NFB in 1992 under the title *Cotton Mill, Treadmill*.

5 La Rochelle, ed., *Denys Arcand*, 2.

6 Arcand, quoted in ibid., 22. The actual budget was $152,266; see Evans, *In the National Interest*, 180.

7 Arcand, quoted in ibid., 10.

8 In his introduction to the *Parti pris* NFB issue, Pierre Maheu argued that the francophone filmmakers seemed to respect the prescribed rules of the 'candid eye' but had succeeded in 'turning against the regime the game it had imposed on them'; Maheu, *Un Parti pris révolutionnaire*, 49.

9 Arcand, quoted in Loiselle, '"I Only Know Where I Come From,"' 140.

10 La Rochelle, ed., *Denys Arcand*, 2.

11 The Frankfurt School (more formally, the Institute for Social Research) was founded in Germany in 1923 by a group of Marxist intellectuals from a number of disciplines. Their initial focus was on the cultural conditions that led to the rise of Nazism.

12 See, in particular, the essays collected in Adorno, *The Culture Industry*.

13 Marcuse, *One-Dimensional Man*, 104.

14 Arcand and Godin, 'Un film didactique,' 34.

15 Newman, 'Interview,' 35.

16 La Rochelle, ed., *Denys Arcand*, 6.

17 La Rochelle, 'Sound Design and Music,' 32–4.

18 Ibid., 33. The 16 mm sound technology could only approximate the effect that Arcand wanted. Looking back in the 1990s, he wished that he had 'modern THX technology to convey just how unbearable it really is'; quoted in La Rochelle, 'Sound Design and Music,' 34.

19 Arcand, 'La genèse du film,' 32.

20 Jones, *Movies and Memoranda*, 153.

21 Arcand, quoted in Bonneville, ed., *Le Cinéma québécois par ceux qui le font*, 37, 39, and in Wright and Magidson 'Making Films for Your Own People,' 220.

22 Arcand, quoted in Bonneville, ed., *Le Cinéma québécois par ceux qui le font*, 37.

23 La Rochelle, ed., *Denys Arcand*, 6.

24 Ibid., 20; La Rochelle, 'Sound Design and Music,' 37.

25 Arcand and Godin, 'Un film didactique,' 33.

26 Ibid.

27 Newman, 'Interview,' 35.

28 Ibid.

29 Evans, *In the National Interest*, 180.

30 Morris, *The Film Companion*, 60–1.
31 Véronneau, 'Alone and with Others,' 17. See also Martin Knelman's comment that 'Arcand's study of the textile industry had led him to the conclusion that the Quiet Revolution of the sixties was an invention of the media: except for the decline in the church's influence there had been very little advance'; *This Is Where We Came In*, 75.
32 Arcand, quoted in La Rochelle, ed., *Denys Arcand*, 22.
33 Evans, *In the National Interest*, 180–2.
34 Ibid., 181. In a brief sequence near the end of the film, originally cut from the film for legal reasons, a group of separatists discuss the relations between their cause and that of the workers.
35 Arcand, quoted in La Rochelle, ed., *Denys Arcand*, 32; Jones, *Movies and Memoranda*, 146.
36 Arcand, quoted in Loiselle, '"I Only Know Where I Come From,"' 149.
37 Newman, 'Interview,' 35.
38 Evans, *In the National Interest*, 182–4.
39 Arcand, quoted in La Rochelle, ed., *Denys Arcand*, 18.
40 Ibid., 21.
41 Harkness, 'The Improbable Rise of Denys Arcand,' 235.
42 Arcand, quoted in Loiselle, '"I Only Know Where I Come From,"' 148.
43 La Rochelle, ed., *Denys Arcand*, 6.
44 Arcand, quoted in ibid., 23.
45 Marcuse, *One-Dimensional Man*, 26, 32.
46 Ibid., 5–6.
47 Arcand, quoted in Wright and Magidson 1977, 'Making Films for Your Own People,' 223; Arcand and Godin, 'Un film didactique,' 34.
48 Marcuse, *One-Dimensional Man*, 3, 190, 254.
49 Arcand, quoted in La Rochelle, ed., *Denys Arcand*, 26.
50 Ibid., 25.
51 Ibid., 26.
52 Ibid., 23.

Performing the Master Narratives: Michael Rubbo's *Waiting for Fidel*

JEANNETTE SLONIOWSKI

There's man all over for you, blaming on his boots the faults of his feet.
Samuel Beckett, Waiting for Godot[1]

In one of the very few articles written on internationally known film-maker Michael Rubbo, Piers Handling poses the following question: 'Why do his films, made by the state film organization [the National Film Board] not get shown by the state television network [the Canadian Broadcasting Corporation]?'[2] Although Handling posed this question in 1984, it is still pertinent today – particularly with respect to *Waiting for Fidel* (1974), Rubbo's sixteenth documentary film. Handling's answer to his own question is that Rubbo's 'subjective' style does not fit the CBC's pretence of documentary or journalistic 'objectivity.'[3] *New York Times* film critic David Denby more pointedly argues that 'most of Rubbo's documentaries have combined exploration of an alien culture and mockery of the observer-explorer (including himself). Awkward, discursive, personal, his style may embarrass audiences accustomed to the smoothly impersonal, authoritative tone of network documentaries and foreign correspondents.'[4]

The CBC's virtual censorship of Rubbo's work resonates throughout *Waiting for Fidel* where, for example, one well-known Canadian media personality, Geoff Stirling, touts freedom of expression in Western democracies while accusing the Cuban government of practising censorship. Rubbo is nothing if not a keen and wry observer of the absurdity of his own position as a 'reporter of the real.' It is his postmodern undermining of traditional, stuffy documentary practice, with its often 'superior' or unthinking imposition of Western values upon other cultures, that makes him unsuitable for a medium that traditionally reassures spectators and contains knowledge within familiar frames of reference. Televisual documentary, which is inherently more conservative than its filmic counterpart, often depends upon traditional and very conventional documentary forms to assure spectators of the truthfulness and dependability of its arguments. Indeed, the institution of televisual newsgathering, reportage, and documentary is built upon this foundation of believability which Rubbo so amusingly undermines in *Waiting for Fidel*.

Bill Nichols has argued that the conventional ethnographic documentary, which is frequently broadcast on television, is marked by a curious ambivalence: a desire to experience and examine the strange, 'exotic,' or unknown, but at the same time a need to contain potentially dangerous strangeness within canonical narrative forms that reassure rather than open the spectator to new, and potentially dangerous, experiences. He calls this ambivalence, after Edward Said, 'Orientalism.' This 'Orientalist' text produces, according to Nichols, 'a viewing subject caught up in a desire for ... oscillation between the strange and the familiar. The satisfaction of the desire to know is deferred in favour of perpetuating this set of staged representations of knowledge.'[5] Although the ethnographic documentary gives the spectator the illusion of knowledge, it does not deliver anything other than the familiar, comfortable subject positions produced by conventional, 'hierarchical,' and politically wrought structures like 'the interview,' 'the informant,' and the 'case study.'[6] This conventional type of ethnographic documentary (like the *National Geographic* special that creates 'an imaginary geography') is a staple on Canadian network television.[7]

A Postmodern Turn

At first glance, Rubbo's *Waiting for Fidel* might seem to emulate these conventional canonical journeys and quest narratives. In the film a group of Canadians including Joey Smallwood, former premier of Newfoundland, media mogul Stirling, and Rubbo himself, an Australian working for the Film Board, travel to Cuba to seek an interview with Fidel Castro. When the promised interview is delayed over and over again, they end up travelling around Cuba, like a trio of ill-assorted, bickering ethnographers, talking to ordinary people about life after the revolution. Like most ethnographic documentaries, the film opens with the conventional 'acts of travel' and 'scenes of arrival' and ends with the equally conventional 'returning here' or separation from the exotic culture and safe return to 'normalcy.'[8] But, as Nichols reminds us, this kind of quest narrative is not ideologically neutral, since 'travel conjures associations with spiritual quests, voyages of self-discovery, and tests of prowess, as well as expansionist dreams of empire, discovery and conquest.'[9]

However, while in traditional ethnographic documentaries these ideological moves are covert, Rubbo makes clear in *Waiting for Fidel* that Stirling and Smallwood's journey to Cuba is hardly innocent. Stirling hopes to sell the interview with Fidel to the U.S. National Broadcasting Company (NBC) for profit, and Smallwood egotistically casts himself in the role of diplomat, the man who will normalize relations between Cuba and the United States. What Rubbo's own motives are remain a matter for speculation – but he does enjoy making fun of his two companions, as well as mocking his own on-screen persona. Rather than giving the spectator the traditional quest, Rubbo gives us a journey of a most peculiar kind, one that is more like Beckett's *Waiting for Godot*, from which the film jokingly takes its name, than a traditional ethnographic narrative.

Not surprisingly given the film's title, Fidel never shows up. We are given shots of him at public functions, but much to the frustration of Smallwood and Stirling – and the amusement of Rubbo's on-screen persona – the proposed interview never takes place. Instead Rubbo films himself and his two companions arguing, debating, and travelling around Cuba in search of a knowledge that they are completely unable, and moreover, often unwilling, to find. At the end of this journey we may be left with, among other things, a sense of the futility of trying to understand another culture – particularly when we make no attempt to recognize the ideological filters though which our understanding works. How fortunate for Rubbo, and for us, that Fidel does not appear. Judging from the questions that we hear Smallwood preparing for the interview, the planned documentary might have been another of those dull, self-serving interviews with great men, so familiar from the nightly round of television viewing. Instead of this, though, we are given an often-hilarious portrait of three Canadian 'clowns' on a quest to learn nothing. Is it any wonder that the CBC balked at showing *Waiting for Fidel*, a film that mocks that most serious, and frequently stodgy, enterprise: the documentary film?

Linda Williams argues that recent postmodern documentaries, like Ross McElwee's *Sherman's March* (1985) and Michael Moore's *Roger and Me* (1989), are in part critiques of cinéma vérité and its unproblematic capturing of 'the truth.' She argues that 'it has become an axiom of the new documentary that films cannot reveal the truth of events, but only the ideologies and the consciousness that constructs competing truths – the fictional master narratives by which we make sense of events.'[10] These humorous, self-reflexive films have much in common with Rubbo's earlier, groundbreaking documentary experiments. As early as *Sad Song of Yellow Skin* (1970) and *Persistent and Finagling* (1971), Rubbo was both showing himself on screen as a kind of documentary anti-hero, like both McElwee and Moore, and commenting upon the complex nature of documentary 'truth' and authorship.[11] Indeed, the 'diary film' or personal documentary, of which Rubbo was an early practitioner, has become far more common as filmmakers question issues of authorship in documentary filmmaking through on-screen personas and surrogate authors. While the emphasis is on personalities and humour (or even entertainment) generated by the on-screen or 'every-man' persona in both the Moore and McElwee films, Rubbo maintains a serious commitment to a politically astute investigation not only of 'the world' but of documentary forms as well – while at the same time questioning his own filmmaking practices and making fun not only of his companions but himself.[12] *Waiting for Fidel*, despite its playfulness, makes some serious demands upon its audience.

Williams goes on to argue that the postmodern documentary, although it is a far less confident rendering of the truth, still preserves the desire to depict 'a truth' even though that truth may only be 'partial and contingent.'[13] Thus, even though Rubbo casts doubt upon the 'master narratives' believed by Smallwood and Stirling, and even himself, *Waiting for Fidel* does teach the audience a number of things, some of which are disconcerting in the extreme. As Nichols observes: 'What we learn in the films of Michael Rubbo, for example *Sad Song of Yellow Skin* or *Waiting for Fidel*, is restricted to what Rubbo himself knows or learns since he places himself in the foreground as inquiring presence. His questions, puzzlements, observations and reflections provide the informative tissue of the film.'[14]

However, Rubbo continuously points out the limitations of his own (and everyone else's) knowledge. In *Waiting for Fidel* in particular, he demonstrates that all knowledge is refracted through the master narratives which his social actors impose upon the world. In a sense, situations exceed what the characters know, and their knowledge, including Rubbo's, is merely an attempt to explain and control reality – and, crucially, to justify their own behaviour. The gap between what people believe and what the spectator might gather about the events on-screen is part of Rubbo's questioning of documentary truth. In the larger sense, he demonstrates that our knowledge is restricted by the master narratives that we bring with us on our journeys. The idea of getting to 'the truth' becomes impossible in a Rubbo film.

Throughout the film, Rubbo shows Smallwood and Stirling walking into situations armed with their own political ideologies, completely unable to agree about what is happening in front of them. For example, when the group goes to an experimental high school, Smallwood sees a model of progressive educational practice; Stirling, on the other hand, sees a sweatshop that robs children of their carefree childhoods. At a construction site where a group of labourers is building a new city, Smallwood is fascinated by the idea of people, from different walks of life, working to construct their own homes, while Stirling, who is shown refusing to take part in this discussion, sits by himself away from the group. All that he sees is an Orwellian vision of demeaning forced labour. With ideological blinkers firmly in place, Smallwood and Stirling survey Cuba and cannot agree about what they have seen. As Walter Truett Anderson quips with respect to this kind of postmodern dilemma: 'If I hadn't believed it, I never would have seen it.'[15] It is almost as though Rubbo has found himself on a desert island with two dyed-in-the-wool modernists and he both watches and provokes them with an amused, postmodernist detachment.

This of course produces an unsettling dilemma for the spectator. Rubbo presents us with a most disconcerting, but amusing, postmodern situation wherein a stable sense of reality disappears behind competing ideologies. Pascal Bonitzer observes that in conventional documentary the combination of the 'voice-off' and image produce a powerful impression of knowledge and a stable, masterful subject position for the spectator. In *Waiting for Fidel* Rubbo's voice/image combinations and disagreements rob us of this kind of pleasure, and, as Bonitzer further argues, 'to recognize the humbuggery in the imperturbable voice-off by laughing is to lift the oppression of the commentary.'[16]

This may in fact be the effect of *Waiting for Fidel*, and perhaps one of the reasons why the CBC might have been uncomfortable with it. Any attack on the authority of documentary may also be perceived by programmers as an attack on much of the other information programming that is broadcast, especially since television documentary is so often dependent on just such authoritative voice-overs. *The Valour and the Horror* (1992), for example, relied heavily on a powerful voice-over narration to convince the spectator of the validity of the film's controversial point of view about Canadian participation in the Second World War.[17] If a documentary is supposed to report 'the truth' objectively, as the CBC would argue, how then can this happen if those present at the event cannot agree on even the most basic of issues placed before them, or if their own mythologies blind them to the smallest of encounters with another culture?

This is perhaps the crux of *Waiting for Fidel*, and Rubbo, to his credit, does not remove himself, as a filmmaker, from this dilemma. Throughout the film, we see Rubbo himself interacting not only with the Cubans but with Smallwood and Stirling as well. He puts himself on screen with the result that we can be as critical of him as we are of the other social actors in this absurd documentary. At one point Rubbo even shows an inmate in a mental institution telling the filmmaker that he might belong in a mental institution more than she does. This is a powerful and humorous undermining of the filmmaker as the final arbiter of truth.

Nichols argues, with reference to *Waiting for Fidel*, which he categorizes as 'interactive,' that documentaries that give the impression of allowing the social actor to speak equally in interview situations in fact do no such thing. He observes that such interactions produce only a 'pseudo-dialogue' and that the documentarian becomes something of a 'ventriloquist.' Ultimately, 'the resulting impression of a pseudo-dialogue disguises the degree to which such exchanges are, in fact, as highly formalized here as they are in other institutional contexts.'[18] But, as I shall go on to argue, *Waiting for Fidel,* through its reflexive highlighting of media issues and its casting of the director as a kind of bumbling anti-hero whom both Stirling and the inmate mock and criticize, does much to undermine the idea of the filmmaker as merely a 'ventriloquist.'

The Filmmaker as Provocateur
Rubbo's role as an embodied, structuring presence is made apparent from the beginning of the film. He begins by referring, in voice-over, to history and sets up a binary opposition between the positions held by Smallwood and Stirling. He tells us that the men have formerly been enemies: Smallwood leading Newfoundland into Confederation, Stirling firmly on the other side. He calls Smallwood the 'socialist' and Stirling the 'capitalist' – setting the ground for a conflict of ideologies. But the structure of the film is not nearly as neat as this playing off of two different worldviews since we see Rubbo himself playing the dev-

il's advocate and pushing Stirling, in particular, into losing his temper two or three times.

Of all the social actors in *Waiting for Fidel*, Stirling is shown to the least advantage. He is a multi-millionaire who owns newspapers and television stations in Newfoundland, and he is, not surprisingly, completely biased against Castro's communism. Rubbo shows him arriving in Cuba with a closed mind and leaving apparently having learned nothing at all. Stirling is also extremely vain as indicated by his rather slick wardrobe. One of the more amusing sequences shows him clad in a small, tight, beige bathing suit, standing on his head on the beach, giving a rather bizarre lecture on physical health. The next shots then take in a discussion on the beach between Smallwood and Stirling. Stirling, it appears, has had a windfall on the stock market – one of those fortuitous gains in the value of gold which only the wealthy ever experience. Smallwood, who is somewhat appalled by the idea of making money by doing nothing, tells Stirling to donate the million-dollar profit to Cuba. Stirling finally says that he is going to reinvest it in his own company. There is a clear clash of values here which might lead to a reading of the headstand as symbolic of an inversion of values, and hence Rubbo's critique of Stirling's capitalism. In the long run, one comes away from *Waiting for Fidel* with a sense of Stirling as a vain, inflexible ideologue with a very bad wardrobe (appropriately enough, he looks rather like Hugh Hefner, publisher of *Playboy* – gold chains, vanity, and all).

But again Rubbo does not make this all that easy. In what is perhaps the central scene of the film, Rubbo reveals himself as a provocateur and he shows us Stirling falling into his trap. This sequence begins with Rubbo telling us in voice-over that he and Stirling are not getting along very well. Apparently – and I say this advisedly, because we are not privy to all of what transpires – Stirling has taken to leaving Rubbo audiotapes criticizing the progress of the filmmaking. As we are shown the tape recorder, a hand, perhaps Rubbo's, reaches around from behind the camera and touches the machine and later turns it off – again an embodied presence from behind the camera structuring the event on screen. There is then a cutaway to a member of Rubbo's crew awkwardly doing a headstand, perhaps making fun of Stirling's earlier behaviour (or again implying another inversion of values since what follows is another disagreement). Just after this, Stirling emerges from the house, as if by coincidence, and gets into a nasty argument with Rubbo – and a most telling argument it is.

Here Stirling reveals his own view of documentary filmmaking and also a great deal about the true extent of freedom of expression in capitalist countries. He is very critical (profanely so) of the amount of film that Rubbo uses. It is clear that for Stirling, economics, not intellectual curiosity, determines what should get on film. With the shooting ratio of 3:1 that he advocates, the filmmaker must go into a situation armed with a script, or at least a very clear notion of what will finally appear on film, since 3:1 leaves virtually no room for experimentation or openness to the potential of an unplanned but valuable situation. Rubbo, on the other hand, with a not-uncommon NFB shooting ratio of 20:1 (or is he subtly egging Stirling on here by whispering 25:1?), can afford to take a more open approach to his subject matter. As Handling notes, the way in which Rubbo approaches shooting, 'arises out of situations, as opposed to trying to control or dominate them.'[19] This is not to say that Rubbo does not control what happens in his films – just that he is perhaps less sure of himself and more willing to let things develop rather than imposing himself totally on them. In this he is quite unlike Stirling, who must barge into the pro-filmic event with meanings imposed on the material before the footage is shot.

Stirling also argues throughout the film that Cubans are not as free as Canadians to say or shoot what they will. But clearly producers like himself place enormous constraints on Canadian filmmakers as well. From his perspective, he who pays the piper calls the tune, so he viciously attacks Rubbo for taking a different view of what *Waiting for Fidel* will ultimately be about. His attack is profane and exceedingly nasty. So much for freedom of expression, for if Cubans are dominated by Fidel, Canadians are dominated by the economics of capitalism; in either case, freedom of expression is severely restricted and one has to wonder about the quality of 'truthfulness' broadcast by people like Stirling – and Rubbo.

Rubbo's relationship with Smallwood is subtler than his continual conflict with Stirling, perhaps because Smallwood is too clever to let Rubbo draw him out, or because Rubbo feels closer to Smallwood's enthusiastic position on the Cuban experiment. At first glance Smallwood appears to be an easygoing, avuncular type who is wildly and uncritically enthusiastic about Fidel and Cuba; Rubbo tells us that Smallwood is interested in Cuba because economic conditions there are not dissimilar from those in Newfoundland. However, there are many subtle hints here that the rather egotistical Smallwood sees himself as nothing less than a Canadian Fidel.

Rubbo tells us early on that Smallwood considers himself a socialist,

Waiting for Fidel (1974), directed by Michael Rubbo. Courtesy of the National Film Board of Canada.

as though this might come as a surprise to us. But as Richard Gwyn, Smallwood's biographer, tells us – and as we can see clearly in the film – Smallwood's understanding of socialism is rather self-serving. Gwyn argues that he was not a socialist in any consistent way but that he was 'a populist and an idealist by instinct, and a pragmatic politician and a propagandist by nature.'[20] He also argues that Smallwood was 'an impressionistic seeker of idols to emulate.'[21] Indeed, Rubbo shows us that Smallwood uncritically accepts whatever he is told in Cuba and that, paradoxically for a socialist and a man of the people, he is a celebrity worshipper – much more so than the Cubans he meets. One might argue that Smallwood's brand of socialism is far removed from governance by the people and more like a kind of populist dictatorship headed by a great man like himself – an idiosyncratic brand of socialism to be sure.

What is most intriguing about Smallwood is the easygoing, open manner that he adopts – a manner that makes him far more likeable than the more belligerent Stirling. He appears to be somewhat concerned by an apparent lack of freedom in Cuba, but is he really concerned or acting for the camera – an obvious question to be asked of such a skillful politician? According to Gwyn, Smallwood was an extremely controlling premier and a vicious, inflexible political infighter when necessary. He argues that Newfoundlanders were often brutalized by Smallwood, and he describes their mixed reaction to his regime:

> Systematic intimidation by a political machine which responded to the will of one man was new and terrifying. Political debate, once a bawdy Newfoundland art form, was driven underground, to be voiced only in taverns and private homes. To oppose Smallwood in public was to risk financial retribution. He used the power of the purse with little restraint. Friends were rewarded and enemies persecuted. If Newfoundlanders feared Smallwood, they did so with good reason.[22]

No wonder Smallwood is less critical of Fidel's apparently hero-centred socialism than Stirling since he perhaps sees leadership as a kind of paternalistic dictatorship as well.

If Smallwood strikes one as a clever actor, what then is the position of the Cubans in the film? Rubbo tells us that all but one of the meetings with them have been scheduled by the government. How freely then do the people speak, and are we in fact speaking to 'the people' or merely to pre-selected 'citizens'? This is something we cannot know, but Rubbo makes it plain to us that the government has authorized these meetings. One thing that he constantly reminds us of is the segregated and privileged treatment that the Canadians are given. He tells us that food is rationed in Cuba and that economic times are tough. He then shows the Canadians staying in the luxurious Protocol Palace #9 – a home abandoned by a wealthy manufacturer after the revolution. The Canadians, as Rubbo points out in several sequences, are served sumptuous foods and wines while the Cubans do without. Clearly Fidel is putting on a show for the foreign media, and, of course, he has sent them to an exemplary school, building project, and hospital. What Cuba, one is prompted to ask, have the Cubans let the Canadians see? And who has seen anything that they didn't expect to see already?

Here the idea of performance, so vexed a question in documentary generally, comes to the surface with particular force. If the people in a documentary film perform for the camera, how then are we to know 'the truth'? Referring to the obviously performative as 'a new mode in town,' Nichols argues that 'performative documentary clearly embodies a paradox: it generates a distinct tension between performance and document, between the personal and the typical, the embodied and the disembodied, between, in short, history and science.'[23] The performative aspects of *Waiting for Fidel* are clear – Rubbo performs the role of filmmaker, provoking and goading his social actors where he can; Stirling performs 'right-wing capitalism,' Smallwood 'socialism,' and the Cubans 'citizenship.'

Thus, although *Waiting for Fidel* is only fifty-eight minutes long, it is packed with irony, humour, and politics, and, as Seth Feldman notes, although nothing happens, 'it is a hard-fought, deeply revealing nothing.'[24] I must confess that I always enjoy seeing Stirling made a fool of in this film. But at the same time I am made aware that my own anti-media-mogul position plays a large role in this. Rubbo's film would fail in its ironic and reflexive examination of ideology if spectators were not made aware of their own biased viewpoints. For if there are clowns on screen, there are also clowns in front of it. Perhaps, in the end, this is what makes Rubbo's films so problematic for the CBC, for to have both convention and spectator made fun of is a risk that a mainstream television network is unwilling to take.

Any documentary that creates problems of believability will be difficult for network television. A film like *Waiting for Fidel* that violates 'the rules' of expository documentary and is both reflexive and obviously performative, may create, in the minds of the audience, a discomfort with the news and documentary offerings in which television networks try to make us place so much faith.

Notes

1 Beckett, *Waiting for Godot*, 8.
2 Handling, 'The Diary Films of Michael Rubbo,' 206.
3 Ibid.
4 Denby, quoted in *Michael Rubbo*, i.
5 Nichols, *Blurred Boundaries*, 74.
6 Ibid., 82. See also Trinh T. Minh-Ha on this point in 'Outside in Inside Out' and *When the Moon Waxes Red*.
7 Nichols, *Blurred Boundaries*, 74.
8 Ibid., 67–9.
9 Ibid., 68.

10 Williams, 'Mirrors without Memories,' 13.
11 For a more detailed discussion of the documentarian as anti-hero, see
    Fischer, *Sherman's March*, and Bernstein, *Roger and Me*.
12 The issue of entertainment and documentary has become a particularly
    interesting one in recent days. Since most documentary films end up on
    television, the 'entertainment' aspect, so inimical to John Grierson, seems
    to be a much greater issue with filmmakers like Moore, whose television
    career developed in the wake of the amazing success of *Roger and Me*.
    Moore frequently seems more like a wisecracking humorist than a serious
    political commentator in his television appearances and it is clear that
    many televisual documentaries are made to compete with fictional dra-
    matic offerings (or even sitcoms). John Corner has noted the innovative
    techniques that documentaries of the 1990s have adopted to make the
    form more popular with larger audiences – devices like reconstructions,
    'do-it-yourself' documentaries, and hidden cameras; *The Art of Record*, 182.
    Rubbo, with his on-screen 'author' and highly charged sense of humour
    around his own work and documentary itself, can be seen as a pioneer in
    this area. Ironically, *Waiting for Fidel* is too potent a critique of a very
    serious and demanding topic (demanding in the sense that the audience
    must know a good bit about Canadian and international politics to get full
    value from the film) to make it the popular success that Moore achieved
    with his far less taxing, but more entertaining, film.
13 Williams, 'Mirrors without Memories,' 14.
14 Nichols, *Representing Reality*, 119.
15 Anderson, *The Truth about the Truth*, 70.
16 Bonitzer, 'The Silences of the Voice,' 329.
17 For a discussion of the CBC and its policy surrounding objectivity and
    accuracy, see Bercuson and Wise, eds., *The Valour and the Horror Revisited*.
18 He makes the same argument for *Les Raquetteurs* (1958), *Chronique d'un été*
    (1960), *Sad Song of Yellow Skin*, and *Wet Earth, Warm People* (1971); *Repre-
    senting Reality*, 52.
19 Handling, 'The Diary Films of Michael Rubbo,' 210.
20 Gwyn, *Smallwood, the Unlikely Revolutionary*, 33–44.
21 Ibid., 254.
22 Ibid., 236.
23 Nichols, *Blurred Boundaries*, 93, 97.
24 Feldman, quoted in Handling, 'The Diary Films of Michael Rubbo,' 205.

Hard Film to Define – *Volcano: An Inquiry into the Life and Death of Malcolm Lowry*

PETER BAXTER

I guess you couldn't really call it a documentary. It's a hard film to define, I don't know what it is. I know it's very long.

Donald Brittain[1]

John Grierson referred to documentary film as the 'creative treatment of actuality.'[2] With these words he provided a compact and suggestive definition that remains a useful starting point for thinking about both the broad range of film practices that the word 'documentary' has come to cover, and the ways in which we distinguish documentary film from other forms. Both issues are implicit in Donald Brittain's expressed uncertainty over how to classify *Volcano: An Inquiry into the Life and Death of Malcolm Lowry*, released by the National Film Board in 1976, co-directed by Brittain and John Kramer. *Volcano* builds an account of its subject from artefacts and personal recollections, from family photographs, interviews with friends and relations, newspaper clippings, and footage of the places where Lowry spent significant years of his life. But the 'creative treatment' of this material results in a film that transcends any simple understanding of the word 'actuality.' In the way it combines words and images, *Volcano* evokes dimensions of Lowry's existence as real as they are intangible, that neither words nor images alone could convey. No wonder the resulting film eludes easy classification.

Brittain regarded a film biography of Malcolm Lowry as almost a contradiction in terms. He acknowledged the difficulty of the project in the 1977 interview quoted above:

I mean his life basically was not dramatic, unlike, say the *Bethune* film [Brittain's 1963 film for the NFB], where we had a man of action and there was a lot happening. Movies have to move.

We were faced with a situation where there was very little movement – just a movement inside a man's body and soul.[3]

The documentary training that Brittain received at the NFB in the early 1950s was not geared toward capturing 'a movement inside a man's body and soul.' In order to enlarge the scope of how documentary was conceptualized, Brittain – like Gilles Groulx, Wolf Koenig, Roman Kroitor, and others – had to push beyond the practices that the Board had institutionalized. Brittain's particular achievement was a matter of creative synthesis rather than radical invention. His greatest works do not so much take off in heretofore unanticipated directions as expand documentary possibilities by a cumulative process, drawing into a single text practices that had emerged at different moments in the Board's existence, in historically distinct periods, and for differing documentary purposes. The Board's first approaches to documentary had been driven by John Grierson's fierce wartime didacticism. In ensuing decades, changes in the Board's official mandate, repeated changes in organization, and changes in the world around it – social, technological, economic – created the conditions for changes in what the Board put on the nation's screens. In 1954, when Brittain began working for the Board, the heroic days of the Second World War production were still vividly alive in the memories of many staffers, though the bulk of Board production consisted of unchallenging commissioned work for government departments. In that year, however, both past and present ways of seeing were being challenged by the first glimmerings of what would become the candid eye movement. All these factors flowed into what was to become Brittain's signature approach to his craft, reaching their fullest development with *Volcano* in 1976.

While editing that film with Kramer in the fall of 1975, Brittain made notes on scraps of paper to remind himself of the objectives he was pursuing: 'illuminate something of human spirit ... images that invoke the joys and agony and banality ... avoid heavy symbolism & still use symbols.'[4] The 'creative treatment of actuality' that is *Volcano: An Inquiry into the Life and Death of Malcolm Lowry* results from the way Brittain and Kramer recapitulated and rearticulated a thirty-year history of NFB practices, in the interests of portraying that invisible 'actuality' that Brittain called 'human spirit.'

The Way to *Volcano*

By all accounts, Brittain had no more than a general idea of what he wanted to shoot on his Mexican locations for *Volcano*. He claimed to have finished reading Lowry's novel only on the flight from Montreal, and to have landed in Mexico in December 1974 principally concerned to avoid shooting any scenes in which evidence of the mid-1970s intruded too jarringly. This was not to be a rigid exclusion. Coca-Cola bottles and pickup trucks of the film's present day coexist with *vaqueros* and open-air butcher shops that might have belonged to an earlier era. What was brought back from the expedition was a mass of heterogeneous material, shot in the town and countryside where Malcolm Lowry had spent less than two years some four decades earlier. Making use of such footage to construct something other than travelogue-ish illustration to a voice-over biographical sketch would demand an approach to documentary filmmaking unthinkable at the Board where Brittain had served his apprenticeship. He remembered his early training in these terms:

> In those days, in the fifties, you had to write documentary films shot by shot so it was good training for anyone who wanted to become a director. For a film on fish spoilage for example, you would start off by putting down something like this – extreme close-up, man's hand, shwish-pan [sic] left to wheelbarrow, tilt up to frame full of fish, dissolve to longshot, then to harbour – all that in detail. And you also wrote the narration on the other side of the page which could be rewritten after the film was shot. The director actually went out with that script and more or less followed it shot by shot, so we were really directing and editing in our heads while we were writing.[5]

To achieve on location what had been envisaged in the writer's head could sometimes involve a considerable effort on the part of the film crew dispatched to do the job. *Setting Fires for Science* (1958), for which Brittain received his first director's credit, was filmed in precise, predictable sequence as scientists prepared and ignited one house after another – abandoned to make way for the St Lawrence Seaway – to gain data about burn rates and patterns. But there were other shoots where a crew's most arduous task was to ensure that filmed 'reality' would match the idea of the film that was to be made. Brittain said that on his first assignment with a crew, acting as location manager, he spent forty-one days shooting a five-minute segment on Cape Breton Island, with most of that time spent simply waiting for the weather to conform to the script.[6]

In the early 1950s, the NFB comprised four production units, each designated by a letter, each with its own personnel, executive producer, and particular subject areas. By the middle of the decade, filmmakers at Unit B began to produce documentaries premised and shot on assumptions exactly the reverse of those that guided most Board productions. Haltingly, film by film, it was realized that the structure of a film could flow from the encounter of filmmaker and subject, rather than follow the preplanned narrative that the filmmaker had been assigned. In *Paul Tomkowicz: Street-railway Switchman* (1954), the third-person narrative commentary that Board productions customarily added over edited images was replaced by the words of the filmed subject himself, recorded during the filming (though spoken by an actor because of problems with the original recording). The result was an immediacy that other Board films of those years sadly lacked. Brittain, who worked on sponsored films during his apprentice years, recalled that he was one of those NFB employees from other units who looked with envy at what Unit B filmmakers were achieving. 'You see a film like *Lonely Boy* and you say to yourself, "Shit, I wouldn't mind making something half decent."'[7] Unit B's experiments spurred his ambition, and the freedom with narrative form taken by the unit's most innovative filmmakers was to become an essential element in the evolution of Brittain's work. Ironically, however, Brittain's first achievement of 'something half decent' didn't come with anything like Unit B's brand of direct cinema, but from a project more reminiscent of the Board's wartime compilations of twenty years earlier, when footage from all over the warring world arrived at the Board's Ottawa headquarters, out of which a coherent film had to be created.

In the early 1940s, Board-produced series such as *Canada Carries On* (1940–51) and *The World in Action* (1941–5) featured documentary films made in the present tense. Wartime production had the official mandate of maintaining morale as well as informing Canadians about the conflict in which the Allies were engaged. The filmmakers' mission was overt, pragmatic, polemical. The films they made bore titles such as *Churchill's Island* (1941), *Women Are Warriors* (1942), *Pincers on Japan* (1943), and *Road to the Reich* (1944). Not many (if any at all) of these films consisted of footage from a single source, and they were often patched together without much compunction about using shots of action from one battle to flesh out the account of another. In the words of then-editor Tom Daly, one day to be head of Unit B, what he and his colleagues were after was 'the *essence* of the real truth *behind* the details.'[8]

What Daly and his people were doing during the war was to be undertaken again, with different purpose, seventeen years after the war's end, when the Board made *Canada at War*, a thirteen-part series that aired on the CBC in 1962. Brittain worked on the project for a year and a half, and received credit as its producer and writer. *Canada at War* was assembled from the vast holdings of wartime footage that remained with the Board after 1945. Even though the war was a personal memory for many thousands of Canadians still hardly middle-aged, no one person's experience comprehended the scope of a war fought on a global scale. The soldiers who spent years as prisoners of war after Dieppe or Hong Kong had different recollections from those of the men who landed on Juno Beach or ferried convoys back and forth across the North Atlantic. Rather than scripting the series in advance (as was standard practice in the early 1950s), or shaping a film out of the encounter with those being filmed (as the candid eye filmmakers were doing, obviously impossible in this case), Brittain's work on *Canada at War* was to bring a conceptual order out of the 'stock shots' that chance had stored in the Board's vaults.[9] To forge a common memory out of a national experience so vast as to escape individual comprehension was an understandable project for the Board to undertake in a period of growing Canadian nationalism. Brittain's participation in the project immersed him in the problems of constructing a narrative out of material that has no intrinsic narrative thread, and of using sound and image in complementary – not redundant – relationships.

Fields of Sacrifice (1963), which followed *Canada at War*, was the first of Brittain's individual films that showed that the compilation form could be raised to a level of conceptual complexity. Commissioned by the Department of Veterans Affairs, *Fields of Sacrifice* was meant to be an uncontroversial, informational, and perhaps vaguely uplifting account of Canada's military cemeteries in Europe. Instead, Brittain combined stock footage with freshly shot material showing Second World War battle sites as they appeared a generation after the conflict ended, and added his own commentary to produce something quite unexpected. The film's structure 'collapses the past and present in a brilliant poetic counterpoint. In black and white, for example, we see a young soldier curled up dead on a beach in France, and then we cut to a colour image of the same beach with a modern-day sunbather curled up in the same position. Meanwhile, the narrator ironically suggests that we shall never forget the sacrifice of these soldiers.'[10]

The combination of heterogeneous film elements was to become characteristic of Brittain's films. Its first full articulation is achieved in *Bethune* (1963), which so closely sets out the agenda to be followed twelve years later with *Volcano* that it may justly be seen as the determining creative experience behind this latter work. *Bethune* marks the definitive turn in Brittain's work: in subject matter toward a focus on individuals, and in form toward a complexity that results from combining distinctly different practices – compilation or archival footage, scripted re-creation, voice-over commentary, studio interviews, actuality film.

Bethune portrays an adventurer who transgressed every orthodoxy that Canadian society of his day held dear. The formal terms of the treatment are largely those which Brittain worked out on *Canada at War* and *Fields of Sacrifice*. There is considerable stock footage of Montreal in the 1920s and 1930s, home movies and photographs of Bethune in his days as an inventive surgeon in Montreal, and – most remarkably – extensive footage of the doctor at the fronts of the Spanish Civil War and the Chinese war against the Japanese. Newspaper headlines, documents, photographs, and letters – all carrying the 'aura' of authenticity and age – contribute to the heterogeneity of the visual material. The compilation form points back to wartime practice, but shows here all the characteristics that were later to mark Brittain's work. Still and moving images from a variety of sources are juxtaposed in striking ways that create conceptual structures, particularly in montage assemblages that work by way of antitheses, either between soundtrack and images or between contrasting images. For example, a long-held shot of a photograph taken in Bethune's study in Montreal focuses on the cacti and other spindly plants on his window sill, against the grey, cold sky outside, while Bethune's words in voice-over address his just-divorced wife: 'Very clear and cold today. Sun shimmering on the snow and the sparrows making a great racket outside my windows.' Cut to a low-angle panning shot of bare tree branches, edged in snow: 'I wish you were here. I'm glad you're relatively happy and well. At least more than when you lived with my petulant irritability. God bless you. Beth.' The relation between images and voice-over implies Bethune's subjective point of view, in the cinematic sense of the term, his presence in the film as a centre of consciousness. The reading of the letter is a re-creation, with emotional inflection, rather than a quotation by a narrator. We know it is not Bethune's voice, but we accept that the reader's tone of weary regret is a valid evocation of Bethune's state at that time. The photograph provides an image of Bethune's world from his literal, visual point of view, as he would have seen – indeed, did see – his apartment through the viewfinder of his camera. But it is the cut from the photograph that is the most daring touch, moving from the artefactual past to a kind of historical present tense. The panning movement of the camera across the branches, from below as if it were the view of someone standing on the ground looking up past the spiky branches to the icy sky beyond, refers us to Bethune's personal desolation on that wintry day when his letter acknowledged the end of his marriage. Brittain often said that to be effective, documentary has to convey an emotion with which the audience can identify: 'I think film, essentially is not intellectual, but a totally emotional thing. Even the most straightforward documentary is all emotion if it's to be good. That's what makes it work. The pacing, the trying to find something that the audience doesn't expect but which is inevitable the moment you turn the corner. It's done with subtle things, it's the tone of someone's voice combined with a certain visual set up against something that went before.'[11]

Bethune uses other material, from different sources, that similarly pushes out from the historical documentation of artefactual footage to complex combinations of elements from different periods and different sources. The film begins and ends with shots of a memorial ceremony for Bethune at his tomb in China. Dignitaries carry wreaths and pause in reverent respect, in a newsreel-like sequence that is clearly contemporary with the making of the film and that is offered to the spectator as the marker of the present time in which Bethune is honoured. From this the film plunges into the chronicle of Bethune's life, to return to the initial ceremony at the conclusion. (*Volcano* will repeat this circular structure.) Knitting the fabric of past and present together are interviews in which people who knew Bethune talk about the kind of man he was. Though these sequences are clearly constructed around questions and answers, the questions and the questioner have been cut, and the interviewees are left to voice their reminiscences to an implicit, unseen, and unheard off-screen interlocutor. The style of their presentation belongs to an age of documentary practice that was being superseded even as *Bethune* was being made. The interviewees are photographed in stilted, studio-bound close-up shots, positioned lifelessly against a little shadowy patch of grey light that belongs to no known real world, but clearly stems from studio-bound documentary production practices, which cut their subjects off from the hurly-burly of life outside for the sake of reason and calm reflection. A few years before *Bethune*, in *Lonely Boy*, the filmmaker's voice – Koenig's or Kroitor's – had already asked Paul Anka and the owner of the Copacabana night club to 'do the kiss again.' Including that off-screen request in the final cut of the film had definitively pierced the sealed space of the on-screen subject, and brought the filmmaker into the conceptual space of the document itself. Although it was made after *Lonely Boy*, *Bethune* uses interviews in a way that belongs to an earlier concept of testimony, one that declines to admit the intersubjective nature of the exchange.

Brittain's films were soon to take a different approach. From the time of his next significant credit, for *Memorandum* (1965), his own on-screen presence – a back turned to the audience, a figure half in, half out of the frame, a voice offering a point for his subject to pick up on – was to become a familiar feature of his films. For *Volcano*, most of the subjects he interviews are shown in identifiable real-world locations – a pub, a schoolroom, along the shore of Burrard Inlet – and Brittain is often palpably there, drawing their memories and impressions from them.

To add further to the mix of elements in *Bethune*, toward the end of the film there is a short but extremely powerful 're-creation' that evokes Bethune's outlook during his last days. Throughout the film, two voice-overs have shared the soundtrack. One is Lister Sinclair's narrative account of Bethune's life and character. The other is that of an actor, Michael Kane, reading from Bethune's diaries and letters. In this sequence, which comes after actuality shots of Bethune's Chinese field hospital – over which Sinclair describes the conditions in which the doctor was working – the film suddenly shifts to another register, from the grainy long shots of the archival footage to a series of alternating, fine-grain, deeply shadowed, close shots: the face of a statue of the Buddha, a lamp, a flame, and a shot of a surgeon's gloved hands at work on a patient's chest, shot from a very low angle so the patient's body fills the lower part of the frame, and part of the surgeon's masked face is just visible in the upper part of the dim frame. Over this series of images, the voice identified with Bethune reads a passage from his diary:

Men with wounds. Wounds like little dried pools, caked with black brown earth. Wounds like torn edges frilled with black gangrene. Wounds expanding outwards. Decaying orchids or crushed carnations. Terrible flowers of flesh. Careful. Better moisten first. Pick the leg up. Where's that fine strong rod of bone now? In a dozen pieces. What fun it was. Now that is finished. Now that's done. Now we are destroyed. Now what will we do with ourselves?

Rather than describing an actual case, Bethune is clearly recording his despair and mortal fatigue. By placing this passage against three overtly symbolic shots – a lamp, the Buddha, a flame – *Bethune* moves out of a 'documentation' of time and place – 'September 1, 1939. Linchu, China,' the narrator says as the voice-over begins – and into an evocation of the emotional heart of its subject.

Bethune is a superb example of how simple elements can come together in complex structures that convey ideas beyond what can be portrayed directly, and how with such structures documentary can transcend the limitation of a realism premised on simple recording. Going beyond just showing physical reality, it can touch its spectators with evocations of how that reality is apprehended, by something we might agree to think of as 'human spirit.'

The Way to the Heart

Volcano: An Inquiry into the Life and Death of Malcolm Lowry opens and closes with lines spoken in voice-over by Richard Burton:

> My secrets are of the grave and must be kept. And this is how I sometimes think of myself: as a great explorer who has discovered some extraordinary land from which he can never return to give his knowledge to the world. But the name of the land is Hell. It is not Mexico, of course, but in the heart.

The passage is drawn from *Under the Volcano*, but is used in a way that differs significantly from its function in the novel. A spectator who has read *Under the Volcano* might realize that Burton is reading a passage from near the end of the first chapter, where the enigmatic main character, a self-loathing, desperate alcoholic referred to most often as 'the Consul,' is being conjured up to take his place at the centre of the story. The sentences are not drawn from the novel's dialogue. They occur in a rambling letter that the Consul wrote but did not send to his estranged wife, Yvonne. The reader of the novel encounters them by, as it were, reading over the shoulder of Jacques Laruelle, another wayward European soul measuring out his days and nights in the fictional

Mexican town of Quauhnahuac, amid its 'eighteen churches and fifty-seven *cantinas*.' Laruelle found the letter folded in a volume of Elizabethan plays that had once belonged to the Consul, who has been dead for a year as the story begins.

Thus, for the reader of the novel, the passage occurs in a context where a network of fictional relationships among characters is already taking shape. For the film spectator, however, Burton's voice is not that of a character so much as it is the voice of the film itself, speaking to the audience about what it has to say and what it has to show them in the images that are to follow. In this difference from the novel, much of the film's conceptual and aesthetic project is established. And that project is audacious, paradoxical, impossible: to document what cannot be documented, to portray in images and sounds what cannot be seen or heard – the hell within, a human heart in disarray.

The first voice-over of the film is accompanied by images of Mexico: mountainous horizons, including a shot of Popacatapetl, in flaming mauves and reds, followed by long shots of a boy padding along a path through tropical countryside, with a turkey for the slaughter slung over his shoulder. But what the voice-over explicitly tells us is that the country to be documented is not represented by the images we see on the screen. The country to which we are beckoned by the speaker, by the film, is 'not Mexico, of course, but in the heart.' Lowry discovered that country of the heart through Mexico, however, and the film will follow in his track, just as for the moment it follows this boy with the bird he casually carries to its death.

This scene is immediately succeeded by three shots very different from what has appeared so far: three close-ups of unidentified people, each speaking English, each giving a different opinion of what caused Malcolm Lowry's death. During this sequence we hear Brittain's voice for the first time, off-screen, uttering a simple question: 'I don't think anyone found out [how he actually died], did they?' Following these three shots, over a lengthy take of actors re-creating a coroner's hearing in what is purported to be a British courtroom, Brittain continues: 'On the fourth of July 1957, an inquest into the death of Malcolm Lowry, a writer by profession, was convened in a coroner's courtroom near the village of Ripe in the south of England.'

For the rest of the film, Burton's voice and Brittain's – clearly distinguishable from one another – will speak from the very different territories set out in these first few moments of the film, conceptual territories already implicitly separated by the colon of the film's title. The source of the one-word main title is, of course, Malcolm Lowry's novel, *Under the Volcano*, where Popacatapetl serves as a recurrent symbol of destructive forces that lie unquiet within the fabric of human life. Burton's territory lies here, in the hidden world – 'not Mexico of course, but in the heart' – that makes itself visible only when it bursts destructively into the open. By contrast, Brittain's voice from the first instant comes from an off-screen interlocutor, someone in the film but outside the frame, the voice of an inquirer directly present to the material world on-screen, but invisible to us. The 'facticity' of Brittain's voice, its connection to the world of verifiable fact – or at least of fact open to verification – is emphasized in the scene of the coroner's courtroom. Here Brittain's voice describes in voice-over what we see on the screen – a hearing in session, with a Union Jack – and adds the date and the location in which it is happening. The voice-over 'supplements' the visual and adds informational details that an image cannot convey. This staged scene simulates the look – and clearly only simulates the look – as if by the self-consciously obvious simulation of a hearing the film were declaring that it will use material evidence and call witnesses to testify, but its real objective is a reality that is invisible, immaterial, that cannot be grasped directly.

A dialectic is thus established: two voices, two sets of images, two versions of the world, one (Brittain's) based on presence, on testimony, on facts and evidence, the other (Burton's) a world that cannot be represented but only indexed, that cannot be directly photographed or recorded but only conveyed in combinations of sound and image. Straddling both versions of the world, the film does not simply balance the one with the other. Rather, it uses the former as entrée to the latter, moving from a level of filmmaking that might readily be acknowledged as conventional documentary – insofar as it brings forward evidence, places events in time and space, seeks possible relationships between causes and effects – into a filmmaking where such material factors are of at most an instrumental interest. Burton quotes passages from a novel; what we see on the screen does not, for the most part, reproduce the content of those passages in visual form. These are not images of Lowry's imaginary Mexico, but images of the real Mexico of forty years after Lowry experienced it. The Mexico of *Under the Volcano* was a fiction 'based on' the fact of its author's residence there. The Mexico we see in *Volcano* is a collage of images that, in conjunction with Burton's voice-over reading of Lowry's words, does not portray the place where Lowry came ashore in his wandering, but

Volcano: An Inquiry into the Life and Death of Malcolm Lowry (1976), directed by
Donald Brittain. Courtesy of the National Film Board of Canada.

refers to that place and *evokes* his hallucinatory experience of alcoholic
self-loathing and paranoia.

The contrast between these passages is powerful. It also risks becoming mechanical, both structurally and conceptually. The documentary
portions provide a secure framework of actual events, set out in time,
from within which Lowry's metaphorical perceptions can be safely
understood as providing intriguing but aberrant departures. It is not
long, however, before distinguishing between the two types of 'see-

ing' becomes increasingly difficult, and our ability to identify with Brittain's detached examination of the facts, while setting ourselves at a safe distance from Lowry's chaotic personal universe, is deeply undermined.

In overall design, after introducing the uncertain circumstances of his death, *Volcano* more or less follows the chronology of Lowry's life: boyhood in Liverpool, public school, a stint on the high seas as a cabin boy. Brittain handles this period with a gathering tension between the outward details of Lowry's life, and notes of unreason, even terror, that point toward that 'extraordinary land' toward which he is moving.

After university and a sojourn in Spain, Lowry – cut off from his family – lands in New York City. The transition is effected by a sharp cut between a shot of an empty deck on the Queen Mary and a telephoto close-up of a laughing derelict sitting on an armchair incongruously perched between lanes of traffic on a New York street. The cut plunges the writer, the spectator, and the two off-screen voices into a single, harrowing, visual world. New York City is portrayed in terms of vagrants talking to themselves or sleeping on the sidewalks, of Bowery saloons, the windows of rooming houses where single men sit reading their newspapers, of the display windows of liquor stores piled with bottles behind their steel grids. With these shots, the voices that had been previously separated in terms of the visuals they accompanied, begin to move closer to each other, so the degree of separation in their points of view begins to disappear. Over a single sequence of views of Bellevue Hospital, the public mental asylum, Brittain's narration of Lowry's admission as a patient is succeeded by Burton's voice, reading Lowry's fearful account of approaching breakdown. Thus, what is on the screen can at one moment coincide with the narrator's voice-over to represent the physical world in which Malcolm Lowry moved about, searching for some kind of peace, and can in the next become the visual correlate of that place – 'in the heart' – where ordinary life is surreal and frightening.

Lowry's anxiety-laden words seem to activate something hidden and menacing in otherwise unremarkable images. By the time the narrative moves to Mexico, shots caught on the fly by Brittain and his crew, that in another context would not be distinguishable from a tourist's home movies, cease to be simple actuality images and become components in the paranoid vision of a man for whom the world around him was a source of constant terror.

One of the most striking moments of the film is a brief passage in which Burton's voice-over quotes the Consul's ruminations on his wife's infidelities. Brittain has already insisted that writing about the Consul was Lowry's way of writing about himself and his own tortured relation to the world. An interview sequence with friends of Lowry confirms that Lowry's first wife, Jan Gabriel, found their marriage intolerable. Cut to Mexican footage of a drunken man staggering vaguely around outside some cantina or other. Brittain, in voice-over, offers the information that Lowry sometimes threw his wife at other men, in order to play the cuckolded husband and bathe in his own humiliation. Then Burton's voice takes up the vocal track, conveying the Consul's cynical, self-pitying contempt for both his wife and her lovers. On the screen there pass shots of a brightly wigged clown, his face bizarrely made up, sucking on a huge baby's soother; then a wholly unconnected shot of two young men on horseback riding in a Mexican street; and then two shots of an elderly man, his back so severely deformed that his chin practically touches his chest, dressed in a bathing suit, wading in a brightly sunlit pool, and tossing a beach ball to someone off-screen. Over these last images, we hear Burton read these words: 'God, is it possible to suffer more than this? Out of this suffering something must be born. And what would be born was his own death. For, ah, how alike are the groans of love to those of the dying. How alike those of love to those of the dying.'

In his taped account of making *Volcano*, Brittain recalls wanting to film a 'Chinese hunchback' in Mexico, since such a character makes recurrent appearances in the novel.[12] No one suitable turned up, however. On the crew's last day in the country, Brittain spotted an elderly man with a crooked spine paddling in the pool at his hotel. Hurriedly filming the man, they found he was a millionaire who was there to relax for a weekend with his grandchildren. The living reality of a man in a hotel pool late in 1974 had nothing to do with Malcolm Lowry's novel, *Under the Volcano*, and nothing to do with the author himself. Even the premise behind the shot, a character in the novel, is hardly pertinent, since it is a reference nowhere raised by the film. What is pertinent, however, is that with the voice-over utterance added to them, the two shots of the elderly man lead to the very centre of Lowry's despair as the film portrays it. For the filmmakers, the Consul and his creator were one and the same. What the Consul expressed, and what the image of the old man exemplified, was the object of the author's fears, the image of his self-loathing, and the focus of fascination out of which the novel had been generated: the human body itself, frail, willful, grotesque, insistent, inescapable except in madness or death.

Early in the film, during the 'documentary' sequence about Lowry's boyhood, Brittain introduced the strand of imagery that achieves its fruition here. His father, who was an enthusiastic body-builder, encouraged his sons' physical development, to mould themselves into models of masculine perfection. To underline the point, he took young Malcolm on a tour of a 'syphilis museum,' making a lesson of the horrifying rot that the body is subject to when carried away by sexual weakness. The photographs of Lowry that recur throughout the film show a man who remained remarkably handsome, and even fit-looking, into middle age. Even so, we understand that he spent the better part of his life showing himself and everyone around him that he was already infected with the rot, the awful decay of mortality. This knowledge is what is implied, of course, by the Mexican celebration of the Day of the Dead – by the worm in the mescal, the glowing liquid with the corpse at the bottom. And this is what comes vividly into the imagination's focus by way of an innocuous film image of a grandfather on holiday conjoined with the fearful language of *Under the Volcano*.

Volcano: An Inquiry into the Life and Death of Malcolm Lowry was released in 1976 and received critical praise far and wide. Most critics rightly gave credit to the creativity that Brittain and Kramer brought to the film's inventive construction. What most did not discuss were the NFB practices going back to the 1940s, brought directly to bear on putting this film together out of interviews, photographs, footage captured often catch-as-catch-can on shoots months apart from one another in four different countries, all of it held together by voice-overs working in two different registers. More than simply holding the images together, the voice-over readings from Lowry's works combine with the film's visual imagery in relations that point beyond what might be simply seen or simply heard, toward the work's true subject: what Lowry referred to as the Hell that lies 'in the heart,' what Brittain, great documentarist that he was, recognized as belonging to an ineffable, intangible reality that he called 'human spirit.'

Notes

1 Brittain, quoted in Riches, 'Oscars in Sight,' 6.
2 Grierson, quoted in Hardy, ed., *Grierson on Documentary*, 13.

3 Brittain, quoted in Riches, 'Oscars in Sight,' 7.
4 Donald Brittain Papers (National Archives of Canada), Box MG 31 D222 Vol. 8, Folder 8-28 ('*Volcano*. Notes'): loose sheet of unlined paper, n.d.
5 Brittain, quoted in 'Writing for the Screen,' 2.
6 See Dorland, 'Rule Brittania,' 12.
7 Blumer and Schouten, 'Green Stripe and Common Sense,' 36.
8 Daly, quoted in Jones, *The Best Butler in the Business*, 36.
9 Brittain, quoted in Dorland, 'Rule Brittania,' 15.
10 Blumer, '*Fields of Sacrifice*,' 28.
11 Blumer and Schouten, 'Green Stripe and Common Sense,' 37.
12 'Brittain, Donald – Interview,' Donald Brittain Papers (National Archives of Canada), Item Number 174191. Third of four taped interviews.

Not a Love Story: A Film about Pornography – Tabloid Rhetoric in Interventionist Documentary

JOAN NICKS

> *The erasure of female subjectivity by the commodification of the female body is ... never quite successful.*
>
> Mary Ann Doane[1]

> *I'm wonderful and articulate, they say. They're even more amazed that I've read so much feminist literature.*
>
> Lindalee Tracey[2]

Produced by the women's studio, Studio D, *Not a Love Story: A Film about Pornography* (Bonnie Sherr Klein, 1981) was the National Film Board's most publicly debated film. For the first time an NFB documentary dared to show the visual spectacle and social actors within pornography and the feminist voices against it. Klein's film was both sanctioned and celebrated, depending upon the critical dispositions taken by those who read the film's problematic documentary approach and feminist agenda. Klein's use of pornographic resources, in a documentary that explores the topic using a rather transparent biblical motif of redemption, is anchored in a journey with her go-between, former stripper Lindalee Tracey (now a writer and documentary filmmaker), who plays interventionist for Klein's feminist cause. Some of the early critiques of *Not a Love Story* took the film to be a moralizing feminist screed, and writers used the occasion as a platform to articulate their own philosophical and ideological positions on pornography, sexuality, and representation.

Lost in the heated debates is a discussion I want to take up here on

Not a Love Story's documentary structure, specifically Klein's employ-
ment of rhetorical devices and imagery, and how the film might be
explored formally and intertextually. I also wish to lend some historical
shape to the place of *Not a Love Story* within the institutional, documentary traditions of the NFB and the now-defunct Studio D (1974–96). My
intention is to problematize the performative social acting of Klein,
Tracey, and other players in the film, its narrativization of pornography's spectacle in which the body is both capital and exhibit, and its
construction of viewing positions in the propagandistic style of *tabloid*
excess. Thus I will draw on contemporary directions in the analysis and
theory of documentary as *ethnography*, and on ethnography's rhetorical
and ideological relations to pornography.

Bill Nichols's discussion of the conventions of television's daytime
talk shows succinctly defines the tabloid-style rhetoric I have in mind:

> The underlying argument, the formal perspective, is more attitudinal: this
> host ... cares about important issues; he or she will explore them conscien-
> tiously; he or she will ferret out evasions and show tact in the face of
> emotional distress; he or she will allow your own surrogate representa-
> tives ... to participate in the dialogue; and we will leave you yet more
> aware of the full extent and possible consequences of the issues even if we
> offer no clear solutions. You may congratulate yourself for watching us;
> we will make you a more informed and empathetic person.[3]

This mode of rhetoric in *Not a Love Story* is put to the service of Klein's
topic, pornography, using an ethnographic process.

In 'Pornography, Ethnography and the Discourses of Power,' Nichols
and co-authors Christian Hansen and Catherine Needham address the
ideological links between pornography and ethnography:

> What does it mean to say pornography and ethnography share a discourse
> of domination? For one thing, they represent impulses born of desire: the
> desire to know and possess, to 'know' by possessing and possess
> by knowing. Each is structured hierarchically. In pornography, male sub-
> jectivity assumes the task of representing female subjectivity; in eth-
> nography, 'our' culture assumes the task of representing theirs. The
> appropriateness of these tasks, though sometimes given a historical con-
> text, remains, for the most part, an assumption, responsibility, or power,
> conferred by dint of membership in the interpreting community rather
> than through negotiation with the interpreted community.[4]

Rhetoric of Reception

With these joint frameworks in mind, let us look at the rhetoric of the interpreting community that controlled viewership of *Not a Love Story*. When the film was conditionally released in Ontario, a prominent label was attached to the film's can, directed at the exhibitor/user: 'Important: This film is not approved for public screenings by [the] Ontario Censor Board. Under law, the user must restrict exhibition to private screenings and refrain from public advertising.' An implicit class bias is embedded in this screening condition, suggesting peep-show viewing but for educated audiences who would not be unduly impaired by seeing the actual pornography used to illustrate the film's message. In an era well before computer access to pornography became borderless and impossible to police, *Not a Love Story* was at once a covert and a respectable documentary object. Its examination of pornography by women threatened the domain of male spectatorship. One effect was that Klein's film put feminism and women's documentary practice to the test: the film's rhetoric, its topic, and its filmmaker(s) would undergo justification, explanation, and refutation.

Noted Canadian filmmaker and critic R. Bruce Elder took offence at *Not a Love Story*'s sin-and-redemption 'theology,' arguing that an empirically based documentary, such as Klein's, has no language (and, by inference, no right) to extrapolate a spiritual theme (the 'divine') from the testimonies of the film subjects' experience.[5] Elder's passionate discussion is laced with hyperbole and parody of the film's religious allegory: 'This mirror opposite of true religion, whose rituals involve desecrating a female, could be none other than Satanism.'[6] But Elder rightly concludes that *Not a Love Story*'s flaws are in its form and coded language:

> *Not a Love Story* has been hailed as a work that is important because it raises pressing issues for discussion. The form of the film makes lies of these claims. The film does not raise issues for discussion; it seals them off from discussion ... *Not a Love Story* is ultimately a theological/moral text masquerading as an empirical documentary. This sort of film is thoroughly objectionable ... I believe that the only language our culture offers us is a language unsuited for discussing theological concepts.[7]

American feminist critic E. Ruby Rich also lambasted and parodied *Not a Love Story*'s 'religious parable,' calling the film 'an exercise in show-and-tell ... Conversion cinema in action.' Like Elder, Rich sees the film to be a 'moral tale' whose social players are barely disguised 'religious actors' (e.g., 'rank sinners,' 'a roster of saints'). Using pornographic jargon, Rich condemns *Not a Love Story* as 'a kind of snuff movie for an anti-snuff crowd.' Yet, she concludes, 'as the first mass-audience film to take up the subject of pornography, *Not a Love Story* is an important work. It opens up the issues even if it closes them down again too soon.'[8]

While the rhetoric of Klein's film is obviously polemical, debates on the film also tended to be polemical, and emotional, laced with liberal defences of free expression or conservative concerns for the public good. Elder's and Rich's passionate critiques of *Not a Love Story* provide a sense of the tenor of the time (early 1980s) when the film was becoming widely known in Canada and the United States. Their arguments are an inviting challenge to any current attempts to reread Klein's film. The popular press was either celebratory or dismissive of the film's feminist agenda against pornography, and the Ontario Censor Board restricted public screenings to 'educational' forums. I was invited to give numerous campus and community presentations on *Not a Love Story* and issues regarding pornography in such oppositional forums as: 'Arts Against Repression,' a visual arts series against censorship; a student-union gender issues forum against the imagery and culture of pornography; a feminist forum on critical and cultural issues within documentary practice; and a public meeting of the local chapter of the University Women's Club, where a panel of women lawyers used Klein's film as a cause célèbre for an anti-pornography petition to the Canadian federal government. Common to all of these forums was an eagerness in audiences to hear how Klein's film *worked as a documentary*. In fact, in the large audience attending the University Women's Club forum, my discussion of the film itself became an intervention into an orchestrated event that was to serve a 'higher' social cause. What interested me then, and now, is that the audience (women, men, and teens, diverse classes) welcomed discussion of the film itself as a documentary and cultural artefact.

Prior controversial NFB films have undergone public debate and sanction, typically on the basis of a film's anti-capitalist or anti-establishment politics, predictably making them historically important and famous even if unavailable to the public.[9] *Not a Love Story* heightened the so-called gender wars over pornography, as well as over the kinds of films that women directors *ought* to make in a period when controlling pornography and denigrating feminism were conjoined preoccupations. This rhetorical conjunction of pornography and feminism creates a *tabloid effect* that can be illuminated by analysis of the links between ethnography and pornography. Though *Not a Love Story* alludes to such links, the allusions are lost to the tabloid sensation of the film's project.

Tabloid Tactics

Not a Love Story begins with the visual imagery of tabloid sensation, as the camera tracks back from a red screen to reveal a heart shape against which a pin-up in satin poses seductively. The film's title is superimposed on this image, both exploiting and effacing the tabloid-style 'girlie' clichés that follow in a string of stills from 'skin' magazines: a woman posed with bow and arrow against a red heart; another posed as a leather-bound femme in studded g-string; another posed in signature *Penthouse* style with a vivid, red, penis-shaped lipstick pressed against her full red lips; a coy blond licking a large, heart-shaped sucker; another peering seductively over the heart-shaped rims of her glasses. On the soundtrack, a pulsing heartbeat underlines the visceral effect.

Accompanying *Not a Love Story*'s title imagery is feminist writer Susan Griffin's commentary on pornography, pulling the imagery and sound into thematic focus – and collision. Griffin's contention is that pornography is a travesty that relegates women's bodies to subservience and their spirits to silence ('the heart [brought to] the knees and if necessary the heart rendered silent'). The collision of bold images and ideological statement creates a *picture-and-headline* discourse to establish the thesis-basis of Klein's documentary. This tactic of colliding image and ideology had a precedent at the NFB in Anne Claire Poirier's highly formal and controversial 1979 docudrama, *Mourir à tue-tête*, on the gendered subjugation of a rape victim.

As NFB filmmakers and feminists, Poirier and Klein laid claim to two explosive topics of the time – women as rape victims and as pornographic objects – and both filmmakers employed the devices of the thesis film. Though Poirier's and Klein's very topics were bolder than any other films in the NFB's history, their respective thesis approaches were not new but rather institutionalized at the Film Board in the Second World War propaganda films produced under John Grierson. In *Not a Love Story*, the thesis justifies the use of tabloid rhetoric just as it necessitates the use of pornographic illustration.

Not a Love Story also adopts the 1960s direct-cinema practice of taking

Not a Love Story (1981), directed by Bonnie Sherr Klein. Courtesy of the National Film Board of Canada.

camera and crew into the field. In direct-cinema fashion, Klein's camera insinuates itself into sites of pornographic production, exhibition, and spectatorship, initially in a Canadian venue, then mainly in American locations. But her point of view can only be driven by a thesis that all pornography represents women's subjugation: in part, as the contestable argument goes, because it is not erotica. Klein begins in a Montreal strip club and a meeting with Lindalee Tracey, who becomes her go-between. With Tracey in tow, Klein's initial destination is New York's 42nd Street porn district, like many NFB direct-cinema documentaries before which moved to the centre of unfamiliar yet populated cultural sites from the safe distance of documentary inquiry, as in *Lonely Boy* (1961), for example. Their sense of mission shapes the documentary structure, with Klein assuming the dual role of outsider-filmmaker, and Tracey the role of insider-companion. In voice-over Klein provides two rationales for her film, rationales being a common rhetorical device in the long history and mandate of NFB documentaries from its inception in 1939. As a convention, a rationale establishes the social purpose of documentary, and, in certain periods of the Board, rationales were sometimes used as a ruse to parody the purposeful, thesis-driven NFB documentary established by Grierson.[10]

In voice-over, Klein declares her personal mission in *Not a Love Story*: to understand 'what's going on inside the [strip club] doors,' prompted, she says, by her role as mother of an eight-year-old daughter (Naomi, now a print journalist who writes about popular culture) who has questioned Klein about the porn magazines visible in convenience stores. Klein's documentary and personal agendas dovetail in the tabloid location of the convenience store's rack of easy-to-access, soft-core pornographic magazines. Tracey becomes a surrogate for Klein's young daughter, eager to take the journey under Klein's documentary wing.

In her memoir, *Growing Up Naked: My Years in Bump and Grind*, Tracey writes of their meeting, her desires, and conditions for the film:

> Doing the film seems like an instant education. I'm not sure what pornography is. Am I supposed to be pornography? I don't think so. I don't like competing with porno films in the clubs and seeing the tits and asses all over the billboards and magazine covers ...
>
> I'm not sure what I'm supposed to be doing in the film, besides going along and watching things. I'm no expert on porn, so I guess my job is to bring another, looser point of view. I don't know anything about making films either, but I know how small the news people can make me. I tell the women [Klein and the Studio D producers] I want all my parts included, the poetry, the home, the performance art. I want to be whole so people know that strippers are complicated and not just bodies. That's my condition, and they agree.[11]

Tracey's references to the reductive practices of 'news people,' and to the skin magazines that trouble her, speak to the tabloidism that is part of Klein's project.

In their discussion of the links between pornography and ethnography, Hansen, Needham, and Nichols suggest that 'sexual actors are watched, while cultural actors are watched over.'[12] Klein brings these two practices of looking together in the opening sequence, in the Montreal strip club where Tracey performs her 'Little Red Riding Hood' act. Tracey toys with her pleased male audience by offering them a teasing woman-child persona, berating their voyeurism but also serving it by the very conditions of expectation and spectatorship in the strip-club arena.[13] In Klein's structuring, Tracey first denounces feminists who have derided her profession, then commands feminist attention as she 'grows' to their values – as the film would have it, through the experience of Klein's filmmaking with its 'mentoring' voices (Susan Griffin, Robin Morgan, Kathleen Barrie). Seemingly, Tracey moves from 'sexual actor' to embrace her (feminist) accusers' positions.

In her memoir, Tracey tells a more informative story, though never directly naming Klein; rather, she refers to 'the two women [who] ask me to join them as a partner on their film journey': 'I like surprising them, but I don't forget they're the feminist enemy, casting shadows on the clubs and on our right to exist. But I want to know them now, to compare their ideas with mine.'[14] As presented in the film, the Klein/Tracey initial meeting focuses on Tracey confidently testifying to the condescension of feminists' remarks about her work as a stripper. She defends herself and male voyeurism by invoking what she terms the 'honesty' of the stripper's arena where she makes her living and finds pleasure in it. Tracey is a working woman who loves her work, though not in the conventional sense of middle-class feminist discourse. In Klein's documentary setup, Tracey's vocal contentions establish a documentary ruse that she will play the film's antagonist, as if pornography's defender. Arguably, despite, or because of, her profession as a stripper, Tracey agrees to be an illustrative lesson on behalf of Klein's film. In Tracey's recollection, she writes, 'I want to get the feeling of it, to the seam between fake and real.'[15]

Klein's documentary strategy plays at and with ideological doubles: her own feminist and documentary interests, and patient understanding of Tracey's assertive defence of the 'immediate love' her male audience gives her. As Rich observes, Tracey, not Klein, is the real 'star' of *Not a Love Story*, but what goes unacknowledged by Klein is her deployment of Tracey as a go-between who also strikes the rhetorical postures of a listener figure within the shooting processes.[16] The documentary compass for the women's journey would appear to be based on debate and female companionship. But numerous shots show Tracey as silent audience for powerful American feminists or framed by their comments and voice-overs. In the presence of Robin Morgan with her passionate anti-pornography stance, Tracey listens raptly and wipes away tears, as if absorbed in a scene from 1940s family melodrama.

Thesis Tactics
Layering pornographic illustration and anti-porn voices, Klein takes a tack consistent with the thesis documentary's thesis/antithesis convention. It is a duplicitous strategy, not because it is uncommon in docu-

mentary but, rather, because in making the first film 'about' pornography, Klein has to attempt to do it all, and she is constrained in this ambition. Her 1970s feminism at once needs to 'show the goods' (pornography) and to flag the social relevance of her project and processes, in tune with Studio D's mandate and in order to speak to *middle-class viewers.* To this end, Klein sets herself up on-screen as an ordinary woman who, as she confides to Tracey, never had to deal with 'all the tits and asses before.' Tabloid interests apparently are outside her cultural scope, while documentary is her working domain. She must convey that she is an adept documentary filmmaker capable of managing her go-between Tracey, a young working-class woman, to meet her goals.[17]

Lacking the licence of making a fiction film, Klein must drive through the documentariness of her project, but her sleight of hand is evident in the film's performative devices. Her on-screen persona as documentary filmmaker and feminist 'sister' to Tracey is marked by her plain talk and appearance and her nonaggressive, but nevertheless performative, presence. What Tracey is being propelled towards is *Klein's* brand of feminist wisdom, and her 'redemption' at the end of the film shows through as contrivance. Tracey's recitation of her own poetry for Klein in a beach setting becomes arch and false, elaborated like a Hollywood film. In retrospect, Tracey writes that the beach scene makes

> it look like I'm bleeding from being a stripper instead of reeling from that day with Suze [Randall, *Hustler* magazine photographer]. Then at the end I'm a snappy, happy, born-again feminist penitent – a bad girl gone good. The film takes credit for my supposed conversion, as if I had no intellectual context before.[18]

This performative strategy is common to melodrama: for example, one operation of the classical (1940s) women's film is that the woman in question is returned to her 'rightful' cultural place, particularly if she is a working-class figure (for example, King Vidor's *Stella Dallas*, 1937; Michael Curtiz's *Mildred Pierce*, 1945).

Documentary Dilemmas in the Field

Part of Klein's role in, and behind, *Not a Love Story* is as researcher as well as committed woman's-issues filmmaker. In voice-over narration, she cites statistics in a matter-of-fact voice that is different from her careful ('big sister') nurturing of Tracey on-screen, or her wry interviewing of porn-magazine publisher David Wells for which she is dolled up in a satin blouse and skilfully trips up his shaky defence that 'market research' shows that the 'greatest turn-on' for men is fellatio. In her statistics-reciting voice, Klein claims that six of the ten top magazines of the period fall into the category of adult entertainment ('skin' magazines). She cites statistics about the products of the porn industry, said to be larger than the combined film and magazine industries of the period. There is nothing of Klein's wry humour or performative roles in her narration, but rather the necessary voice and exposition of a documentary filmmaker who knows her topic because she has done her homework as a researcher. Her reportage-narration is delivered 'above' the shots of New York's sleazy 42nd Street porn district, enforcing the tabloid look of it all.

Klein's most problematic operation as documentary filmmaker in the field occurs in the scene where Suze Randall photographs Tracey as if Tracey were a centrefold porn figure. In interview, Randall is only informational about the history of porn, noting the shift in 1969 from *Playboy* to *Penthouse* and the evolution in Larry Flint's *Hustler* magazine from 'pussy' to gynecological 'spreads.' She uses the language of pornography, and unlike Klein with her voice-over statistics, she is a tabloid persona – somewhat unexpectedly, an English woman who is giggly and gossipy. She is the opposite of feminist Kate Millet, who explains to Klein that the United States' puritanical roots have made the culture receptive to pornography over 'erotica' (which she herself favours and creates in the drawings she shows Klein). But Millet's rhetoric (erotica is 'for it,' and porn is 'against it') doesn't illuminate the distinctions that the terms are supposed to convey. It is in structurally following Randall that Millett's ease, articulateness, and 'natural woman' persona become a corrective to Randall's apparent lack of substance. Randall is shown to be unanalytical about her role in pornography (it's all 'play-play' and shouldn't be taken 'too seriously'). In the company of Randall, both Klein and Tracey appear to be stuck in a tabloid narrative, discussing allowable angles by which erect 'dicks' can be photographed for popular 'skin' magazines and the aesthetic arrangements by which vulvas are made to resemble 'flowers.'[19]

Tracey's posing for Randall is edited into *Not a Love Story* as the film's penultimate scene, so its function is climactic, as if following the classical Hollywood narrative paradigm, and salutary, as if a moment of documentary truth. In light of the movement of Klein and Tracey's journey together, during which prominent American feminists, as well as psychologist Ed Donerstein, have all had their scenes and says on pornography, Tracey's posing for Randall constructs a problem for the film that Klein never resolves.[20]

In earlier sequences, when Klein puts herself in the position of paying male spectator-customer, in a New York peep-show emporium, she attempts to redress the problem of the male gaze in pornography. Instead of requesting porn display from sex workers who sit behind glassed cubicles waiting for clients, Klein interviews them about how they feel in their work (degraded). Rich is right to argue that Klein's position in these sequences does not give us the sex workers' perspectives *on* the male voyeurism the women serve: 'Doesn't such a shot turn the viewer into the male customer normally occupying that vantage point?'[21] Arguably, Klein partially disrupts the male viewing position by seeking *opinions* from the women who otherwise only function as pornographic displays. But in the scene where Randall photographs Tracey, Klein puts herself, and us as viewers, into a more questionable viewing position and fails to problematize her camera's voyeuristic position. The preparation of Tracey's vulva (we get a close-up, if briefly), as photographer Randall calls for 'pussy juice' and 'pussy light,' is intercut with a shot of Klein (serious-faced) safely behind the cameras and lighting sources. Tracey poses easily for Randall and with a degree of self-effacement and humour, but Klein's position echoes the one her camera takes in the film's first scene, when Tracey taunts and amuses the male customers who put money into her hands for her parody of spread-leg 'box' shots. In both instances, Klein positions herself and us as passive voyeurs.

Tracey's and Klein's rites of passage as documentary go-between and documentary filmmaker ultimately fit the colonizing mode of ethnography, concluding with Susan Griffin's moral lesson, which is extended in the film's epilogue (Klein and Tracey on the beach). Griffin is the linchpin between Tracey's 'arrival scene' as Randall's – and Klein's – porn-inscribed subject, and the film's epilogue. Shot in sunlight, Griffin offers that, inside, a woman 'knows that she can't be objectified ... that she has another vision,' rehearsing the thesis of her book *Pornography and Silence* (1981). Tracey is shown to smile in agreement, a feeling she carries into her appearance and disposition in the epilogue, but especially in the reading of her own poetry for Klein. Klein's strategy effects Tracey's revelation and redemption. But, the key question is: revelation and redemption from what to what? By my argument, Tracey's revelation and redemption proceed through tabloid rhetoric and the fields of pornography to feminist polemic.

The sun-drenched naturalism of the beach in the epilogue, with Tracey in white t-shirt and bikini bottom, carries traces of the aesthetics of Poirier's *Mourir à tue-tête* in which the dead but redeemed rape victim is draped in white, on a bier and ethereally lit by a 'holy' shaft of light from a high window. However, Poirier's excessive imagery evokes a doomed protagonist. Klein, on the other hand, constructs formulaic, Hollywood-like closure in *Not a Love Story* and a positivist feminism for her go-between. If anything is 'snuffed,' as Rich writes, adopting porn-rhetoric, it is the tabloid discourse into which the film has had to immerse itself.[22] Klein offers a new day, and feminist discourse is that new day. In ethnographic terms, Tracey's Otherness has been overcome by feminist discourse. Like a grown-up confessing to an older sister, Tracey confides that she felt 'weird' about Klein and the NFB crew witnessing her posing for Randall's camera. She has experienced what it means 'to fall off knowing what you are ... feeling sick' but is glad to have endured for she now knows what pornography is about. Tracey's new day is writ large, in the recitation of her poem (a kind of personal mission statement), and the sentimentally optimistic song ('I'm much more than this/I have an image of my own') that plays on the sound-track through the closing credits.[23]

If we look backward at *Not a Love Story*'s structure, Klein does make it apparent that Tracey represents the film's litmus test. She nurtures Tracey to her own ideological positioning through their rapport, for example, in their warm embrace before a rack of 'skin' magazines. Tracey confides that what she is seeing in New York is getting to her emotionally, but adds that her foot is still in the 'money barrel' as a stripper. Here in the field, the film reminds us of its tabloid beginnings at the magazine rack in Montreal. In New York Tracey instructs Klein to ask her how she feels at the end of the week, which becomes a narrative foretelling of the epilogue, when Tracey will express her feelings with certainty. The short New York scene comes at a key point in the struc-ture, as punctuation underlining the documentary's ethnography and reiterating the film's ideological rightness: redemption requires testing in the field, and revelation becomes proof of the rightness of the test – and the tester.

Tracey's initial, rhetorical test in yet another porn district (in Califor-nia) has her standing on a soapbox, a performance-art gesture that draws a hostile crowd (mostly men), who berate her and her anti-porn poem. A black man shouts that she's 'downing them' (women sex workers), and a smirking white man gestures expressively for Klein's camera but directed at Tracey, holding up a fist to show off his swastika tattoo. This sequencing becomes 'proof' of the film's thesis, for in the next scene Susan Griffin likens pornography to a blank screen: 'that screen is women's silence.' But as a vocal woman in the film's crisis structure, Tracey's accusatory soapbox rhetoric predictably provokes the nasty male responses it receives from men guarding a territory at risk. What is questionable here as documentary (as in ethnography) is Klein's ethics, for she never contests her on-screen presence as, for example, former NFB filmmaker Michael Rubbo did in developing interventionist documentary strategies a decade earlier.[24]

Conclusion

One issue that *Not a Love Story* raises for women's documentary is how feminist discourse can become propaganda and specifically the degree to which film can, or should, represent the mentorship that Klein takes on, pointing a young woman, and thus viewers, in the direction of her ideological, creative, and critical ethic. One way to historicize this issue is to recall that feminist film theory and agendas of the 1970s helped to shape women's filmmaking stratagems, with strong and often inviting prescriptions and models setting out the kinds of filmmaking that women directors *ought* to take up.[25] Under the early leadership of executive producer Kathleen Shannon, Studio D's mandate took up women's issues through documentary production. The cause drove the projects, and a documentary and ideological sameness prevailed.

Critic Elizabeth Anderson has raised an underlying problem with Studio D's mandate in her rhetorical question, 'Are these films, in effect, a form of collective cultural therapy – a comfortable, distant way for audiences to sample the lives of people who exist at the margins of the national community?'[26] In her memoir, *Slow Dance* (1997), Klein, who writes from the healing perspective of her long rehabilitation after a stroke, makes a similar point about her filmmaker's work as cultural labour:

> Watching *Not a Love Story* after so many years, I see that it's really about voice – or lack of it. The dialogue about pornography and erotica has evolved since 1981 and become more complex, but *Not a Love Story* was part of breaking women's silence, opening our eyes and our mouths. Seeing it now in Israel, I realize the coherence of my life's work. It wasn't a series of unrelated films, but variations on a related theme: speech vs. silence, peace vs. violence, solidarity vs. isolation.[27]

One general criticism of *Not a Love Story* is that it isn't strong enough. In part, this is due to the softness of Klein's role as an intervening documentary filmmaker addressing a controversial topic. She engages minimally in conversation or debate with the film's feminist 'talking heads.' This is most noticeable when she sits on the floor listening to Robin Morgan, who is surrounded (and embraced) by her husband and young son at the end of her passionate anti-pornography statement. Morgan weeps at the very moment she says that the battle ahead is 'like making a real renaissance in the middle of insanity ... in a Bosch world.' She concludes that women must confront men with their 'shame' not their 'guilt' – for she 'loves men too much' not to have faith in their ability to be resensitized. Klein plays listener throughout, as does Tracey, without confronting Morgan about an implication in her ardent speech, which is that women should remain men's (and culture's) nurturers – correcting, sensitizing.[28]

In retrospect, Tracey frequently attests to her need, as a stripper and as a woman, to please men and male audiences and, importantly, to befriend the other strippers she worked with. Her recollection of the experience of first seeing the film, with the filmmakers, is striking in its condemnation:

> Months go by and then the women from the National Film Board show me the film. I'm stunned. They huddle around me, wanting me to like it, needing me to. I have to stop myself from shaking. How do you tell someone you like that you feel betrayed and sickened? ...
>
> The 'educational' film gets a prestigious screening at the Toronto Film Festival, and another is scheduled at a benefit for *Ms* magazine in New York. I wake up one morning to a huge photograph of me from the Suze shoot in *The Globe and Mail*. It crushes me – I feel exploited, the same way the filmmakers say pornography exploits other women.[29]

What Klein's construction of Tracey works towards on screen is ideological solidarity and ethnographic progress out of rhetorical contradiction. *Not a Love Story* is a documentary of its time, but still capable of provoking attention and debates for audiences and in the media.[30] And, it has garnered a place for Klein in Canadian cinema that her other documentaries likely would not have done.[31] But it builds a 'sisterhood' of feminist sentiment that could only exist in Klein's seamless structuring of a thesis documentary out of fieldwork and talking heads. This is particularly so because *Not a Love Story* is a Studio D film with the double mission of serving the NFB's documentary purpose and a women's-issues mandate.

Notes

1 Doane, 'The Economy of Desire,' 23.
2 Tracey, *Growing Up Naked*, 190.
3 Nichols, *Representing Reality*, 130.
4 Ibid., 209.
5 Elder, 'Two Journeys,' 238.
6 Ibid., 241.
7 Ibid., 242.
8 Rich, 'Anti-Porn: Soft Issue, Hard World,' 62, 64, 74. Midway, the language of Rich's article changes mood and substance, from smart journalese to sharp treatise on the issues concerning pornography that feminists were debating in the period.
9 The banning of Denys Arcand's *On est au coton*, his 1970 NFB documentary on exploited workers in Quebec's textile industry, is a prominent example of such censorship within the Film Board. See Jim Leach's essay in this volume.
10 The French Unit's *Les Raquetteurs* (1958), with its initial definition of snowshoeing, is an example from early direct cinema of the rationale as ruse.
11 Tracey, *Growing Up Naked*, 190–1.
12 Nichols, *Representing Reality*, 212.
13 In her own documentary, *Abby, I Hardly Knew Ya* (1995), Tracey acts out emotionally for her own camera, lamenting a missing male, her unknown dead father.
14 Tracey, *Growing Up Naked*, 189–90.
15 Ibid., 198.
16 Rich, 'Anti-Porn: Soft Issue, Hard World,' 63.
17 Historically within the NFB, Klein's rhetorical approach in *Not a Love Story* may again be likened to the more formal structural precedent in *Mourir à tue-tête*; Poirier's reflexive docudrama is structured around a victim-protagonist but pivots ideologically on the on-screen debates and strategies of the fictional women filmmakers (a director and her editor) editing the film-within-the-film. Poirier's film is a feminist treatise in the guise of dialogue, on a highly charged and gendered topic. While Poirier's two women filmmakers are consistently serious and driven by 'their' film

project (*Mourir*'s film-within-a-film), they also intentionally and formally exploit their fictional protagonist in the very processes of defending her and showing the universality of her trauma and suicide.

18 Tracey, *Growing Up Naked*, 201–2.

19 'Flowers' is a term that Tracey uses some sixteen years later in her memoir, quoting an older stripper who described her own genitalia as such; *Growing Up Naked*, 8. In the film, Tracey uses the term to name the fiction being applied to her sex in the process of being prepared for a porn-'spread' shoot for Randall.

20 Tracey describes her distress, and Randall's, when the photography session was over: 'I follow Suze into the bathroom and find her heaving in great, shaking sobs. She tells me no one's ever complained before, that they've always said they [the models] were having fun. I feel sorry for her. Who am I to judge how another woman makes her money. So all I can do is say how it affects me'; *Growing Up Naked*, 199–200.

21 Rich, 'Anti-Porn: Soft Issue, Hard World,' 65.

22 Ibid., 64.

23 Klein's simplistic closure fits the tradition of Griersonian good-news propaganda, concluding with a freeze-frame of Tracey, floral lei around her neck, reaching towards the sun. This is reminiscent of such Griersonian Second World War propaganda films as *Wings on Her Shoulder* (1943), which ends with a group of smiling women in Canada's armed forces gazing skyward to 'the men who fly.' Tracey writes in her memoir that the filming of the beach scene seemed 'so beside the point, this is not a film about me, but I go along. Maybe people need to know how porn feels. I did'; *Growing Up Naked*, 200.

24 Rubbo's persona-driven, on-screen interventions and use of go-betweens began with the activist women in *Persistent and Finagling* (1971), a film that well preceded Studio D and its stake in feminist ideology. See Jeannette Sloniowski's essay on Rubbo's *Waiting for Fidel* (1974) in this volume. Tracey herself would continue to exploit – with the heavy-handedness of realist melodrama – the conventions and rhetoric of a performative documentary persona in her double role as intervening director and emotive daughter in *Abby, I Hardly Knew Ya*.

25 For example, Laura Mulvey's oft-reprinted article, 'Visual Pleasure and Narrative Cinema' (1975) and Canadian critic and filmmaker Kay Armatage's early documentaries *Jill Johnston, October 1975* (1977) and *Striptease* (1980).

26 Anderson, 'Studio D's Imagined Community,' 55.

27 Klein and Blackbridge, *Slow Dance*, 314.

28 Tracey recalls a troubling perspective that prevailed in the shooting processes of *Not a Love Story*, specifically how the famous American feminists,
but not Tracey, were filmed: 'We film Robin at home, we'll film all the
feminists that way, in their own worlds, surrounded by their trinkets, not
swallowed up in ugly places like the porn girls. Robin reclines on her sofa
with her husband and son ... charming and welcoming'; *Growing Up Naked*,
193.
29 Ibid., 201–3.
30 For discussion on *Not a Love Story*'s reception at a film festival in Israel in
1989, where Klein is treated as a 'media star,' see Klein and Blackridge,
Slow Dance, 311–14.
31 Wise, '100 Great and Glorious Years of Canadian Cinema,' 31.

Voyage en Amérique avec un cheval emprunté: A Journey of the Mind

MARION FROGER

Nous sommes nés à quêter la vérité, il appartient de la posséder à une plus grande puissance. (We are born to seek the truth; it brings to the possessor a greater power.)

Montaigne, Essais

Voyage en Amérique avec un cheval emprunté (*Travels in America with a Borrowed Horse*, Jean Chabot, 1987) is part of a National Film Board series conceived and produced by Eric Michel, and devoted to *américanité*. This series comprised six documentaries, all produced between 1986 and 1988. Its goal was to encourage filmmakers to consider Quebec's place in North America, to put *québécitude* into perspective by exploring the *américanité*, more or less conscious and more or less well understood and accepted, within it.[1]

However, *américanité*, a concept more abstract than 'Americanization' or 'acculturation' and even the 'globalization' it implies, proved to be a difficult subject for a documentary. Indeed, conceiving a film around such an abstract concept was a real gamble. Was it assumed that the filmmakers would become economists, sociologists, or historians in order to define Quebec's relationship with the United States; or philosophers in order to describe the relations of the self and the other; or even ethnographers in order to describe the common founding myth of North American cultures?

In their contributions to the series, Sophie Bissonnette (*L'Amour ... à quel prix?*, 1988) and Micheline Lanctôt (*La Poursuite du bonheur*, 1987) ventured onto this terrain with the production of two social and economic reports. In classic fashion, their commentaries take possession of the images, name or explain them, and incorporate them into the political discourse of the filmmakers, which thereby gains visual confirmation. Jacques Godbout (*Alias Will James*, 1988) and Herménégilde Chiasson (*Le Grand Jack*, 1987) chose to address the question of *américanité* by making it tangible, literally giving it a face: the faces of Will James and Jack Kerouac, both Québécois by birth but who subscribed in their writings to that dreamt or mythical 'American America' that may be more meaningful to non-Americans than to Americans themselves. Behind the term *américanité*, the directors saw a search for identity and made it the basis of two essentially biographical films in which each writer's career symbolizes and reveals the motives and desires of a collective Québécois consciousness.

The two most original endeavours were those of Jean Chabot and Jean-Daniel Lafond (*Le Voyage au bout de la route ou La Ballade du pays qui attend*, 1987). Both used the 'travelogue,' as Chabot calls it, as a form of intellectual exercise. However, it is Chabot who offers a thorough exploration of the formal work needed to follow the progress of abstract thought in the documentary image. This point is of particular interest. The Candid Eye seems far away indeed. It is not a question of letting the images speak for themselves, or of concealing the formal aspect of the documentary behind the least manipulative possible form of editing. But neither is it a question of returning to the classic, controlling documentary discourse that exposes *its* truth and imposes *its* analysis; nor of yielding to the journalistic lure of an objectivity that refuses to take a point of view. In the manner of Chris Marker's essay films, Chabot opts for absolute subjectivity by writing a monologue in the first person that takes the place of the commentary, left vacant since the advent of direct cinema.[2] He chooses fiction instead of documentary, appears on-screen as the protagonist, and creates an improvised tour of America.[3] He eschews statistics and observations in the field to give free rein, in his words and images, to the memories, fantasies, and hallucinations that will provide the main building blocks of his thought.

A Cinematic Essay
It is understandable then why the option chosen by Chabot proved perplexing to some viewers. There was a strong temptation to pay attention only to the protagonist's discourse and to find in it the filmmaker's whole proposition. In this discourse, Chabot appears to be

worried about the fragility of the francophone culture in an unfavour-
able demographic and linguistic context; more generally, his character
wonders about the Americanization of the world that he associates
with neoliberalism, sets up an opposition between national culture and
American hegemony, raises the old bugbear of American political im-
perialism, denounces the global reach of economic and human exploitation in the wake of American capitalism, finally establishes the system's
aggression toward all cultural traditions, and seems unable to imagine
the emergence of viable cultures in the context of a globalization marching to the drum of large corporations. Chabot takes care not to develop
the subject in a theoretical way or to delve into the political, social,
psychological, and even psychoanalytical implications of this account.
He will be reproached for the absence of analysis, for not going beyond
simple opinion. From this perspective, the formal aspect of the film
seems to be secondary: intended only to make Chabot's discourse
pleasurable, even though it may have the opposite effect. The monologue, uninterrupted except by a few inner silences, may put people off,
and the fiction of this man in flight, because of his fear of impending
fatherhood, may interest nobody.[4]

We miss Chabot's point if we focus only on the discursive content of
his monologue and dismiss questions of form as of marginal interest.
On the contrary, Chabot's formal work is central, as Ian Lockerbie
stresses in an article on the reflexive documentary in Quebec; if he
undercuts the discursive treatment of Americanization, if he thereby
deprives himself of all credibility (using a monologue, resorting to
fiction, departing from the 'objective' documentary image in favour of
memories, fantasies, etc.), it is for the sake of another way of thinking
with which the filmmaker experiments in his essay film.[5] *Américanité*,
from this point of view, is less an idea to develop, illustrate, and so
forth, assuming its validity, than an empty concept around which Chabot
moves, finding a way – in this very emptiness – to question himself
about his own thought and about the fragility of this thought. This
blend of scepticism and reflexivity has characterized the essay form
ever since Michel de Montaigne defined its 'ever-changing' principles,
and Chabot adapts these principles to his own purposes. He seems to
want to shift the debate on the essay to the completely new terrain of
the reflexive documentary.

Studying Chabot's film thus provides an occasion to reformulate the
question of a possible *cinematic development* of thought. It could be that
this film involves a subversive experiment with traditional discursive

forms, a thought aspiring to 'speech' – a demonstration or account of the experience of thought – rather than an argument.[6]

As a first step, the question can be turned around to identify the forms of thought that the film does not reproduce, for example, argumentative thought that requires analysis based on figures and examples. It is thought of this kind that characterizes the research report, concerning the demographics of the Québécois population, that Hélène Bourgault prepared for Chabot during the preparatory stages of *Voyage en Amérique*. Chabot is very careful to avoid reproducing verbatim the arguments and conclusions in this report. He chooses only the information that interests him, that is to say, anything that might be included in the preoccupations of his character, a Montrealer anxious about the future of his life-space. He scatters this information throughout his monologue *without once presenting it as an argument*. It wanders around in the text just as it haunts the character's mind, like a statistic whose figures he has forgotten.

This dispersal of information, this argumentative volatility, contrasts with the methodical rigidity of Bourgault's report. The film's interior monologue tracks down a thought and discovers the impossibility of finding an answer to the question of identity. Without an answer, the methodology of exposition and demonstration, which is the basis of the didactic and omniscient commentary of classical documentary, makes no sense. And it is therefore easy to understand why Chabot abandons it. Isn't this a sign of thinking in an *essay*, that it constantly ventures into the unthinkable, remaining and even justifying itself in its interrogative form?

Thinking between Text and Image

Let us return then to what Chabot offers us in *Voyage en Amérique*. He offers us a risky, lonely venture, beyond the American border, motivated only by the need to think. The route thus corresponds to a movement of thought that seeks to be initiated and made concrete in the *experience of looking*. All that the film's protagonist needs is images, images that he gleans, invents, and remembers. It is this special collusion between image, movement, and thought that I would like to investigate in this study. By yielding to the sense of sight while passing through a *territory*, Chabot banks on being able to fix the direction of his character's thought and to offer it, no longer in traditional discursive articulations, bound to written expression, but in the literal representation of his journey, and above all in closer proximity to what makes him think: images, then, gathered along the way that the man begins to read, but also images emerging from the discourse, around a memory or a fantasy that he can't get out of his mind and that inscribes itself on everything he sees.

Let us look more closely at what goes on between the text and the images. Neither argumentative nor informative, the text of the monologue involves more than just its narrative aspect. Once the reasons for departure are explained, the story of the journey is abandoned and replaced by an internal monologue that attempts to capture the ideas that appear along the way. These ideas appear through the gaze of the protagonist at the landscape; they are captured by the text, in the images that it, in its own turn, is able to evoke. In this way, the text functions as a search for verbal images that have been forgotten in the argumentative exercise of speech, and the film as a search for missing images, virtual images that purely documentary images cannot convey. The text will trouble the documentary image, and the documentary image will disturb the noble linearity of the text.

I will give some examples of the special relationship established between the images and the words. First, words seek to make images from the past reappear, mental images – not visible on the screen, imprecise, changeable – that 'haunt' the character. In effect, the text brings personal memory and historical recollection into the present to *create* an image, over and above the documentary images that occupy the screen:

> With my father, with my uncles, we would often go to see the machines working, to see a few simple cogs in the system, without ever trying to understand how the whole thing worked, any more than we could hope to in those places where we watched trains passing, planes taking off, locks opening, and boats leaving.
>
> I am once again a little boy of four or seven. With my uncle Richard, I am going south on a very windy or rainy day.

A verbal image is superimposed on a film image: Iroquois playing baseball, says the monologue, while the screen shows a wasteland. The violent and inexorable disappearance of civilizations has found here, as a symbol, a simple documentary image that gives it all the weight of reality.

I will also note that the monologue is concerned to reveal *visions* of the present and of the past as well as purely imaginary visions that the documentary image cannot show. There is also the aptly named 'apocalyptic fantasy' that the protagonist describes over the most banal images of the frontier.[7] The idea is to bring into view the implications and tendencies of everyday life, what is happening under the visible surface of things.

Finally, the text has its origins in the crucial images that release not only words, but the journey itself: such is the highly enigmatic image of *in utero* life that opens the film, an image of annunciation, a promise, an image of that which exists without being born, an image neither virtual nor real, an image of the 'non-reality of beings,' that Chabot will find again during his journey:

> I well recognize the old obsession with returning to the non-reality of beings, of things, of places inside each individual. To go back to the origins of everything and of oneself, both to find one's true face again and to escape everything that disintegrates and fades in the course of time.

The main goal of the trip is to reveal what is invisible in the filmed images, which for Chabot also consists of images – mental, virtual, intellectual, faded, and so forth. All that is, and all that is presented to the camera, is made up of a multitude of images that must be redeemed: 'Here, there, birth, death, it is nothing, almost nothing. Like a sudden presence in the landscape. A simple movement of wind in the trees.'

If the text starts out like a classic narration, that is to say in the past tense, the film's images disturb its linearity and temporal continuity: when the present tense replaces the simple past or the imperfect, we move out of the narrative mode in the strictest sense. It is the image on the screen that requires this change of tense. It is the same at each stage of the journey: 'Every time I leave the city, it's always the same adventure, the same journey that begins again'; 'For a long time I drive, I think, I listen to the news'; 'I stop at the CRTC control centre'; 'At Customs, childhood memories are declared, they are the only things that will not pass.' When the image provokes an idea, the present tense is used once again: 'the whole landscape is about to disappear,' says the voice at the end of a 360–degree panning shot of a border zone, as it is 'everywhere else on the planet.' When the image gives rise to a feeling, it is also expressed in the present tense: 'Sometimes I feel like I am a member of one of the last generations before the deluge.' There is, in effect, a verbal as well as a visual montage, which segments the narra-

Voyage en Amérique avec un cheval emprunté (1987), directed by Jean Chabot. Courtesy of the National Film Board of Canada.

tive sequences in the text and in which music functions like the fades in the visual track. This verbal montage implies a new temporal structure. Tenses become signs that connote images: the past tense of the narration leads the film image back to the past just as the present opens the image to the presence of the world:

> I'm drifting, a journey in stages, a reminiscence: sometimes I even went back to them. They had survived the epidemics of the Middle Ages, the famines, the deportations, the religious wars, the Inquisition. They had embarked on unsafe ships, for long weeks on unknown seas towards menacing and hostile countries, territories to explore, cities to found, families with fifteen children to feed, battles to fight, defeats and wounds to heal, conquest and survival.

> In American cities, there is always violence in the air. In the streets of Tehran tonight, they will shout: 'Death to America.' In the streets of Bogota, Lima, Kinshasa, Saida and Beirut, the same clamour is rising.

The present tense and the passage from 'I' to 'they' and then to 'we' releases the intellectual or emotional aspect of the documentary image.

No longer disembodied images of the world, but images of the world that 'I,' 'they,' 'we' inhabit, of the fragile reality of the world people have created:

> What will we lose, what will we win? Perhaps the absence of suffering, test-tube babies, distant wars in space ... and man ... man .... He is not there. He is elsewhere, beyond. He consumes and he waits. Far off, in countries that are being eaten away slowly by the inexorable erosion of acid rain and its poisonous retinue. Here, for example, 75 pounds of fluorine dust per hour, I forget how much that is in a year, that the wind carries most often towards the northeast: Quebec, Canada, and then where?

> I, rather, we, are millions drowned, blown to bits. In the scheme of things, *I* do not exist. Kodak exists in a seven-million-square-foot factory in Rochester. General Motors exists. IBM exists. Nabisco, Boeing, Texas Instruments exist. General Foods, CBS, Gulf and Western, United Fruit, United Technologies, ITT, Alcoa, United Steel, Bechtel, NASA, Exxon, Bandit, Xerox exist. The end of the second millennium when the individual gets closer and closer to being infinitely small.

The text does not seek to bring out a symbolic image as such and never engages in the process of interpreting the images through which it is communicated. Rather, the image is the source of the text. This is the case for the final vision of the native country, a disused factory that the protagonist explores and over images of which is heard the following:

> All of a sudden, like an apparition, I had a grand vision of my native country left far behind me. This strange, uncertain country that often gives the impression of having been hit by a neutron bomb, with its huge expanses of wasteland, its factories abandoned by foreign companies as soon as government subsidies have been swallowed up, its shut-down cities and regions, razed to the ground, polluted, emptied, exploited to the limit of their resources and then left to take care of themselves.

The Progress and Trajectory of Thought: The Travelogue

The narration does not state what must be seen, but *the reason for going to see it*. It is a discourse provoked less by the images seen, than by the *act* of seeing. Throughout the film, the words seek to materialize a vision, neither more nor less than the face of change, of a process of 'becoming' that would otherwise evade all attempts at capture.[8] Evoking the text from the image, and conversely the image from the text, is the method used to avoid the impotence of text and image alone to present this figure or the concept of becoming. There is a tendency to believe that the image illustrates the text or the reverse. In fact, the image is the origin of the text, its raison d'être. It launches the process of verbalization. What launches it, what restarts it, what concludes it are images. The image of life *in utero* begins the man's journey, and the vision of the state of Quebec announces his return. Two powerful moments in the film are: *the image of the ultrasound*, voiceless, leaving us with a fragile heartbeat, and *the image of the disused factory*. Between these two images, a journey has taken place, a journey that will flow into a movement of thought.

This will be my second point, which I would like to introduce through this observation by Gilles Deleuze:

> Perhaps all study of travel is encompassed by four observations, one by Fitzgerald, the second by Toynbee, the third by Beckett, and the final one by Proust. The first asserts that travelling, whether on islands or in wide open spaces, is never a complete break because one brings along one's own Bible, one's childhood memories and one's everyday discourse. The second is that travel is the pursuit of a nomadic ideal, but as a kind of pathetic wish, since the nomad, on the contrary, is the one who does not move, who does not want to leave, and clings to his own poor land, a central region ... According to the third observation, that of Beckett, 'we do not travel for the pleasure of travelling, that I know of, we are stupid but not to that extent' ... So, at the end, what is left but to verify, to try to verify, something inexpressible that comes from the soul, from a dream or a nightmare? ... The true dreamer, said Proust, is the one who seeks to verify something.[9]

When the documentary becomes a 'travelogue,' it brings sounds and images back from the journey, it re-creates its movement and duration in the film's space-time. It is on its own preferred ground. This means that there is a real journey, that made by the filmmaker while research-ing locations and which he repeats while filming, and an ideal journey, crossed and inhabited by the reflections, ideas, memories, and so on, that it has provoked. Chabot's scenario, dated June 1986, is thoroughly imbued with the journey already completed while scouting locations. This is shown in two ways: in the summary description of places already visited, but mainly in the evocation of images that Chabot hopes to film and that will be able to reproduce the feelings and ideas arising from a lived experience.

It is, then, neither the story of a journey of initiation, nor the original subjective experience, inner quest or discovery of the world, that matters: 'I have done this for a long time. Driving off in the car with no particular destination for the simple pleasure of thinking freely on the road.' The journey implies a thought process that proceeds through the penetration of a landscape and the film an articulation of this thought that proceeds through an arrangement of images and sounds marking its trajectory. The film offers the space-time of this movement, and not the outline of an argument. Chabot invites us to travel and not to decipher signs. He does not conceive the images of his film as tableaux of which the protagonist will propose in voice-over a more or less relevant interpretation. Instead, it is the movement and direction of thought that he proposes to bring to life in the relations between images and sounds that construct a site on which this movement and this trajectory can be actualized.

Chabot does not want to *read* his documentary images as *symbols* or *indexes* of *américanité*. *Américanité* is for him less a general idea designating a cohesive group of features characteristic of an increasingly universal culture than a process of 'becoming' that he interprets nostalgically, in terms of disappearance. Thus, Chabot will, in the end, insist upon the impossibility of seeing what will become of the landscape. Significantly, some trails proposed in the scenario disappear, including the comparison of the dominant values of the communities that he will discover, those of an American, a Québécois, an Indian, and an Ontarian.

The filmmaker's route, without a precise destination, is gradually motivated by a thought process that seeks to verify something. The film's protagonist wants to see America as it is, deserted, empty: he wants to verify the nightmare of an *américanité* which has from the depths of the historical past represented the future in terms of destruction and loss. His thought is indistinguishable from the documentary trajectory that seeks to make things visible, not just to record and document them. At the end of his quest, Chabot will find the true face of *américanité*: the disused factory taking us back to industrial development and its ravages, to individual impotence (the protagonist hammers on the doors and shutters that block the entrances to the factory) in the heat generated by an angry voice that derives precisely from the history of the Québécois people, the story of an agony that speaks for all the agonies of America and elsewhere. Chabot thus brings back from his journey a thought that exists only in this final image that he set out to find, to verify. It is in this image that his thought is rooted, and it unfolds along a completely different trajectory from that of a written text.

People and Territories: Signs of Disappearance

A journey implies a territory to cross, a territory to discover. Documentary thought, as Chabot develops it, lays siege to territories, seeking to escape from them or, conversely, to mark them out. This will be our final topic: what happens in *Voyage en Amérique* to the earth and to the territory. Deleuze again acts as a guide to unravel Chabot's ideas:

> If there were a modern political cinema, it would be on this basis: the people no longer exist, or not yet ... *the people are missing* ... This truth was absolutely clear in the Third World, where oppressed and exploited nations remained in a state of perpetual minority, in a collective identity crisis. Third World and minorities gave rise to authors who would be in a position with regard to their nation and their personal situation in that nation, to say: the people are what is missing ... Art, and especially cinematographic art, must take part in this task: not that of addressing a people, which is presupposed already there, but of contributing to the invention of a people. The moment the master, the colonizer, proclaims, 'there are no people here,' the missing people are a becoming, they invent themselves, in shanty towns and camps, or even in the ghettos, in new conditions of struggle to which a necessarily political art must contribute.[10]

How does this trajectory of thought manifest itself in cinematic space-time? The latter is complex; it articulates different kinds of space, earth, and territory that have different temporalities in a single landscape: the first ahistoric and primal, the second historic and transitory. The earth is the birthplace, the primal ground that ties man to the universe and shows him where he belongs. In the images of the film, the earth is an invisible presence, 'the non-reality of things.' The wind in the trees, in the reeds, in the grass, constitute recurring images, as if Chabot wanted to film the breath, the soul, the invisible reality behind things, the breathing of the universe: 'It is the whole universe that we hear breathing.' In the end, the earth is the sacred place of all births. The film's last words are an evocation of the earth, murmured in a woman's voice: 'This child who is coming will put an end to all your absences. You have finished seeking your roots. You have finally come down to earth. That can't be sought, it is constantly inventing itself. Yes, as we know, something watches and endures.'

As for the territory, it is the visible aspect of the landscape. With good reason, because the landscape is ultimately nothing more than a collection of the marks, or expressive features, of each territory. If the earth is one, territories are many, some clearly marked off from the others, others overlapping. They possess strong expressive features that identify them: francophone territories, anglophone territories, national territories, provincial territories, farming territories, urban territories, border territories, and so forth. The trajectory of the film's thought penetrates deeply into these spaces where the landscape takes shape. The film will list no fewer than a hundred places, a hundred landmarks. But by examining them closely, Chabot notices the erasure of the marks, the disappearance of territories.

The disappearance of territories coincides, on this American earth, with the disappearance of the people: the old fur traders, the Mohawks before the Conquest. At the forefront of these missing peoples are the Québécois, who folklorize themselves south of the border and Americanize themselves on their own earth. *Américanité* is in fact this displacement of territory. What is implanted in minds and appears in landscapes is the new territorialization of the large corporations – 'I do not exist, General Motors exists' – with the result that, at the end of the film, the protagonist has no choice but to retreat to the only territory available to him: the family circle. The completely interior territory of modern individualism has transformed peoples into crowds of exiles.

The film's protagonist might have met Canadians, Americans, Québécois, men or women who can say where they belong, who still believe that they are part of a community, of a people. But these meetings did not happen. If there were such meetings, it was with ghosts: ghosts of sedentary Mohawks, fur traders, trappers, the adventurers of the first European immigration whom the monologue attempts to revive by making their presence felt in the landscape. But 'ghosts' also refers to living beings, men and women as unchanging and predictable as the town halls and churches in the villages through which the protagonist passes, and which Chabot films from afar, like monuments.

It appears from the scenario that Chabot wanted to film territories, concentrating on the landscape's expressivity, but he discovers in the lived experience of the journey a more profound movement, a state of becoming that sweeps everyone along, even Americans. The only remaining territory, as we have seen, is that of the family. The protagonist's return to his city of Montreal, to his pregnant wife, can only be a retreat, an improvised reterritorialization, waiting for the people to come who will replace the missing people, hence the hope represented by this unborn child.

Chabot's thought is itself without territory; it is pure trajectory. It also is disappearing and leaves only the cinematic trace of its passage – and not the written trace of the idea of *québécitude*, since *québécitude* is itself, like any identity, carried along by the process of becoming. The end of the film coincides with the interruption of this trajectory, with the retreat to the family. It is not a question of a retreat to traditional notions of identity with all the political connotations that one fears. Some critics did, in fact, interpret in this way the final image of the multiethnic crowd on rue Sainte Cathérine in Montreal, accompanied by a phrase of the monologue concerning the disappearing peoples. However, the film encourages us to think otherwise, not to seek the meaning in what is said, or in the traditional association of image and commentary. It invites us to follow a particular train of thought, beginning with an escape, then unfolding, losing its way, while the thought is in search of itself, choosing roads at random, to finally escape, to disappear in the final retreat, not without having verified an intuition, a nightmare under the circumstances, about the future of the people, and the people of Quebec in particular. This is the moment of the *vision* of Quebec in that disused factory, at the end of the road, in a nondescript location in the northern United States.

I will conclude by emphasizing that *Voyage en Amérique* shows us an image of thought rather than the thought's content. The image in question presents a thought with neither order nor reason, defying discourse and attempting to find a certain spontaneity in the confusion of an improvised journey. It is a thought in the process of becoming that, in and of itself, accepts its own impotence: Chabot tackles an unanswerable question that remains unanswered.

As for the idea brought back from the journey, that of the disappearance of territories and peoples, it gains its value only from the initial disruption and the suffering and anger felt along the way, which make the protagonist aware of the urgent need to think. The testing of thought counts more than its result.

Finally, Chabot seems to have been seeking a place where he could think, a place for thought. Where does one go when one thinks? This is the question that a reflexive documentary cinema poses: in its unwavering search for a place to think that the real world never offers, the cinematic essay constructs one by means of montage and style, while not wanting for all that to lose contact with the real world. Chabot seeks the moment of coincidence between the place of thought and the real world as if this constituted the mission of documentary. He thus leaves in search of his own thought, in search of what is hidden in his thought, in search of what hurts him, this secret that disturbs him and that brings the documentary gesture back to reality through the suffering of the world. Neither direct cinema nor thesis film, *Voyage en Amérique avec un cheval emprunté* establishes some rules for the travelogue and adapts them to the demands of an uncertain, uneasy thought, to the production of a cinematic essay that a Montaigne would not have disowned.

Notes

1 I refer here to the initial proposal and the brochure about the series, from which the following is an excerpt: 'If it is impossible to foresee the effect of freer trade between the USA and Canada on French culture in our country, these economic negotiations should nevertheless encourage us to reflect upon the North American dimension of this culture. *Américanité* is a European dream born from the new relationships between Western civilization and American nature. The "American way of life," its products and references, have gradually transformed Canadian culture into a peripheral culture ... Historically, Canada, for political reasons, remained for a long time more closely tied to Europe than to the USA, but since the end of the World War II, we have witnessed the slow and inexorable integration of our French and English cultures into *américanité*. What does this mean? This program will attempt to explain the situation with respect to children, youth, artists, our urban lifestyle, and our relationship to the nature of *américanité*, frequently covered up for good and sometimes bad reasons.' Pierre Véronneau has discussed the paradoxes involved in such a program; see 'L'Américanité, les paradoxes d'une notion.'

2 A single interview with a Mohawk Indian, a few words spoken on the spot, the voice of Yolaine Rouleau – his companion in the film as in life – are all that interrupts him. Chabot writes in the 'L'Hypothèse Marker': 'Marker represents the most remarkable outcome of a perfect French tradition: to be in the middle of the world, everywhere on the planet, and to take possession of it (this is not a play on words) through the commen-

tary. This imperious use of speech reveals itself as the driving force behind the act of filming in Chris Marker.'

3 Chabot appears on screen, but his monologue, heard in voice-over, is spoken by the actor Gilles Renaud.

4 The use of the conditional tense here emphasizes the fact that, with regard to reception, we can refer only to the reactions of critics, whose representativity is far from firmly established.

5 Lockerbie focuses on the films of Fernand Bélanger, produced by the NFB at the same time, but sees in them the emergence of a new reflexive style that is also Chabot's: 'This recourse to meditative self-interrogation quite naturally leads to a complex structure. In place of linear and sequential construction found in the Grierson model and in direct cinema, recent documentaries assume a splintered form similar to postmodern literature. Discontinuity is accentuated by a mixture of genres in numerous films ... Certain works are sometimes so complex that they can justifiably be called self-reflexive. They attract attention to their own formal characteristics and we get more enjoyment out of them the more we grasp the processes used to produce them'; 'Le documentaire auto-réflexif au Québec,' 124–5.

6 The *cinematic development* of Chabot's thoughts depends not so much on knowledge, but on questioning. Chabot already introduced this idea in the scenario: *Américanité* is not for him a concept from the social sciences that he has been asked to expound. *Américanité* is a question: 'But what does this really mean? I don't know, I can't say. It is, in fact, a word that I have received as a question; and it is also as such that it has stayed in my head, as a question. As the highest point in a pyramid of questions ... And where there is a question, there is a search. That is, something that is sought more than it is found'; *Scenario of June 1986*, second part, page 10.

7 'One day, in the United States, the simultaneous occurrence of a big traffic jam in the New York area and a railway strike prevented a group of air traffic controllers from reaching a large airport. Worn out by stress and fatigue, the controllers made mistakes which in turn caused two 747s to collide and fall on a high-voltage electric wire. This burden on an already overtaxed electrical system caused a blackout, which lasted for several days. People in offices lit fires to keep warm. Fires broke out. Firefighters could not reach them. The telephone networks were jammed as fifty million isolated people tried to contact one another. More and more, people set out on foot in the snow. It grew colder. The dead were abandoned left on the road. Survivors soon found themselves ravaged by illness and famine. All provisions exhausted, they tried to seize whatever food and shelter they could. The tens of thousands of firearms sold in

America were pressed into action. In homes, all reserves were depleted. In hospitals, the number of deaths due to hunger, cold, and lack of care grew. At a certain moment, the military seized power, but it was already too late. They were themselves victims of the general paralysis. A few weeks later, when things had painfully returned to order, millions of corpses scattered through the towns and the countryside began to spread epidemics and plagues worthy of the Black Death, which destroyed two-thirds of the European population in the Middle Ages. An "apocalyptic fantasy," but two hundred years ago a whole other civilization collapsed on this very soil.'

8 In the scenario, Chabot explicitly diverts the theme of *américanité* towards a problematics of becoming: 'I see things changing. Becoming. In motion ... My eyes have always sought out something that is not yet there but is coming ... To see things changing, that is definitely the subject. The world that surrounds me just as it is itself as the movement of history changes it ... The only subject. Time passing, the world changing.'

9 Deleuze, *Pourparlers*, 110.

10 Deleuze, *Cinema 2: The Time-Image*, 216–17 (translation modified).

Queer Cinema at the NFB:
The 'Strange Case' of *Forbidden Love*

JEAN BRUCE

According to Annamarie Jagose, 'Queer describes those gestures or analytical models which dramatise incoherencies in the allegedly stable relations between chromosomal sex, gender and sexual desire.'[1] As broad and potentially inconcise as this definition seems to be, when queer techniques are strategically employed the results are often recognizable, if not easily quantifiable. Queering is an activity, as well as an analytical model, that invites us to reconsider the most central and highly held values of a society; queering makes the ordinary appear strange and can provide an opportunity to rethink the logic of the sexual hegemony of social and political institutions. As an aesthetic strategy, its unhinging potential is enormous. I will argue that *Forbidden Love* (Aerlyn Weissman and Lynne Fernie, 1992) is an example of queer cinema writ large, in part for the way it challenges the stable sex-gender-desire relationship, referred to by Jagose, at every turn. My reading of the film is that it foregrounds these 'incoherencies' at a textual level precisely because they are a part of the film's discursive context. Textual and contextual elements start to become blurry.

Forbidden Love has both a historical and dialectical relationship to women's cinema; to the politics and aesthetics of the lesbian postmodern; to the institutional framework of the National Film Board; and to Canadian culture in the 1990s, generally. These formal and discursive arrangements involving the style, subject matter, and the conditions of production and reception of the film, including its spectatorial address, all contribute to the queerness of *Forbidden Love*.

Queering the NFB
Forbidden Love has the dubious honour of being one of the last films

made by the women's unit, Studio D, as well as the first overtly lesbian film made at the NFB. Lynne Fernie suggests that the NFB's working processes, at the time *Forbidden Love* was conceived and produced, are largely responsible for its success. She cites Studio D, an overtly feminist space within the NFB with its visionary leader, Rina Fraticelli, as a major factor in allowing women to work, in large part, in a creative and supportive environment: 'You got the resources and support from people who really cared about making films and who have worked in film for years.'[2] The result is a film, at first modestly proposed as a women's history film, that has won numerous awards and recognitions.

The research and development phase of the project, which precedes the formal presentation of any film proposal at the NFB, was, in the case of *Forbidden Love*, a necessarily lengthy process. Talking to 'the subjects,' searching the 'archives' for evidence of a lesbian cultural history in Canada involved a degree of digging and primary research that would not be quite so daunting today (in part because of the film itself). The thoroughness of the research is what contributes not only to the credibility of the film, but also to its confident stance on the subject matter it depicts.

The central problematic is twofold: on the one hand, the film's aim is to negotiate some kind of satisfactory relationship between personal and cultural notions of lesbian identity in Canada, and to validate that identity. Yet, on the other hand, it disrupts any implied stability of this subject position, refusing to posit lesbian identity as a ticket to the world beyond the frame as though the film were capable of carrying forward its ideal time and space. In other words, *Forbidden Love* engages in a kind of queer utopian juggling act that attempts to strike a balance between its postmodernist aesthetic strategies and (modernist) lesbian sexual politics. The film depicts two fantasies of an ideal lesbian mise en scène: the pleasure and the politics of sexual subjectivity. Hot sex and the promise of romance in lesbian heaven are depicted in the pulp fiction parts, while the film captures a historical fragment of the lives of Canadian lesbians through their 'unashamed stories' in the documentary portion of the film. In so doing, *Forbidden Love* becomes queerly utopic; it both negates and confirms, offers and denies a coherent sexual subjectivity.

Forbidden Love flirts with the audience in the manner of its *address* and suggests a lesbian spectator position. Independent of the 'real' identities of individual spectators, the film at first teases the audience with the fundamental promise offered by its parody of the documentary mode, reeling us in under the pretence that we will know more about the subject of the film, i.e., lesbians, than we did before. Although presented as a parody, this implies an intention that fits with the educational mandate of the NFB. In exchange, however, *Forbidden Love* makes palpable the more salacious elements of its address by linking the desire to know of the documentary with the desire for the 'real' representation of sex in the lesbian pulp genre sequences of the film. This strategy undermines what Bill Nichols calls the 'discourses of sobriety' associated with the instrumentality of the documentary.[3]

By appealing to the pro-filmic event it references, a (classic) documentary film typically permits viewers to engage in voyeuristic activities unencumbered by guilt. This is, in part, due to the lofty promise of attaining knowledge about the real world outside the film frame, an implicit separation of the mind from the body. In *Forbidden Love*, however, the conventionally cool and hot registers of the documentary and the pulp fiction are often mismatched. The film refuses to sacrifice the heart to the head. So, for example, while we might expect (to enjoy) the 'heat' of the love-making scene in the pulp fiction portions of the film, we might not be prepared for the characters to take a pose and stare directly into the camera as they do at the end of each vignette. This effectively 'cools off' the audience by confronting us, albeit playfully, with our lustful looks. Moreover, because these sequences alternate with the documentary interviews, achieving the sexual 'payoff' is also deliciously delayed and prolonged.

These textual strategies make us acutely aware of our voyeuristic complicity, and thus our potentially multiple or 'queer' identities. The desire to *know* is thus intimately linked with sexual desire, and as neither desire is neatly separated from the other, the blur between them implicates the spectator in a politics of looking. The result is that *Forbidden Love* manages to be pro-lesbian for lesbians and non-lesbians alike, but their positioning as spectators, indeed their access to the stories, will necessarily be different. Perhaps this is a matter of the postmodern film's knack for irony, or its seeming ability to do what Linda Hutcheon calls 'speaking with a forked tongue.'[4] In contrast to Laura Mulvey's account of the classical positioning of the spectator as always-already male, *Forbidden Love* opens up another form of spectatorship that may indeed be one realization of Mulvey's theory of a dialectics of 'passionate detachment.'[5] A queer spectatorship, such as the one I am suggesting, may be merely one that does not exclude lesbians. In this case, however, the film includes the non-lesbian while also functioning, in the NFB tradition, as a way of gently informing outsiders about a 'different' culture.

'Full' is, I think, an appropriate word to describe the style of *Forbidden Love*. As I have suggested above, the film's complex treatment of the subject matter, deployed by the documentary and melodramatic modes, constitutes a politics of style that is part of its rich analytical potential. Even the film's opening plays knowingly with the conventions of the institutional style of the NFB by satirizing both the Board's logo and its tendency to warn viewers in writing about the usually tame contents of its films. This tactic helps to convey the NFB's image as 'nice and inoffensive,' but the logo of the fluidly moving figure, who presumably represents the ideal, non-gendered, and multicultural Canadian, is the first image to take a 'shot' from the filmmakers. The logo is accompanied by the sound of a honkin' saxophone solo; the music later includes drums and a hot electric guitar riff. Together the image and soundtrack suggest that the film already offers contradictory positions for its spectators. On the one hand, it briefly conforms to the opening of any NFB film and to its political (if not aesthetic) mandate of correctness – to interpret Canada to Canadians – no matter how diverse we may be. On the other hand, the musical style of the soundtrack suggests that this film may be 'hotter' than expected, and, in retrospect, it serves to remind viewers that some of the people who were groovin' to that sexy urban music known as r & b were dykes.

The NFB logo is followed by the disclaimer, 'Unless otherwise stated the people who appear in this film should not be presumed to be homosexual ...' The music then fades as one inter-title is replaced by another: '... or heterosexual.' In the first inter-title, the form and message are consistent with the middle-class liberalism that could be argued to be the Board's overriding ideology, given the style and subject matter of many of its documentary films. The warning carries an aura of sobriety that reassures the viewer about the seriousness of the film and the worthiness of the subject. The inter-title is thus connected to the film's title, suggesting that the film will be a serious (albeit vicarious) look at 'perverse desire.' *Forbidden Love* is, after all, a topical, educational film. However, this film also remains within an arguably subversive tradition that is also part of the legacy of some of the units of the NFB.[6]

The identification techniques set up at the beginning of *Forbidden Love* are a part of its reflexive, postmodern pastiche of film genres. The interview-style documentary favoured by feminist filmmakers in the 1960s and 1970s, some within the NFB, is intercut with a filmic version of the lesbian pulp melodrama of the 1950s and 1960s to create a new hybrid style that is more than the sum of its aesthetic parts. This particular stylistic treatment of the subject matter, besides suggesting a historical and aesthetic continuity, makes the film both playful and serious, as well as engaging and distancing. The parodic mode permits a wide-ranging critique of the ideologies that have traditionally informed these identification techniques, yet the film is truly reflexive and thus not above scrutiny itself. *Forbidden Love*'s evocation of the documentary film's discourses of sobriety suggests that these discourses are purposeful, ideological apparatuses implicated in the historical containment and pathologizing of sexuality.

The rhetorical strategies adopted by both scientific discourses and classic narratives have together lent a legitimacy to exploring the 'problem of lesbianism.' This is a common feature of the classic documentary film: to objectify and therefore distance the relationship between active agent and subject matter. By clearly positioning the 'investigator' and the 'investigated' on either side of the apparatus, the film suggests an unequal power relationship that also effaces the prurient look into the world of the other. The documentary impulse of science, or indeed the scientific impulse of documentary, along with the pulp fiction novel of popular culture have offered two possible sources for locating and learning about lesbians. In order to explain (away) the lesbian, or to mete out poetic justice, 'the story' has often had the same ending: 'the lesbian gets her due ... marriage, insanity or ... suicide.'[7]

None of these options has been altogether satisfactory to the lesbian herself. The daily struggle of keeping body and soul together was not usually accurately reflected in these novels. Ironically, some of the women in the documentary portion of *Forbidden Love* explicitly link their burgeoning sense of a lesbian community to the pulp novels. They compare their own lesbian identities with those suggested by the tortured fantasies of the novels. In retrospect at least, some of the women actively read these stories against the grain. Rather than simply learn the lessons offered by such homophobic texts by resolving their own lives according to the outcomes of the novels, the women portrayed in the film were clearly selective about what to accept or reject. They negotiated their lesbian identities in relation to what was offered by popular culture and, if occasionally they took away the knowledge that at least there were other 'freaks' like them out there somewhere, that also meant they actively sought out and created a lesbian subculture. To do so must also have meant gaining a temporary respite from a comparatively more hostile world, or at least the women's stories suggest this.

Their reading strategies indicate that while the hegemony of science and psychoanalysis may still be alive and well, these women, in reading the novels against the grain, seized upon an instance of discursive instability. As Michel Foucault argues: 'Discourse transmits and produces power; it reinforces it, but it also undermines and exposes it, renders it fragile and makes it possible to thwart it.'[8] Revising elements of the interview-style documentary in combination with the lesbian pulp novel is a strategy that permits *Forbidden Love* to valorize lesbian history and experience. This overtly revisionist practice celebrates the pleasures of lesbianism without making the lesbian pay, and refusing to empiricize or imperialize her desires.

Nichols argues that 'documentary opens up a gap for the viewer between the representation and its historical referent,' which suggests an awareness on the part of the viewer of their differences and of the documentary's tendency to suppress that knowledge.[9] But whereas Nichols discusses the style and ethics of proximity to the subject as either a kind of tactful cinematic distance or comfortable viewing position, the queering of the documentary/melodrama undermines this safe, proprietary mode. The body of the lesbian is neither invisible, nor a highly visible object of voyeuristic pleasure; this body is indexical, historical evidence of disavowal as much as of desire.

Women's Cinema, Queer Cinema

The historical and critical conditions of counter-cinema conventions and their links to feminist film theory and practice provide another example of the discursive relationship between text, context, and spectator. Feminist critiques of the patriarchal structures of Hollywood cinema began from the position that if a woman's place is always as a cultural outsider, then any pleasures she receives must be 'against the grain.' This has been seen as a practice of conflicting or inappropriate readings of culture that has produced either masochistic[10] or unruly cultural consumers in women.[11] But it might be further argued that these conditions provide a queer discursive space in which a film such as *Forbidden Love* is only the logical outcome. *Forbidden Love* is ironic and unusual, multiplying the effects of its postmodern artistic practices such as pastiche and parody. Notwithstanding the complexities of the screen–spectator relationship, the film addresses the lesbian spectator directly, or treats the spectator as though 'it' were a lesbian.

Yet, tempting as it may be, *Forbidden Love* refuses to create a world in which the presumed desires of its addressees are put ahead of its political aims. One of the film's implicit goals, in recovering parts of lesbian culture, is to remain connected to both the history of feminism and women's cinema. This might present a dilemma for a film made in the early 1990s, when the spoken or unspoken pressure to arrive at theoretical consensus and political solidarity on the subject of the then burgeoning and sexy-sounding sub-genre of feminist, gay, and lesbian theories known as 'queer theory' may have been substantial. There certainly was much discussion of queer theory's terms of reference and its relationship to women's cinema.[12]

In rethinking a definition for women's cinema in 1990 while reflecting on films made by women in the 1980s, Teresa de Lauretis attempts the daunting task of accounting for the many components that define women's cinema as it has emerged over a specific historical period as both practice and attitude.[13] This task is likely to have been more difficult – and perhaps all the more interesting and satisfying – in the giddy theoretical context offered by queer theory. De Lauretis concludes that there are any number of 'guerrilla tactics' – discursive possibilities, specific textual strategies, and counter-cinema audiences – that contribute to the ambiguity of the term 'women's cinema,' and, while these ambiguities may sound not unlike the incoherencies referred to by Annamarie Jagose, de Lauretis does not subsume them under the 'queer' umbrella.[14] Rather, she takes some of the central ideas concerning women's cinema proposed by earlier critics and recontextualizes them for the 1980s. She cites some of the contributing factors for consolidating women's cinema as the 'mutual support and interchange between feminist film critics, scholars, festival organizers, distributors, and filmmakers' who together comprise a critical mass. De Lauretis moreover argues that '"women's cinema" is not just a set of films or practices of cinema, but also a number of film-critical discourses and broadly cast networks of cinema-related practices that are directly connected with the history of feminism.'[15]

Among the many postmodern aesthetic strategies, multiplicity, reflexivity, parody, and intertextuality are the most prominent in *Forbidden Love*. Together these produce what Patricia White might call a 'narrative with a vengeance.'[16] White tackles de Lauretis's psychoanalytic approach to feminism and cinema in which de Lauretis claims that the most interesting works disrupt the Oedipal narrative and instead 'stress the duplicity of that scenario and the specific contradiction of the female subject in it.'[17] Focusing on a more elaborate or complex sexuality may thus invite new research and analysis on the strange case of heterosexuality as well.

White is, I think, calling for a queer theory of sexuality in which psychoanalysis is 'outed' as a discourse that cannot fully explain heterosexuality any more than homosexuality. Psychoanalysis is effectively 'put in its place' historically and culturally as 'merely' one of the more popular Victorian discourses preoccupied with producing rigid sexual categories by applying standards that define everything beyond a narrow, symbolic realm as deviant.

The Oedipal trajectory, disrupted, is precisely what is at stake in *Forbidden Love*. It is a narrative with a vengeance for its excessiveness, for the manner of its address and the identification techniques it deploys, and in particular for the way in which these strategies refer to but refuse to adopt an Oedipal trajectory and resolution. Like the opening credits sequence that I referred to earlier, the next sequence addresses this notion of heterosexual presumption concerning spectatorial address and identification. It employs the tactics of give and take, or setting up the expectations associated with one story and 'satisfying' them with another. The sequence opens with a long shot of a truck in a vast landscape. The 'washed out,' almost sepia, quality gives it the character of overexposed film stock; it is an 'outdated' image. It thus locates the moment depicted firmly in the past and, judging by the costumes and music, this is likely the late 1950s or early '60s. On the now explicitly diegetic soundtrack, the song 'Tell Laura I Love Her' is announced by the disc jockey. The relationship of the image to the soundtrack might suggest that the song refers to the heterosexual romance of the couple in the image, since 'the couple' acknowledges it with a knowing look. The song (by Ray Peterson) is referred to by the disc jockey but not performed in the film. As the young woman gets out of the truck, her boyfriend gently cautions her about the woman on the train platform.

In this context, it might be safe to assume that the conflict has been between the two women, and that they have perhaps been vying for the young man's love, particularly as the woman at the station is quickly identified as 'Laura.' The song itself recalls a fairly typical conceit of the melodramatic modes from both film and music genres of the 1950s, a musical subgenre characterized, in part, by the figure of the masochistic male torch singer.[18] Because the song is not actually performed in the film, its status as a secure marker of heterosexual love is questionable. Given the song's new reference within the context of the film, the heterosexual presumption upon which the 'joke' relies is completely undermined. The affair, which has ended, is clearly revealed to have been between the two women, and one of them, heartbroken, must now leave town.

This sequence demonstrates that heterosexual romance is a reference point, not something to be taken for granted. In retrospect, the couple's anxious reaction to the song's title – their 'knowing look' – indicates the fragility *not* the stability of their union. By extension, their status as the only heterosexual couple depicted in the film (whom we never see before or after this sequence) suggests that heterosexuality itself is a social fiction that requires the constant cultural propping up that the song ostensibly provides. Moreover, the suggestion that the song as a cultural product and an ideological apparatus could be 'consumed' by both lesbians and heterosexual men, however differently, is also underscored by the revelation that Laura and the woman were romantically involved. The song is indiscriminately deployed as a marker of romance; it could easily have been 'their song,' and the heterosexual couple's reaction to it, given the context that is developed in the sequence, suggests its malleability.

Rather than manoeuvring or negotiating unfriendly texts, the appeal of a narratively queered counter-cinema is that it opens up those incoherencies between sex, gender, and desire to which Jagose refers. Narratives establish conventions easily, but foregrounding incoherencies is a kind of textual strategy of irony and excess that is difficult to conventionalize and contain, and thus it would seem to have much to offer queer cinema. By alluding to the textual strategies associated with the classic narrative and redeploying them in a reflexive manner – in this case, the context of queer cinema – both the subject of lesbianism and the lesbian subject become visible.

Forbidden Love continues to underscore the caveat that homosexuality is no more 'real' than heterosexuality. However much such definitions codify human interaction, they are the product of social discourses imposed on reality through language and convention. Thus the women bid their tearful good-byes, but these are also artificially and excessively emotional, even for melodrama, particularly since the film has yet to invite the spectator to become invested in the film's narrative resolution, or to identify in any way with these characters. The sequence ends with a close-up on a locket that the other woman has just returned to Laura. Laura protests, but eventually waves good-bye with the locket in her palm. The gesture appears very wooden, and the image then becomes highly saturated with colour. The camera tracks out while it freeze-frames Laura's direct address gaze, and shrinks the image to create the effect of a paperback book. The long shot is then digitally altered as it dissolves into the cover of the lesbian pulp novel, *Forbidden Love: The Unashamed Stories of Lesbian Lives.*

As spectators of conventional narrative cinema, at the beginning of this sequence we might have expected that 'dispensing' with Laura at the end would have been a means of dealing with 'the problem of lesbianism,' and that once she left town, the narrative would take up its proper function by returning to the concerns of the heterosexual couple. This is clearly not the case. The film dismisses the couple not Laura. Furthermore, the washed-out sepia tone with which they have been associated now suggests their very drabness, while the narrative 'chooses' to follow Laura's more colourful adventures in the exciting underground of the lesbian bar.

The 'hot' and 'cool' emotional temperatures, or the wrestling between the classic narrative and the subject matter of the film, underscore the tensions in keeping with the melodramatic mode of the film.[19] And while it does so playfully, the effect is to convey an anxiety that something unforeseen may yet happen. Everything, however amusing, is not all fun and games for lesbians. This nagging sense of ill- or unresolved tensions in the film has at least two purposes, both of which are potentially subversive, serious, and playful. First, the tension foreshadows the interview featuring Ann Bannon, a writer of lesbian pulp novels, who acknowledges the difficulties of writing for the often tragic narrative resolution that the genre imposed. Second, it imbues the film with another kind of tension that is later expressed as an erotic charge taken up in the revised pulp fiction sequences. While Bannon claims that, unlike many of the lesbian protagonists in the popular fiction of the period, 'some of her women survived,' this film's ending suggests another possibility. Our protagonist, Laura, has not only survived, but judging from her 'successful' entry into lesbian subculture (underscored by the playfully romantic commentary of the female voice-over narrator celebrating her affair with the woman she meets at the bar), chances are she will actually flourish.

There are at least two purposes for revising the pulp formula in *Forbidden Love* itself. The happy ending of pulp romance in the film can be seen as a means to reconstruct the aesthetics of melodrama for lesbian political revision.[20] The utopic revising of the fictions thus becomes a marker of the 'progress' of the real history of lesbians and

Forbidden Love: The Unashamed Stories of Lesbian Lives (1993), directed by Aerlyn Weissman and Lynn Fernie. Courtesy of the National Film Board of Canada.

lesbian culture. However, the parodic mode these portions of the film engage does not completely allow the spectator to forget that this is indeed a conscious revision, a fiction we as spectators agree to participate in for the duration of the film. The tension that results from these competing strategies makes identification problematic for everyone. The most overt of the techniques is perhaps the previously mentioned direct address gaze combined with the freeze-frame that ends each section of the pulp melodrama parody of *Forbidden Love*. This strategy both invites spectators in and keeps them out by making visible the processes of identification; the direct address gaze thereby undoes the voyeurism of spectatorship with one hand while offering it with the other. This gaze is the gaze of the lesbian protagonist(s). Her/Their desires and ours are aligned; thus our mutual voyeurism is 'outed' and made complicitous in a tenuous erotics of identification.

Forbidden Love is an example of postmodern parody that reexamines ways of knowing knowingly, and takes issue with those forms (documentary and melodrama) stylistically. Thus the film works in the way theorists of the lesbian postmodern such as Robyn Wiegman suggest is true of postmodernism generally. Following Lyotard, she claims that 'the postmodern doesn't transcend the modern; it rereads the modern, not from beyond but from within.'[21] Examples of postmodernist cinema such as *Forbidden Love* thus contribute to a confrontation between discourses – Lyotard's *'grand récits'* – that, however embedded within a history of unequal power relationships, are here aesthetically challenged, providing what Foucault suggests are stumbling blocks, points of resistance, or a starting point for an opposing strategy.[22]

Such films rely also upon a tradition of political/feminist filmmaking, as well as the work of critics, and a leaping critical mass of lesbians who together, and in excess, challenge the dominance of grand cultural narratives with their own 'little stories.' The cinematic strategies of identification thus resonate outside the film as a politics of identification, though not necessarily as a strict identity politics. *Forbidden Love* demonstrates that there is both strength and pleasure in identifying with a community of like-minded, desiring women. However, the various strategies the film sets up, such as the structurally layered address of the melodrama and the documentary, impose a critical distance and engage us in a dialectic between the pleasure of identification and a new-found pleasure of criticism.

Defining 'The Lesbian Postmodern' in Cinema

Spectators who are particularly marginalized within sociopolitical discourses (perhaps because they are part of a sexually subordinate group such as lesbians), arguably make especially astute cultural analysts and 'wilful' spectators. This may be because they must engage in an ongoing process of (re)negotiating a tenuous position as cultural consumers of exclusionary representations. According to Penny Florence, this marginality or alterity invites lesbians to 'perform complex manoeuvres when watching films that make it possible to gain pleasure against the grain of representational and narrative structures.'[23]

It could thus be argued that lesbian spectators, in particular, manoeuvre with a high degree of agility within and outside the dominant discourses of gender and sexuality. This presents at least two – sometimes competing sometimes complementary – positions for the lesbian spectator. One acknowledges the exclusive nature of heterosexual romance upon which much of mainstream cinema rests, and another admits that in order for any film to be understood, the lesbian spectator must be familiar with those very modes of social discourse and cinematic address. A third or queer position results from the relationship between these two that acknowledges her adept skills as cultural negotiator and survivor: the lesbian spectator is in some ways always a cultural guerrilla. She is constrained by cultural exclusion and may take pleasure in the wilful act of reworking scenarios to include her. Films about sexuality and gender – in other words most (if not all) films – are thus susceptible to unruly lesbian readings or aesthetic treatments.

Postmodernism tends to valorize multiplicity, reflexivity, parody, textual and sexual ambivalence. In those texts that are postmodern and directly involve sexuality and gender, the availability of lesbian readings is especially highlighted. However, as Wiegman suggests, a merely 'facile embrace of contradiction, multiplicity and flux' is insufficient for claiming a politics of postmodern lesbian aesthetics.[24] Laura Doan argues that films exist along a continuum of postmodernist–lesbian to the degree that they 'enable an interventionist or transformative politics.'[25] They foreground the complexity and instability of the categories of gender and sexuality by employing defamiliarizing cinematic strategies.

These films achieve the queer goal of destabilizing or intervening in and multiplying sexual subjectivity, but do not stop there. It's not as though you can take lesbian sexuality and postmodernism and place them side by side to get 'The Lesbian Postmodern.' When you put them together, the first kind of transformation that occurs is between them. Both lesbian sexuality and postmodernism are changed by their association with the other. Together, they do not simply provide spectatorial experiences that please everyone, *even* lesbians. Rather, the Lesbian Postmodern marks an opportunity for the politicization of postmodernist practices. In this case, melodrama and documentary are deployed as agents of postmodernity. As an explicit example of cultural questioning – queering or query – lesbianism becomes a means to both anchor and unmoor the relationship between politics and culture in a manner consistent with, but also deviant from, postmodernism.

There are numerous textual devices that can be deployed for political purposes. In the documentary portion of *Forbidden Love*, the interview style suggests that the women's lives are both ordinary and extraordinary. The women are depicted in conversation with the off-screen filmmakers. Their conversations are sometimes edited together so as to create a conversation among the women interviewed, but the situations they face are also shown to be unique to them individually. At the same time, it becomes clear that these lesbians are constrained by many of the same issues that affect other (heterosexual) women's lives at the same historical moment. A new conversation emerges from this layering of conversations through editing and connects the women's stories. This functions as a rhetorical strategy, a common feature of documentaries which Nichols suggests is 'the means by which the author attempts to convey his or her outlook persuasively to the viewer.' Nichols explains that, in strategies such as these, success or failure is achieved through evidence and artistic proof, or 'factual material recruited to the argument' and 'the quality of the text's construction.'[26] In this case, however, to get caught up in these 'recruitment' or rhetorical strategies is to align oneself overtly with these lesbian women, not only with their struggles but their desires.

Since the women remain individuals, neither their stories nor their desires can be contained as a group and dismissed; the film is evidence of the reintroduction of their stories to the larger historical and cultural context from which they were previously excluded. Likewise, however overtly the rhetorical devices are presented, they are depicted within, and not outside, familiar representational forms of documentary that also have historical resonance and relevance to both lesbian culture and feminist filmmaking.

Together the combined styles of melodrama and documentary exceed the constraints of either the classic or modernist modes taken individually. The film is thus stylistically 'queered' since the juxtaposition of the two styles neither is delivered nor can be taken as 'straight.' In effect, the film overlays stereotypes about lesbianism onto these familiar generic conventions. These expectations are modified, undermined, or completely discarded by mixing the two styles. The implications of mixing the expectations of one genre with the outcome of the other go well beyond attaching certain conditions and values to the conventions based on the new subject matter. 'Queerness' itself is also expressed (or outed) as an excessive aesthetic value: excessively sexual, and in this case, excessively woman-centred. For example, *Forbidden*

Love includes many references that are directed to many audiences simultaneously. This audience is not only an 'ideal' or general Canadian audience; in some cases the references are quite specifically addressed to lesbian spectators. Thus sometimes non-lesbians are initially excluded, and some of the references are never explained. The payoff for the lesbian spectator is in seeing her desires represented on-screen.

Conclusion

Susan Rubin Suleiman reminds us that to conceive of art as a strict political platform rather than as a forum for debate locates the notion of resistance firmly within texts (or films) and 'not in their readings.' Suleiman cites Stanley Fish's argument that 'every reading of a text, no matter how personal or "quirky," can be shown to be part of a collective discourse and analysed historically and ideologically as characteristic of a group, or what Fish has called "an interpretive community."' Suleiman also challenges the hierarchy of the 'correct reading' that she claims valorizes certain readings at the expense of others. She sees this as operating hegemonically to block new interpretive and discursive strategies that seek to define what a thing *is* (in this case postmodernist culture), and then names what it can *do*.[27] This approach to culture ignores the long history of women as cultural consumers who have 'stolen' pleasures from a variety of cultural sources and used them for their own (queer) purposes.

According to Linda Hutcheon and Gayatri Spivak, 'in jokes' such as those found in *Forbidden Love* can function to redress the 'lost' history of the ex-centric while voicing a complaint about the way things are now.[28] The film is thus a kind of representational metaphor for a cultural salvaging process that is locatable as both lesbian and Canadian. This film performs a kind of doubling or juggling act; a double-voicing/double-imaging to both connect and dissociate itself from the mainstream of culture through the use of hybrid film styles. The complexities of a politics of identity and postmodern aesthetics are thus related, but not identical. For however tempting it may be to conflate feminism and anti-homophobia in acknowledging the many things they share in common, their relationship is not, as Craig Owens and Eve Sedgwick have reminded us, 'automatic or transhistorical.'[29]

By examining some of the queer aspects of cultural discourses – those instances of discourse that raise incoherencies but do not adequately address or settle issues of (lesbian) sexual politics – notions of both film textuality and potential viewing situations are inevitably opened up. A queer reading, against the grain, to steal pleasure is also an implicit politics of interpretation. This is one place where the politics of identity and the aesthetics of resistance coincide. Together they produce, as the end-title of *Forbidden Love* suggests, 'another fragment, another telling, as we break the silence of our lives.'

Notes

Versions of this essay appear as 'Querying/Queering the Nation,' Armatage et al., eds., *Gendering the Nation*, and as 'Querying or "Queering" the Nation: The Lesbian Postmodern and Canadian Women's Cinema,' *Canadian Journal of Film Studies* 5, no. 2 (Fall 1996). Both of those essays also deal with *La Vie rêvée* (Mireille Dansereau, 1972). This essay is a greatly revised and expanded analysis of *Forbidden Love*.

1 Jagose, *Queer Theory*, 3.
2 Interview with Lynne Fernie.
3 Nichols, *Representing Reality*, 3–4. According to Nichols, 'documentary film has a kinship with those other nonfictional systems that make up what we may call the discourses of sobriety. Science, economics, foreign policy, education, religion, welfare – these systems assume they have instrumental power; they can and should alter the world itself, they can affect action and entail consequences' (3).
4 Hutcheon, *As Canadian as – Possible – Under the Circumstances!* 10.
5 Laura Mulvey, 'Visual Pleasure and Narrative Cinema,' 18.
6 The tradition is long and wide. Subject matter has often been broadly interpreted in the topic-driven documentaries produced by the NFB, especially Unit B, the French Unit, and Studio D.
7 Zimet, *Strange Sisters*, 27.
8 Foucault, *The History of Sexuality*, vol. 1, 101.
9 Nichols, *Blurred Boundaries*, 48.
10 Mulvey, 'Visual Pleasure and Narrative Cinema.' See also Johnston, 'Women's Cinema as Counter Cinema.'
11 See, for example, Florence, 'Lesbian Cinema.'
12 See, for example, the debates in Bad Object Choices, eds., *How Do I Look?* especially de Lauretis' 'Film and the Visible,' and the subsequent questions and commentary. The anthology represents a selection of papers and discussions from the conference of the same name, held in New York, October 1989.

13 De Lauretis, 'Guerilla in the Midst,' 9.

14 De Lauretis herself is partly responsible for the status of the term 'queer' employed in its new, non-pejorative manner. B. Ruby Rich ('A Queer Sensation,' *Village Voice*, 24 March, 1992) is also cited as having 'reinvented' the term queer and applied it to film and video. However, the article referred to (by filmmaker, Greta Schiller) in Wilton, ed., *Immortal, Invisible*, postdates at least two other prominent references to the term: Bad Object Choices, eds., *How Do I Look?* and de Lauretis, 'Queer Theory.' In any case, Rich also expresses her own concerns about the use of the term 'queer' in subsequent articles. See, for example, Rich, 'New Queer Cinema,' and Wilton's reference to it in the introduction to *Immortal, Invisible*. De Lauretis, like some other feminist theorists/critics, eventually abandoned the term 'queer.' According to Jagose, de Lauretis did so 'on the grounds that it had been taken over by those mainstream forces and institutions it was coined to resist'; *Queer Theory*, 127.

15 Ibid., 129.

16 White, 'Governing Lesbian Desire,' 86–7.

17 De Lauretis, quoted in ibid., 86.

18 The almost, but not quite, falsetto voice of Ray Peterson is reminiscent of other male torch singers of the day, notably, Canada's Paul Anka. In this film, it could be argued that the boyfriend fills the role of the male masochist suggested by the song's generic reference since he sits anxiously (and idly) by while his girlfriend actively deals with Laura.

19 This idea is in keeping with the socially critical 1950s Hollywood melodrama analysed in Elsaesser, 'Tales of Sound and Fury.'

20 Doan, *The Lesbian Postmodern*, x.

21 Wiegman, 'Introduction,' 13.

22 Lyotard, quoted in Benjamin, ed., *The Lyotard Reader*, 132–3; Foucault, *The History of Sexuality*, vol. 1, 101.

23 Florence, 'Lesbian Cinema, Women's Cinema,' 127.

24 Wiegman, 'Introduction,' 14.

25 Doan, *The Lesbian Postmodern*, x.

26 Nichols, *Representing Reality*, 134.

27 Suleiman, 'Feminism and Postmodernism,' 324–5.

28 Hutcheon, *A Poetics of Postmodernism*; Spivak, *In Other Worlds*.

29 Sedgwick, quoted in Owens, *Beyond Recognition*, 219.

'This Land Is Ours' – Storytelling and History in *Kanehsatake: 270 Years of Resistance*

ZUZANA M. PICK

Alanis Obomsawin, a filmmaker from the Abenaki nation, begins her documentary *Kanehsatake: 270 Years of Resistance* by saying that 'the story you will see takes place near Montreal in Kanehsatake, a Mohawk village near the town of Oka, and in Kahnawake, a Mohawk reserve south of the city at the Mercier Bridge.' With these lines, she locates herself and the film within the storytelling tradition that is the cornerstone of First Nations' knowledge, culture, and history. This chapter explores the centrality of this tradition in Obomsawin's practice and, through an analysis of the film and of its production and reception, outlines its contribution to Native historiography.

Kanehsatake: 270 Years of Resistance reconstructs the momentous confrontation between Natives and the Canadian state in Oka in the summer of 1990. Mohawks mobilized to protect the Pines, a burial ground in a white pine tree forest bordering the town, against the expansion of a nine-hole golf course. With the intervention of the Canadian army, the protest took on the characteristics of an armed uprising and received extensive television coverage. Acts of solidarity took place at the Oka Peace Camp, and Native communities across the country set up blockades. With the release of *Kanehsatake* in 1993, the Oka showdown regained political currency, albeit temporarily. While acknowledging the film's Native point of view, critical responses predictably focused on factual accuracy or distortion and revealed the precarious nature of public opinion on land claims and self-determination. Obomsawin's film offers an opportunity to non-Native Canadians to understand the significance of the land in First Nations' history, culture, and community. And it is in this spirit that the film will be approached.

Filming the Events: Conditions of Production

In interviews Obomsawin has stated that she began working on *Kanehsatake* on 12 July 1990, one day after a contingent of the Quebec Provincial Police arrived in Oka to enforce an injunction at the request of Mayor Jean Ouellette and the Municipal Council. The police stormed a barricade which had been set up on 10 March by Mohawks from Kanehsatake, Kahnawake, and Akwesasne, on Chemin du mille, an unpaved road leading to the Pines and the Pine Hill Cemetery. Following the attack, in which Corporal Marcel Lemay of the Quebec Provincial Police was killed, Mohawks backed by the Warrior Society set up two other barricades in Oka and blocked the roads on the southern shore of the St Lawrence River leading to the Kahnawake reserve and the Mercier bridge, beginning a standoff that lasted seventy-eight days.[1]

Obomsawin explained to Karen Margison that during the first week she recorded sound and, until cinematographer Roger Rochat could join her, Zoe Dirse operated the camera. Afraid that the police might confiscate the material, she had it delivered every night to the National Film Board. When it became obvious that, even with her press accreditation, she might be denied access to the area, she decided to rent a room in Oka. On 12 August riots broke out in Chateauguay, a suburban community south of Montreal and the Mercier bridge. The Quebec Provincial Police confronted an angry mob of white residents blocking a small bridge across the St Lawrence Seaway near Valleyfield in protest against the one-month-old closure of the Mercier bridge. Three days later, at the request of Quebec Premier Robert Bourassa, the Canadian army took up position near Oka, and on 20 August the army replaced the Quebec Provincial Police and the Royal Canadian Mounted Police on the barricades in Kanehsatake and Kahnawake. At that point, Obomsawin was staying overnight in the Pines behind the Mohawk barricades and had two rotating crews, one shooting during the day and the other at night.[2]

On the evening of 1 September, the army advanced into the Pines, forcing the Mohawks back from the Highway 344 barricade. They retreated into an alcohol and drug abuse treatment facility, known as TC, on the shore of the Ottawa River. Only a handful of journalists, as well as Obomsawin and her cinematographer, were allowed to remain on the TC side of the barrier set up by the army. Once the cinematographer left, she filmed with an 8 mm video camera supplied by her crew. After the telephone lines were cut, she communicated by cell phone with the crew on the other side of the razor wire. Obomsawin was the only filmmaker able to document the last days of the standoff. Though she left the TC on 24 September to avoid having her tapes impounded, the march of Mohawk women, children, and men onto Highway 344 on the next day was filmed by a man with whom she had left a video camera and by herself on a 16 mm camera. She returned later to Kanehsatake and Oka to record additional interviews.[3]

The work on the film was very difficult, and ultimately traumatic. Obomsawin worked in a highly militarized area, directed crews at separate locations, and faced high-stress situations everyday, including police and army intimidation. She said, 'I slept outside in the sand, just half an hour at a time, because helicopters were going by. There were many times when I'd wonder if I was going to come out alive.'[4] What happened at Oka affected Obomsawin personally as well. She spoke of the experience as one of 'going back into the repression of my childhood days. I saw and heard a lot of things because I was there a long time. The racism was so apparent. I felt disgusted, to tell you the truth. Everything that was going on there made me return to a really ugly time in my life.'[5]

After a long postproduction period that involved working with over 100 hours of exposed film, *Kanehsatake* was first shown on Channel 4 in Britain on 12 July 1993. Advance screenings in Winnipeg and Banff were followed by a Canadian premiere at the Toronto International Film Festival in September, where it received the Toronto-City Award for best Canadian feature. It was shown on national television on 31 January 1994, but only after the Canadian Broadcasting Corporation introduced a new policy to accommodate documentaries 'with no pretence of being impartial.'[6]

Documenting the Events: Narrative Form and Native Worldview

For over three decades, Alanis Obomsawin has worked as an activist, performer, storyteller, and filmmaker. Her films are political interventions that document the enduring traditions of Natives and their struggles for survival within a history of discrimination and dispossession. Obomsawin's films convey a Native worldview grounded in the actual world and based on the sacred meaning of all aspects of life and the interdependence of beings and things. This worldview constitutes the organic link between Native traditions and Obomsawin's documentary practice.

In *Kanehsatake*, the narrative elements of documentary (voice-over narration, interviews, observational shots, and found footage) are recoded to articulate a worldview based on interdependence and reciprocity. This recoding operation entails, on the one hand, the grounding of the film's discourse in a symbolic system that embodies values, beliefs, and identity, and locating its representation in images that illustrate the intricate balance between the natural environment and its human inhabitants. On the other hand, this operation involves a nonlinear patterning of narrative elements to reinvoke the poetry of oral traditions. While incidents follow chronologically, the elements are organized to represent space as an experience of oneness and time as a cyclical experience of what the sacred power has taught humans to do since 'time immemorial.' Insofar as *Kanehsatake* reconstructs and mediates the participants' explanation and experience of the events, this recoding is put at the service of Native historiography. From this perspective, history is, as Linda Pertusati explains, 'the unbroken thread from the past and a path to a collective future. It is a source of obligation and sense of responsibility that influences perceptions or lenses through which people interpret subsequent events. It is a source of identity ... as well as a motive and strategy for action to protect that identity.'[7] The film conveys what history means to the Mohawk nation.

The pre-credits segment illustrates the film's recoding operation and its historiographic agenda. It uses drawings of the Mohawk territory to situate geographically the story to be told, and establishes, through interviews and observational shots, the circumstances leading to the 11 July police raid. The matching shots that end this segment shift the linearity of the exposition to foreground the spiritual meaning of the hillside burial ground overlooking the Lake of Two Mountains. The first is a lateral tracking shot from the golf course to the Pine Hill Cemetery gate and serves to map spatially Obomsawin's narrative of Mohawk opposition since the 1930s to municipal development. The second is a tilt down from the tree tops to the headstones, ending with a close-up of a ceremonial feather, and is accompanied by Native chanting. It visualizes the Iroquois name of the Pines, Onen'to:kon which means 'under the pines,' and establishes it as a sacred site where the above and the below are joined so that spirits and humans can come together to experience the unity of the cosmos. As Pertusati explains, the Pines 'is more than a place where [Mohawks] bury their dead. It is also a place from which they draw their spiritual strength and communal identity, where they practice the Mohawk way of life.'[8] To the extent that this representation is central to the film's historiographic project, it is sustained throughout in observational sequences depicting the everyday relationship of Mohawks with the land.

The centrality of tradition amid conflict is confirmed when Loran Thompson (Oneida) teaches children the Iroquois language while walking in the Pines. Later sitting around a picnic table in the TC, he gestures to the children to plug their ears ('Do this ... War is really annoying') as an army helicopter flies overhead. The same sense of harmony and confidence to go about ordinary tasks is conveyed when equipment is carried away during the army's advance with Robert Skidders 'Mad Jap' (Akwesasne) eating pizza, when the engagement of Cathy Sky (Kahnawake) and Dennis Nicholas 'Psycho' (Kanehsatake) is celebrated in the TC, and when food is prepared and shared during the last days of the showdown. The complementarity of sacred belief and defensive action is expressed by Joe David 'Stone Carver' (Kanehsatake) recalling the danger posed by army flares over shots of Warriors who rush into the bush and haul water from the river to extinguish the fire. The concern to preserve the Pines is contrasted with the indifference of the military, who scar the landscape by driving tanks on unpaved roads and hammering metal rods into highways. Their zeal to set barbed wire in the river beside the TC verges on the comical and prompts David to react by saying, 'Don't they realize that we are going nowhere?'

In addition to signs of militarization, *Kanehsatake* shows the traces left by colonialism on the landscape. Panoramic shots illustrate the carving up of the Mohawk territory into a checkerboard design of farm fields and suburban homes. The hillside view of the river from above the Highway 344 barricade highlights the commanding position of the Sulpician church. This recurrent shot is a reminder of what is at stake: the aboriginal right over the Kanehsatake territory which Mohawks have never relinquished and which is at the core of '270 years of resistance' of the film's title.[9]

The identity of the Warriors as defenders of Mohawk sovereignty and custodians of the Pines is visually reinforced. During the interviews, their bodies are framed by the trees (Tom Paul 'The General,' Eskasoni, Nova Scotia), by the sandy knolls giving Kanehsatake its name 'where the sandy crust dunes are' (Brad Laroque 'Freddy Krueger,' Regina, Saskatchewan), and by the wooded views of the river (Larry Thompson 'Wizard,' Akwesasne). Moreover, the interview showing Obomsawin sitting next to 'Wizard' is split into two parts to place in the present, through shots of the army's advance on the St Germain road and later on Highway 344, his narrative about the traditional covenant to protect the sacred land through military action.

Kanehsatake reconstructs significant moments like the signing of the 12 August agreement between the Mohawk negotiating team and federal and provincial government officials to initiate peace talks. While presenting its various phases, the segment emphasizes ritual over protocol. Through the mise en scène, every gesture asserts its historicity because it is embedded in the memory of actions performed numerous times before, such as the procession led by John Cree over the original barricade, the prayers and speeches, and Obomsawin's voice-over reading of the three Mohawk preconditions. The symbolism of the Pines is reinstated when Joe Doem (Kahnawake) says, 'These barricades are just the physical manifestation of the barricades that have existed between our nations since contact occurred in the western hemisphere almost 500 years ago.' This convergence is echoed in the visual and aural elements bracketing the historical segment. Obomsawin's comment, 'the irony is that the army helicopters are landing behind the Sulpician church where the trouble began 270 years ago,' is preceded by matching shots of army helicopters, one carrying Mohawk warriors to Kahnawake to discuss the reopening of the Mercier bridge and the other landing behind the church. At the end, the words, 'in July 1990, this sad legacy continues,' are placed over a shot of a young man standing beside a police cruiser to parallel the preceding archival photograph of members of a Quebec Provincial Police squad in full uniform.

Obomsawin's skill as a storyteller is most effectively rendered in this historical segment. Placed twenty-eight minutes into the film, it is narrated by Obomsawin and illustrated by a variety of visual materials. It focuses on the pre-contact period, the displacement of the Mohawks to Kanehsatake during the French regime, and two land claim petitions during the British regime in 1787 and 1868. More than an exposé of dispossession and colonial domination, this segment validates Native historiography. Its imagery represents time as cyclical, where whatever has happened before will happen again, and its exposition draws on Native oratory. The watercolour sketches by Bob Verrall of the wooded river landscape symbolize 'time immemorial' and highlight what occurred in the beginning of time. Those of the Lake of Two Mountains and the church symbolize the temporal aspects of Mohawk history, their estrangement from the land when they were forced to migrate, and Europeans encroached on their territory. The engravings and diorama reconstructions depicting Native life carry the awareness of how colonial images can be appropriated for First Nations' history. The two speeches in this segment are historical reenactments. The first, spoken by a male voice, describes the Two Dog Wampum Treaty Belt presented to Sir John Johnston, Superintendent of Indian Affairs, in 1781, and reproduces the traditional oral recital of the Great Law of Peace. The second is a speech by Chief Sose Onasakenrat, known as Joseph Swan, confronting the Sulpician priests in 1869 and is accompanied by archival photographs of families in a Mohawk community. It concludes with the following words: 'This land is ours – ours as a heritage given to us as sacred legacy. It is the place where our fathers lie; beneath those trees our mothers sang our lullaby, and you would dare to take it from us and leave us wanderers at the mercy of fate?' This interconnection of knowledge, culture, and environment is the driving force behind this historical segment and, with the recoding of narrative elements to represent space as sacred and time as cyclical, is central to the interpretative framework of the film.

Representing the Events: Storytelling and Politics

Kanehsatake is foremost a film about the conflict between First Nations and the Canadian state. While it exposes the showdown at Oka as another instance of colonialism, it manages to negotiate the difficult path between politics and solidarity. Obomsawin's approach to human emotion creates a space for empathy. By drawing on the expressive universe of Native storytelling, the film represents the affective and political dynamics of the events and their effect on protagonists, observers, and bystanders. The disruption of everyday life is recorded, not always through conflict, but through incongruity and paradox. Cutaway shots in interviews are not digressions but images that convey the meaning of human life in a dangerous world. The film places belligerence and serenity side by side, as when shots of the Chateauguay riots with the infamous burning of a Mohawk effigy precede farm animals foraging in the Pines and a masked Mohawk behind a barricade relaxing on a lawn chair. The analogy is refocused when Oka resident Luc Boivin says, 'in fact, you have to really, really ask yourself who's the most mature in this whole affair?' The cat lounging on a step and the couple of seniors on a bench swing underline Boivin's remarks on the official disregard of dissenting voices in Oka and his objection to historical fallacies about Natives. This human and animal analogy is broadened by Obomsawin's voice-over comment that 'many Mohawk residents of Oka and Kanehsatake have left fearing another attack' over shots of a porcupine walking on a sidewalk and under a car. This moment may exemplify the filmmaker's ability, as Donna Sinclair puts it, to 'tell the story with a joyful sense of the absurd that frequently sustains Native people at times of stress.'[10] Yet, it also becomes a metaphor of wisdom whereby the porcupine, like the Mohawks in Oka, realizes the perils that lurk behind the placid surroundings.

The face-to-face encounters between Warriors and soldiers emphasize the military dimensions of the conflict. As in the peace-signing segment mentioned earlier, the symbolic meaning of gestures and actions resides in the unbroken continuum of spirituality, everyday life, and warfare. During the military advance on 20 August in Kanehsatake, for example, equal weight is given to the ceremonial gestures of Native spiritual leaders from Mexico, the foresight of a child who takes a photograph, and the belligerent postures of 'Psycho' and Lieutenant-Colonel Pierre Daigle. Each action has a moral dimension because it asserts individual responsibility as a response to chaos. Here, historicity is a resisting agency that contests victimization because it consciously participates in the construction of individual and collective identities.

The army occupation of the Pines on 1 September has an epic dimension. Shot by two crews, one located in the rear of the original barricade and the other on Highway 344, these sequences capture the battle readiness of the army and the resolve of the Mohawk warriors, yet individualize the protagonists. Major Alain Tremblay makes a dramatic entry: he appears in a clearing on the dirt road flanked by soldiers with green painted faces, army vehicles behind them and helicopters above. Notwithstanding the well-rehearsed show of force, bewilderment is exposed in cutaway, close-up shots of camouflaged soldiers patrolling the Pines on the lookout for Warriors. On the highway, Richard Two Axe 'Bolt Pin' (Kahnawake), a lonesome resister on a golf cart, interrupts the advancing column, and 'Mad Jap' the strategist acts as an intermediary between the Warriors and the military. Yet the hero is Jenny Jack (Tlinkit, British Columbia) as the pacifier driving back the impulsive young Warriors in an all-terrain vehicle. This image, like those of negotiator Ellen Gabriel (Kanehsatake), confirms the courage and authority of women as peacekeepers. As the soldiers dismantle the 'Main Gate' (as the Warriors call the Highway 344 barricade) and roll out the razor wire, the film establishes the stage on which the drama

Kanehsatake: 270 Years of Resistance (1993), directed by Alanis Obomsawin. Courtesy of the National Film Board of Canada.

will unfold: a narrow strip of land separating the Warriors, their spiritual leaders, a few journalists, and Obomsawin's crew from the army.

At fifty-eight minutes into *Kanehsatake*, the imagery changes. In night sequences, the chiaroscuro effect of searchlights and log fires distorts and renders everything colourless, except for intermittent flickers of brilliance. The landscape acquires a spectral, dreamlike quality signalling a perceptual shift. At the beginning of the narrative about Randy Horne's beating, Obomsawin announces: 'The sun is going down. The warrior's silence speaks of death. Some of them have made their wills. Another night in TC.' The shots of the ghostly forest and the army post replicate those of the shooting incident that killed Corporal Lemay and, by means of matching swish pans, construct a metaphor of terror.

While symbolism confirms the place of spirituality amidst the chaos, it also enhances affect and identification. Behind the makeshift curtain put up as a shield against the army search lights, Kahentiiosta (Kahnawake) sings a lullaby to her young child near an ominous-looking army flare, and a Warrior chats on a cell phone with his child under the watchful eye of a sentinel. With Obomsawin's remarks, 'Shadows on the wall, is this the end?' the imagery aligns itself to Native vision quests where humans confront mortality. The silhouette figures of the Warriors, backlit tree branches, and multicoloured skyscapes underscore this foreboding with their poetic quality. Yet, the death that Obomsawin evokes is not the end of life but the passing from one life to another. The bleached-out and grainy-looking daytime sequences reveal the turmoil of this transitory state. Experiences sway between anger and melancholy during the rituals performed by the Oneida spiritual leaders, Terry Doxtator, Bob Antone, and Bruce Elijah, to appease the belligerent Warriors. The testimonies by Joe David 'Stone Carver' and Tom Paul 'The General,' now with their faces uncovered, are accompanied by the heartlike beating of a drum. While their words articulate the prevailing mood of those last few days, the rhythmic sounds convey the strength that comes from spiritual traditions.

The film's reconstruction of the march out of TC is narrated by some of its protagonists. It is a montage sequence integrating images shot by different crews and interviews recorded subsequently with 'Bolt Pin,' Marie David (Kanehsatake), Lorna Delormier (Kahnawake), Donald Hemlock 'Babe' (Kahnawake), and Lorraine Montour (Kahnawake/ Akwesasne). Like the agreement-signing segment discussed earlier, its significance goes beyond the immediacy of incidents and testimonies. It creates a space for empathy because it is simultaneously an account and a meditation on how the events were experienced. The dramatic dénouement of *Kanehsatake* reaffirms its historicity. Images draw on symbols embedded in history and evoke the poetry of oral tradition using the trees and the leaden sky as lyrical backdrop for the Warrior and Iroquois Confederacy flags, the drifting smoke of burning fires, the helicopter suspended high above the river, and the silhouettes of children. Their epic dimension constitutes the film's legacy to Native historiography.

While this segment deploys the spiritual metaphors of preceding segments, it valorizes fearless confidence and collective action. The compositional and rhythmical effects, together with the graphic textures, expand the expressive range of ritual and memory, during the evacuation arrangements, the trek through the dark forest, the skirmishes on the road, or the departure to Farnham military base. The shots on the road, for instance, are edited to the flashes of reporters' cameras. The sporadic bursts of light brighten the sombre, grey shading of bodies and landscape, freezing gestures and interactions to visualize the metaphor, articulated by Two Axe, of being in 'a twilight zone.' While images of chaos and violence prevail, this segment also underscores defiance in the ceremonial actions of spiritual leaders and the enraged reactions of women in Oka. Moreover, the meaning of their gestures resides in the understanding of self and destiny expressed in a Warrior's assertion that 'the circle is not finished. It's not finished.'

By invoking the Sacred Circle of Life, *Kanehsatake* asserts the cultural ethos that informs the film's representation. Its symbolic meanings are reasserted in the closing sequence that records the first anniversary march on 11 July 1991. While the camera identifies some of the protagonists of the Oka showdown, its scope is commemorative as it follows the walk through the town of Oka and up the hill towards the barricade on the Chemin du mille. By retracing the topography of the events, the camera underscores the enduring symbolism of the landscape, even in the shot of players on the golf course. By summoning the words of Chief Sose Onasakenrat (1869) heard in the historical segment over shots of the marchers in the Pines, the film reinscribes the experiential memory of time. Reinforced by the vital power of tradition, this memory is articulated in a short statement by Tom Paul 'The General' and conveyed by the songs of the spiritual leaders, the emblematic presence of the white pines, and the gulls feeding in the river. In the brief scenes during the final credits, the film affirms the temporal aspects of life and the 'timeless' understanding of cyclical time. Each transposes experience into ritual and recaptures the moment as timeless, through shots ranging from the close-up of leg shackles to the victorious gestures of Mohawks leaving the St-Jérôme courthouse and the tilt up from the burial stones to the tree tops.

The last shot of the final credits is of a Mohawk cornhusk mask, shown earlier as a visual preamble to the military escalation following the breakdown of negotiations. Backlit by the fading daylight, the mask's visionary power is reinforced. It belongs to Mohawk narrative traditions and represents the legendary world of supernatural and spiritual beings that roam the earth to protect humans. Like the False Face masks used in healing ceremonials, it recalls that the Mohawks have a long heritage of facial expressions symbolizing power. The presence of the mask in the film draws on this heritage to challenge the government and media characterization of the Warriors, who were depicted as faceless terrorists in numerous photographs. The image of a masked Warrior staring down at a soldier became the icon of Oka, as exemplified by the picture of Brad Laroque 'Freddy Krueger' and Private Patrick Cloutier taken by Shaney Kamoulian for Canadian Press. Hence, the imagery in *Kanehsatake* fulfills a double function, one recuperative because it draws on the cultural and symbolic heritage of Native traditions, and the other political because it subverts the racialized typologies of colonialism.

Documentary Process and Critical Responses to *Kanehsatake*

While challenging official narratives, Obomsawin's film also documents how narratives of the event were constructed. By focusing on the roles of the government and of media and film crews (including her own) in this process, the film provides a context for the imagery that Canadians have come to associate with the events at Oka. Shown on television screens, often with Warriors and journalists watching, the official pronouncements expose in an ironic way the manipulation of public opinion. A shot of CBC reporter Tony Ross, for instance, filing his report over the phone, contradicts claims about a Mohawk arsenal. This short scene invalidates one of the reasons given for bringing in the army in the broadcast statements by Robert Bourassa and Prime Minister Brian Mulroney. Since these announcements follow testimonies of police intimidation, they demonstrate the duplicity of Bourassa's claim that the army was called in to protect society 'against people who do not believe in democracy.'

The obvious differences between simultaneous incidents recorded by different crews on film and video provide insights into the documentary process. When these materials are edited together, as in the sequence discussed earlier of the army advance in the Pines, they create a broader narrative context while foregrounding the production process. Moreover, the inability to shoot certain episodes is explicitly acknowledged through the optical effects used for the reconstruction of the 11 July raid and the beating of Randy Horne.

Obomsawin's presence in the film anchors her role as participant. In some cases, she appears in episodes related to journalists and film crews. When reporters are allowed to approach the razor wire by the TC and an unidentified man speaks about the army interference, Obomsawin is among the group requesting help from their colleagues outside. The close-up of soldiers, holding rolls of film thrown over the wire and later impounded, frames her holding a boom mike in the background. Other scenes shot inside the TC area convey her empathy and identification, as when Ted Cash negotiates with the army to get his asthma medication, and Albert Nerenberg and Robert Galbraith recount how they sneaked behind army lines in broad daylight to document the last days of the standoff.

Kanehsatake exposes not only the difficulties faced by journalists, described by Native writer Doug Cuthand as being the result of 'army censorship and lack of cooperation,' but also the limitations of their accounts, since 'the reporters did not understand the issues and philosophies behind the barricades.'[11] Hence, what differentiates the film from mainstream reporting is its autonomy, scope, and point of view. Not being bound by journalistic criteria of 'objectivity' and as a permanent staff director, Obomsawin could count on the NFB's tradition of creative independence and the absolute support of producers and crew members. Her comment that the confrontation at Oka 'had to be documented by a Native person' explains the placement of events within a broader historical and cultural framework.[12] In addition, as many reviewers agreed, she brings a distinctive voice, emotional outlook, and political commitment. The result is that, as Ronald Wright states, 'the film transports the viewer to the barricades and the camps, achieving a powerful immediacy and devastating logic.'[13]

The critical responses to *Kanehsatake* focus on the events by reflecting on what they have meant to Canada rather than simply emphasizing what J.R. Miller has identified, in commentaries about Oka, as the 'specific, local and immediate factors.'[14] The dominant issue in the English-language press was the film's importance. Reviewers emphasized that it exposes the shameful handling by the government of Native land claims and provides historical background to the conflict. Generally positive, reviews described it as a history lesson and, in Richard Cawley's words, 'a reminder of the long history of broken promises and shady dealings with ... First Nations communities throughout the country.'[15] According to Cam Fuller, 'the film easily wins your support for the Native's land claims and you leave this story in awe of their determination.'[16] For some reviewers, the issue was how Canada is understood as a nation, and Elissa Barnard called it 'a dramatic, damning and frightening film' that every Canadian should see because it is a 'struggle of the soul between anger and patience for something it believes in, and a probing into what Canada is and for whom.'[17]

The reception of the film reveals important differences between English Canada and Quebec. While English Canadians seemed inclined to accept a Native point of view, in Quebec there was animosity, if not outright hostility, to what Obomsawin had to say. *Kanehsatake* was first shown in Montreal at the Festival du Nouveau Cinéma in October 1993. Some reviews provided only information and quotations from interviews, with the most negative comments directed at the film's point of view and militant position. If there was some admiration for Obomsawin as a Native filmmaker, reviewers like Odile Tremblay censured her for 'wearing two hats: that of a militant for the First Nations' cause, and that of a journalist pretending to deliver an objective account and retrace the history of a crisis.'[18] For critic André Roy, the film's position endangers its credibility because the characterization of the Mohawks exclusively serves a Native cause and 'rejects any possibility of reconciliation.'[19] In contrast, Franco Nuovo expressed admiration for the film and for Obomsawin because 'she sheds her own light on the blunders and exposes the differences that often lead, in times of crisis, to intolerance.'[20] Others found the portrayal of Quebeckers objectionable: 'we seem like a band of brutal racists and square like an axe. Not very flattering.'[21] A few, like Eric Fourlanty, praised the film, because of 'the compassion it shows for the violation of our rights, the clamour of the scorned Oka citizens, the absurdity of an army worthy of a banana republic.'[22] In a sense, Obomsawin foresaw these negative responses in Quebec when she stated 'there are people [in Quebec] who will hate it, who will not like to see again the scenes of racism.'[23]

The seventy-eight-day standoff at Oka was a defining moment in Canadian history. It confirmed in more ways than one the colonial relationship that has existed for over five centuries between the Canadian state and the First Nations. It also confirmed long-held assumptions about Native grievances and Mohawk militancy. Even three years after the event, the film could still become a vehicle for discussion. The critical responses described above reveal the lack of consensus around a film that, as Jerry White states, 'offers a substantial, biting critique of the way in which nationhood has been defined, which is an especially important point of dissent in a country like Canada, which prides itself on the looseness and diversity of national identity.'[24]

Conclusion

Kanehsatake provides non-Native Canadians with an opportunity to understand the significance of the event for First Nations' people, but, as Doug Nepinak pointed out in his review, it has a special meaning for Natives:

> From within us, [the film] draws the outrage that never goes away. We remember the admiration we felt for the band of women, men and children who changed the way Canada sees aboriginal people ... Be on the

lookout for this scorcher. It is recommended to all those who wish to remember, because forgetting is a step backward.[25]

But foremost, the film validates history and locates identity in tradition, thought, and culture to imagine a Mohawk nation grounded in the spiritual connection with the land. In Obomsawin's work the creative process finds expression in storytelling. Storytelling creates bonds and defines identity, celebrates life and entertains, sustains and critiques history, and reinforces cultural and religious continuity. Storytelling illuminates the role of humans and expresses the rhythm and vitality of life experiences, and, as Marjorie Beaucage states, it 'comes from being in the world, from experiencing life rather than measuring or controlling it.'[26] Because it is an activity that preserves and creates, Native artists, writers, and filmmakers see themselves as storytellers, as carriers of histories and keepers of collective and individual memory.

The stories Obomsawin tells in her documentaries validate culture as an experience of history. Yet her storytelling is as much about remembrance and retelling as the sharing of power through exchange and responsible action through moral guidance. This alignment to the moral imperatives of storytelling explains her extraordinary ability to create empathy and affect. This ability also enables dialogue between herself, the people she films and those who see them, Native and non-Native. As she has said, 'I am really a bridge between two worlds.'[27] By using film to start a conversation, her work invites participants and viewers to engage with and commit themselves to understanding themselves and others because they are too, at some point, implicated. It is this impulse towards dialogue and engagement that explains her multipositioned approach to documentary and, because it blurs the boundaries between the educational, agitational, and poetic, calls for a different critical framework.[28]

Kanehsatake conveys Obomsawin's outrage and admiration for the courage shown by the Warriors during the long confrontation. She provides insight into the many stories and the numerous ways in which the Mohawks, the people of Oka, and the journalists experienced the events because, as she has stated, 'there are many stories to Kanehsatake, or Oka, or Kahnawake during the crisis – thousands of stories.'[29] As in her other films, the elements of documentary become components of storytelling to create a narrative and a visual space that represents knowledge and social experience and reclaims traditional and contemporary stories.

Notes

With many thanks to Westwind Evening Woman for her encouragement to write about Obomsawin's work, her patience with my queries, and her advice. And to Bernard Lutz, of the NFB, for allowing me to consult the press files on the film.

1 For a detailed account of the events, see York and Pindera, *The People of the Pines*.
2 Marginson, 'Talking Heads,' 10.
3 Ibid., 10–11.
4 Baele, 'An Eye on Oka.'
5 Alioff, 'Dream Magic,' 6.
6 Atherton, 'CBC Aims to Revive Documentary.'
7 Pertusati, *In Defense of Mohawk Land*, 37.
8 Ibid., 85.
9 Ibid., 21–37.
10 Sinclair, 'Film Review,' 53.
11 Cuthand, 'Documentary on Oka Standoff Is a Must-See.'
12 Obomsawin, quoted in Greer, 'Mohawks and the Media,' 20.
13 Wright, 'Cutting through the Razor Wire.'
14 Miller, 'Great White Father Knows Best,' 369.
15 Cawley, 'Film Reminds Us of Failures and Broken Promises.'
16 Fuller, 'Documentary Probes Wounds of Oka.'
17 Barnard, 'Filmmaker Explores Oka Crisis.'
18 Tremblay, 'Alanis, Pascale et Antonin ...'
19 Roy, 'Non Réconciliés,' 74.
20 Nuovo, 'Les Cowboys et les indiens.'
21 Tremblay, 'Alanis, Pascale et Antonin ...'
22 Fourlanty, 'États de crise.'
23 *La Tribune*, 'Accueil controversé au Québec.'
24 White, 'Alanis Obomsawin,' 26–7.
25 Nepinak, '*Kanehsatake: 270 Years of Resistance*.'
26 Beaucage, 'Aboriginal Voices,' 215.
27 Obomsawin, quoted in Petrone, ed., *First People, First Voices*, 200.
28 White, 'Alanis Obomsawin,' 32–3.
29 Obomsawin, quoted in Greer, 'Mohawks and the Media,' 19.

Hyperbolic Masculinity and the Ironic Gaze in *Project Grizzly*

BRENDA LONGFELLOW

Produced in 1996 by the National Film Board and directed by Peter Lynch, *Project Grizzly* premiered at the Toronto Film Festival to wildly enthusiastic reviews. A surprise hit on the festival circuit, it won Best Ontario Film at the Sudbury Film Festival, was released to over fifty theatrical screens in Canada (principally repertory houses and cinematheques), and went on to become one of the top-ten-grossing feature films in Canada that year. Cut down to a forty-two-minute version and broadcast on CBC's *Witness*, the film received one of the program's highest ratings (600,000 viewers). All this is highly unusual for a Canadian film, but for a documentary to attain such popular status is extraordinary.

Certainly, the association between audience popularity and documentary has been rare, even somewhat scandalous within the history of documentary practice in Canada. The role of the NFB was conceived by John Grierson precisely in opposition to the debased pleasures of popular culture. The 'tawdry,' 'vulgar,' and 'facetious' distractions of 'entertainment movies' would be left to Hollywood; Canadians would be directed to the sober task of making documentary films of moral and political purpose.[1] While the NFB has evolved a range of heterogeneous styles and practices since Grierson, the concept of documentary as a committed and pedagogic form has, with few exceptions, continued to predominate within the institution.

What then to make of a film like *Project Grizzly*, which is so unapologetically constituted as a popular entertainment? According to Michael Allder, the producer and initiator of the film, *Project Grizzly* was always conceived as a 'non-fiction movie' intended for theatrical release and, as such, was shot in super 16 for a blowup to 35 mm.[2] Clearly, the orientation towards packaging documentaries as 'non-fiction movies' is inextricably linked to the recent institutional history of the NFB, which over the last decade has been displaced as the centre of documentary production in Canada. Steady budget cuts, downsizing, the dissolution of technical services and laboratories in Montreal, coupled with the proliferation of an independent documentary sector, created pressures within the institution to produce a more coherent and distinct public profile. Abandonment of distribution in the non-theatrical sector and a concentration on creating a bigger broadcast profile have been among the major responses. Limited theatrical releases have been another.[3]

What I want to do in this paper is analyse the 'popularity' of this Canadian film while examining some of the textual and extra-textual causes of its entertainment value. Let me hazard a hypothesis: I believe that the popularity of *Project Grizzly* is constituted in two very distinctive modes depending on the class and regional habitus of the spectator. This doubleness of spectatorial response, moreover, is cued by a primary textual difference between the *explicit* pro-filmic world of a northern, working-class hinterland, the hyper-masculine world of scrap metal dealer, Troy Hurtubise, and the *implicit* metropolitan gaze of the film director which frames and, inevitably, appraises Troy's world through the specifically cinematic codes of montage, music, and the orchestration of mise en scène. Each of these 'levels,' to use a spatial metaphor, implies a discursive universe composed of collective values, cultural knowledge, and taste dispositions, and each cues a significantly different reading strategy. It is this doubling of the text, the interaction and relation between these levels, that produces both *Project Grizzly*'s textual playfulness and its powerful sense of irony.

Documenting the Popular

Project Grizzly follows the antics of Troy Hurtubise, a self-styled bear researcher in North Bay, Ontario, who is on a mission to reenact a close encounter with a grizzly bear he calls The Old Man. To that end he designs a series of high-tech suits variously named Ursus Mark I, II, III, constructed out of titanium, chain mail, and Japanese rubber that he tests in all manner of ways, including throwing himself off the Niagara Escarpment, stepping in front of an 18-ton truck going 50 kilometres an hour, and being rammed with a 300-pound log. One hundred and fifty thousand dollars later and seven years after the first attack, Hurtubise claims he is ready to test the suit in the field.

I have provided a very generalized definition of the pro-filmic events represented in this documentary. The film – and this is, perhaps, its biggest deviation from classical conceptions of documentary – is fully narrative, interventionist, and self-reflexive. Not only are numerous sequences obviously staged, but the principal dramatic event, Hurtubise's would-be encounter with a grizzly in the foothills of the Rockies, is deliberately choreographed by the film production, which subsidizes and arranges the transport of Hurtubise, his posse of seven men, and a small arsenal of guns and ammunition to Alberta. While NFB documentaries have long transgressed the border between the fictional and the real, and while the staging of sequences has been a convention of even the most hypothetically realist of documentary practices, what is significantly different in *Project Grizzly* is that the fictional mediation is deliberately constituted through the deployment of the icons, genres, and mise en scènes of American popular culture.

As Lynch reports, 'the film itself was constructed along the lines of a Western; we found that dispensing with much of the documentary baggage freed us to fashion an action-based narrative ... Scenes were blocked out in advance so that he could act out his story unencumbered ... I was going for a greater truth than the truth of incident or circumstance,' he continues, '[so] I just basically set up as many strategies as I thought suited the needs of this story and pushed them as far as I could take them.'[4] Lynch avows he set out to work on several generic levels at once, and this is commonly repeated in all reviews: 'Canadian western, a reinvention of the action-adventure genre, a mythic quest and a metaphor for standing up to American culture.'[5]

The marshalling of the tropes of American popular culture, however, only arrives with a powerful sense of dissonance and with a distinctly ironic flavour. The 'standing up to the American culture' that Lynch lists as one of his intentions has everything to do with the disruption and bracketing of the surface similarity of appropriated cultural forms. In this sense, the textual strategies of *Project Grizzly* are closely aligned with postcolonial and feminist work that deploys mimicry as a strategy of critique and subversion, a 'making strange' in order to reveal the persistence of difference.[6] To appropriate an insight from Luce Irigaray, 'to play with mimesis is ... to try to recover the place of [one's] exploitation by discourse without allowing [oneself] to be simply reduced to it ... If [Canadians] are such good mimics, it is because they are not simply reabsorbed in this function. They also remain elsewhere.'[7]

In *Project Grizzly* the irretrievably seedy landscape of North Bay stands in for our enduring national 'elsewhere.' Indeed, the humour and irony of *Project Grizzly* are absolutely dependent on the central visual juxtaposition the film establishes between the prosaic, everyday life in North Bay, and the epic (American) grandeur of Hurtubise's mission. While the prosaic is established through the deliberate choice of locations in North Bay (a metal scrapyard, a Country Style Donuts shop, town dump, and bar parking lot), the epic is visually articulated through the classic landscape panoramas of mountains and uninhabited vistas of the Rocky Mountain foothills.

There are few other towns or cities in northern Ontario where this contrast would work in quite the same way. Originally developed as a transportation and lumbering centre, North Bay experienced a short boom period. Unlike Sudbury (where I was born), whose economy prospered around the single extractive industry of mining and which developed deep traditions of unionization and working-class militancy, North Bay got a NORAD base and developed service industries, primarily oriented around providing wilderness experiences for tourists from the south. Today you only have to drive down the main drag in North Bay under the banner 'Gateway to the North' past rows of dilapidated resorts who had seen their heyday in the fifties, past strip malls and ubiquitous American junk food chains to witness North Bay's stunted history. Predominantly white and lower middle class, life in North Bay is fuelled by a deep and abiding resentment against the south and all the south stands for: privilege and wealth. While the Chamber of Commerce in North Bay has lately initiated a campaign to attract information technology industries to North Bay (a principally non-unionized workforce), the area remains one of high unemployment and low wages.

Like Sudbury, however, North Bay is a culture fundamentally divided between male and female spheres of work and pleasure. For someone growing up in this environment, one's most profound observation of the world is that schism, so aptly captured in the immortal words of Stompin' Tom Connors' 'Sudbury, Saturday Night,' where 'the girls are out for bingo and the boys are getting stinko.' It is also a culture where, apart from serious drinking, activities in the 'bush' – hunting, fishing, and snowmobiling – are dominant forms of leisure activity for men. It's hard to impart the deep significance that northerners attach to the 'bush' as a real and psychic territory of freedom – freedom from domestic and work responsibilities and freedom from female presence. It's a place where male social relations are forged through a style of masculinity that frequently borders on the militaristic – camouflage outfits, guns, knives – and where an interest in culture (outside of video rentals) is taken as a sign of effeminate or inveterately snobbish orientation.

Ironic Detachment

My unease with *Project Grizzly* has to do with the way in which this working-class culture is framed by the film's metropolitan and ironic perspective. As Linda Hutcheon has pointed out, irony inevitably involves an 'appraising edge,' and it is that edge with its necessary evaluative judgments that tends to position working-class culture in *Project Grizzly* as a perpetual ethnographic 'other.'[8] Let me insist, however, that the issue here is not voyeurism or the exploitation of innocents, the kind of ethical debates that commonly come up in documentary discourses. *Project Grizzly* is completely produced with the full awareness and exhibitionist ambitions of its subject, Troy Hurtubise. The process according to all reports was 'intensely collaborative.'[9] A born raconteur and garrulous showman, Hurtubise is clearly an all-too-willing accomplice in the performance of his eccentric persona, as his numerous appearances on Canadian radio and television and his interviews with print journalists demonstrate.[10] The representation of this performance, however, is framed by a particular attitude expressed in the film's choice of music, visual style, and genre.

In *Project Grizzly*, the ironic perspective is developed through broad and eclectic genre quotations which range from cyborg science fiction, to nature documentaries, to boy's own adventure tales. These intertextual references are the source of the film's considerable and frequently cited 'quirky' humour. From the wide panoramas of men on horseback, to the faux Sergio Leone music track of twanging guitars, the film's revisionist Western style (Lynch refers to it as a 'northern') deliberately tropes on the mythic genre films of John Ford and Clint Eastwood. At the heart of this intertextual play, of course, is the subject himself, Troy Hurtubise, a walking pastiche of American popular culture if there ever was one, with his guardian angel red beret, Davey Crockett buckskin jacket, bowie knives, and his propensity to read Hollywood films as if they were scientific evidence. Hurtubise, in fact, derived the idea for the Ursus Mark series of titanium bear-proof suits from Paul Verhoeven's 1987 hit *Robocop*, and in one sequence even appears as Robocop's Canadian doppelganger, lumbering through the North Bay Drive-In in full Ursus Mark regalia as the Verhoeven movie plays on the large screen.

It is certainly no coincidence that the predominant generic citation in *Project Grizzly* is the Hollywood western, given the ways in which that

Project Grizzly (1996), directed by Peter Lynch. Courtesy of the National Film Board of Canada.

genre has been so inextricably linked to the imagining of the American nation with its deeply retrograde constellation of ideas about heroic individualism, expansionism, and violence linked to moral purpose. It is also a genre in which the gendering of the American national subject is transparently revealed through the central protagonist's habitual performance of a hyperbolic masculinity. In its appropriation of these most mythic and imperialistic genres of American culture, *Project Grizzly* establishes a benchmark against which the Canadian deviation will be measured – and found hilariously lacking.

In *Project Grizzly*, Troy Hurtubise's would-be performance of heroic masculinity always arrives with bold quotations marks around it. While American western and action/adventure films naturalize the spectacle and exhibitionist display of the male body through a textual emphasis on swift, brutal, and goal-directed action, it is perhaps Hurtubise's very garrulousness and the ever-widening gap between his inflated sense of purpose and the bumbling ineffectualness of his actions that produces the humorous deflation of generic expectations. Indeed, the image of Hurtubise's hyperkinetic, chain-smoking, long-johnned body is so firmly located in a prosaic real that it can only deflect the kind of deep mythic idealizations of masculinity performed in the seamless American fantasies of *Robocop* or *Dirty Harry*.

This ironic de-mythification becomes obvious through a slightly more obscure potential intertext – the no-production-value television series *Super Dave* (currently repackaged as a feature film) in which Dave performs various manic stunts (being shot out of a cannon, jumping rows of barrels on a motorcycle), a show whose slapstick antics are echoed in the whacking and thunking sequences where Hurtubise tests his suit against a ten-ton truck and a gang of surly Hell's Angels.[11] The aggressive low-brow 'dumbness' of these sequences, their flaunting of a broad physical comedy, relates them to the taste predilections of what Pierre Bourdieu has called the popular aesthetic and what Constance Penley, for one, sees as a critical assertion of 'white trash sensibility.' I'm not sure everyone would follow Penley in reading white trash (which for her reaches its apogee in the raucous political incorrectness of Beavis and Butthead or Howard Stern) as a singular political corrective to the 'false decorum' and repressed fury of the new right. But her insight that this sensibility stems from a 'masculinity that perceives itself to be under attack from all sides, a masculinity no longer sure of its godgiven privilege and sense of entitlement' seems to say something essential about Troy Hurtubise, working-class hero and denizen of the regionally disadvantaged hinterland of North Bay.[12]

I'd like to return, though, to my unease with the way the film delivers Hurtubise as an ironic spectacle. As Hutcheon points out in *Irony's Edge: The Theory and Politics of Irony*, unease is the most common emotional response to the textual and ethical ambiguities evoked by irony precisely because of the way in which 'the scene of irony involves relations of power based in relations of communication.'[13] In its inherent duplicity and in its fashioning of a dialectic between the literal and the meta-textual, irony is often understood, according to Hutcheon, as a means of positioning its spectators/readers within a hierarchy of value: 'In a negative sense, irony is said to play to in-groups that can be elitist and exclusionary. Irony clearly differentiates and thus potentially excludes: as most theories put it, there are those who "get" it and those who do not.'[14] From Hutcheon's point of view, however, it is not the practice of irony itself that creates such distinctions: 'irony happens because what could be called "discursive communities" already exist and provide the context for both the deployment and attribution of irony.'[15] This is not, she insists, simply an issue of cultural competencies dividing those who read for 'depth' from those who cannot climb to the 'heights' of superior knowledge. Discursive communities (always multiple and overlapping) are constituted around varying concerns, 'interest, or simply knowledge (of context, norms or rules, intertexts) that enable the participants to perform "moves of indirect communication."'[16]

Hutcheon's notion of the variability and contingency of discursive communities provides, I believe, a very useful complement to Pierre Bourdieu's insight that particular reading practices, cultural knowledges, and preferences are intimately linked to a particular educational and social habitus. In his exhaustive sociological study, *Distinction: A Social Critique of the Judgement of Taste*, Bourdieu locates economic class as the central arbiter of a social distribution of taste, arguing that a key signifier of bourgeois perspective is an aesthetic preference for artistic work that involves critical distance, multi-levelled reflexivity, and, above all else, ironic detachment.[17]

While any theoretical poaching from Bourdieu has to acknowledge the 'tacit functionalism'[18] and 'lurking determinism'[19] that posits a direct analogous relation between class and taste formation (a tendency that has a great deal to do, I suspect, with the peculiar heritage of the European educational system), his focus on 'ironic detachment' as a crucial symbolic marker of economic and social privilege provides an entry for thinking through the power relations (of reading and performance) embedded in *Project Grizzly*.

One particular discursive community – reviewers and critics writing in major metropolitan newspapers – clearly 'got' the film's ironic intentions and read it as a dissertation on the foibles of Canadian national identity. The consistent repetition of headlines like 'Archetypally Canadian' (*Festival Listings*, 6 December 1996–30 January 1997), 'Distinctly Canadian' (*POV*, Winter 1997), and 'Ultra-Canuck Docu' (*Variety*, 14–20 October 1996) more than emphasized the homogeneous pattern of reception in these quarters. Geoff Pevere, the dean of the mondo-Canuck school of criticism, opened his column on the Toronto International Film Festival avowing, 'You'll trudge a long way before finding a better metaphor for contemporary national experience than Troy Hurtubise' (*Globe and Mail*, 7 September 1996). For the most part, what defined the reading strategies of these reviewers was their ability to draw clever intertextual links. 'A *Field and Stream* excursion into the absurd,' quipped Brian Johnson (*Maclean's*, 16 September 1996); 'a bargain-basement *Robocop*,' wrote Carole Corbeil (*Toronto Star*, 17 September 1996). Cervantes' *Don Quixote* was the primary literary intertext, and the image of a fool tilting at windmills was appropriated as an axiomatic statement of Canadian identity, with Hurtubise standing in as a 'Hoser Quixote' (Peter Roffman, *Festival Magazine*, 10 January 1996). Only one reviewer, Cameron Bailey of *Now*, provided some qualifications to the film's alleged assertion of national identity, noting that the Canadian psyche which Lynch so aptly chronicled is 'white' and 'male' (*Now*, 9–15 January 1997) and, I would add, hyberbolically so.

At the risk of sounding cranky and humourless, my irritation with the film and its critical reception stems precisely from the fact that in the narcissistic mirroring of clever critic and the ironic discourse of the film, difference is completely marginalized. To be sure, the 'national subject' conjured up in this mirroring only exists in its mondo version as ironic joke and caricature, but even (and, perhaps, most particularly) in this mondo turn, national identity remains in exclusive dialogue with whiteness, maleness, and straightness. What I believe mondo tries to do is to negotiate a way through the contemporary world of proliferating differences by positing a common cultural experience and affliction. As Pevere and Greig Dymond put it in their *Mondo Canuck: A Canadian Pop Culture Odyssey*: 'the cultural conditions of Canada, a country where everybody watches TV that comes from somewhere else ... [produces] Canada [as] a nation of chronic, ironic, detached observers.'[20] What interests mondo is not subcultures but pop culture; not queer nation but suburban nation. As Pevere and Dymond suggest:

What if for a moment, we were to drop that conventional Canadian middlebrow disinclination toward popular culture ... to suggest that Canada is every bit as distinct in its approach to schlock as it is to art, and that the former may indeed reveal vastly more of a national distinction than the latter. That it is possible to see as much of ourselves (if not more) in Mike Myers as it is in Margaret Atwood.[21]

While this democratization of national taste formations must be seen as an advance over the 'largely Arnoldian concept of high culture'[22] informing institutional and historic discourses of Canadian identity that equate the popular with the barbaric ruin of civilization, I think there is something telling in that substitution of Mike Myers for Margaret Atwood that continues to reify whiteness and maleness at the centre of an imagined national identity.

Cultural Negotiations

I started out this paper arguing that *Project Grizzly* implicated two different reading strategies and discursive universes. Up to this point I have only discussed one of them: the one characterized by an ironic consciousness that is seemingly shared both by the filmmakers and by the majority of reviewers who wrote on the film. The other is constituted by the unique social environment of Troy Hurtubise and North Bay. Indeed, I would like to argue that a primary determinant of reading formations and discursive communities in English Canada is the profound difference between north and south, between metropolitan audiences and those of the hinterland. And while this difference is not produced exclusively through it, the simple fact that outside of major metropolitan centres and university towns, cinemas located in the strip malls of the hinterland only exhibit Hollywood films, has a major impact on taste formation.

In direct contrast to the aesthetic preference for ironic detachment associated with middle-class culture, Bourdieu suggests that a popular aesthetic is governed by a desire for 'passionate involvement.' 'This stems,' he argues, 'from a deep rooted demand for participation, which formal experiment systematically disappoints. The desire to enter into the game, identifying with the characters' joys and sufferings, worrying about their fate, espousing their hopes and ideals, living their life, is based on a form of investment, a sort of deliberate "naivety," ingenuousness, good-natured credulity.'[23]

What did those spectators in Sudbury who voted *Project Grizzly* 'best

Ontario film' see when they watched the film, or those seventy North Bay spectators who, according to the *North Bay Nugget* (1 March 1997) 'braved the heavy snow recently to attend the local premiere of *Project Grizzly* at the North Bay Arts Centre'? In an uncanny reiteration of Bourdieu's theory, Paul Smiley, one of the spectators interviewed by the *Nugget* claimed, 'I really liked his character and the passion that he had for what he was doing. I liked his energy and spirituality too.' His sister Gail added, 'there is such a building of frustration throughout the movie. I felt that was really a reflection of his character at the end.'

I think that what Bourdieu adds to our theories of cinematic spectatorship is a crucial refinement on the notions of negotiation and agency developed so persuasively in cultural studies. Reading at the level of content, for Bourdieu the primary mode of popular aesthetic experience, does not reduce spectators to the role of unthinking dupes of mass culture but, precisely, provides a way to read agency into the desire for emotional and ethical engagement.

With that in mind, I want to return to that movement *en abyme* that *Project Grizzly* stages around Hurtubise's relation to American popular culture. One way of reading the scene in the North Bay drive-in where Hurtubise, encased in his Ursus Mark suit, lumbers past the giant image of *Robocop* would be to marshal Mary Ann Doane's theory of female spectatorship as narcissistic over-identification. And that might well raise some very interesting issues around the gender, class, and regional dimensions of national spectatorship. Doane argues that the female spectator, because of her culturally marginalized position, lacks the necessary means and signifying abilities to enact the 'proper' distance between subject and object that a developed Western society privileges as a mode of cultural consumption. Too close to the image, the female spectator, rather than modelling her desire around a heterosexual object choice, chooses to become the image, imagining the image as a narcissistic ideal of the self.[24] Now I believe there is something very useful here in this notion of spectatorship as a process of becoming 'other,' something that implicates agency at the heart of the problematic.

Clearly, *Project Grizzly* is not as invested in this notion of agency as it is in ironizing the visible difference between the two bodies, the one, Troy Hurtubise, a lesser 'bargain basement' version of the Hollywood other. But there might be another way of thinking the difference between these two bodies in relation to what Michel de Certeau (following Bourdieu's lead) calls 'the tactical.' In other words, what might be a source of ironic play to a middle-class spectator might just be understood as an instrumental means to address marginalization, 'a practice that brings into play a "popular" ratio, a way of thinking invested in a way of acting, an art of combination which cannot be dissociated from an art of using.'[25]

Fashioning himself as epic hero (with all of its attendant contradictions) has, at least, to be seen as a means Hurtubise employs to win recognition, to escape the boredom and banality of North Bay life. And this self-fashioning, for him, is simply not ironic. After the premiere screenings of *Project Grizzly* in Toronto and Vancouver, Troy confessed his hurt and his bafflement at the laughter of metropolitan audiences. In an interview with *Vancouver Sun* reporter Marke Andrews, Hurtubise elaborated on what he perceived was the audience's misunderstanding of the film: 'There's also the whole preservation aspect. I've spent each waking hour of my life [concerned with] the preservation of the grizzly-bear habitat. This was all missed. I don't know where the laughs come from ... In certain parts of the film, it doesn't make sense to me. I try to explain to people ... while you're laughing, you're missing the narration. When you see those trucks hitting me at 50 kilometres an hour ... this is eight years of research.'[26]

I am using this exchange not to position Hurtubise as a victim (he seems to have sufficient quantities of male ego not to require our paternalistic sympathy) but to again foreground the very clear differences in the discursive worlds and reading strategies that cross each other in *Project Grizzly*. It seems to me that one of the unacknowledged sources of that metropolitan laughter has to do with the prejudice built into middle-class culture around the professionalization and monopolization of knowledge. Hurtubise's liberal use of pseudo-scientific discourse (Psi factor, close quarter study) and his insistence that he is conducting 'research' and that his posse of chain-smoking, gun-toting boys are his 'research assistants,' can only be read, in a metropolitan context, as 'amateur.' The ironic discourse in the film uses this prejudice to great effect, showing Hurtubise conducting 'close quarter bear research' – in the town dump in Mattawa. But the persistent undermining of Hurtubise's scientific pretensions is also a way of reinforcing those class divisions between, as Bourdieu puts it, 'practical partial, tacit know-how (common sense) and theoretical, systematic, explicit knowledge (a division which tends to be reproduced even in politics) between science and techniques, theory and practice, conception and execution, the intellectual and the creator ... and the manual worker.'[27] It is also a way of maintaining the insider privileges of the ironic text, of maintaining, for the metropolitan spectator, the smugness of ironic detachment.

Some Concluding Ironies

Six months after the film was first released, Hurtubise went into personal and professional bankruptcy mostly because of 'Project Grizzly' debts. 'I've lost everything,' he said. 'They're going to put my suit up for auction. They think it might be worth something because of the film.'[28]

According to Michael Allder, the producer, the film did not do well in distribution in the United States, despite being publicly endorsed by Quentin Tarantino as one of his favourite films of 1997. And, irony of ironies, there was a dark rumour circulating among the hordes of filmworkers eager to sign on to any American production parking its trailers on the streets of downtown Toronto: Jim Hensen's production company might be remaking Hurtubise's story as a fiction film.

Notes

This essay first appeared in the *Canadian Journal of Film Studies* 8, no. 1 (1999).

1 Grierson, quoted in Morris, 'Backwards to the Future,' 18–19.
2 Author's interview with Michael Allder (12 May 1998). While certainly not a genre, the entertainment documentary may have been Allder's stylistic imprimatur during his time at the Toronto office of the NFB, where he produced the theatrically released documentaries *The Powder Room* (Ann Kennard, 1996) and *Drowning in Dreams* (Tim Southam, 1997).
3 These new directions were announced by Louise Lore at a Canadian Independent Film Caucus meeting in 1996.
4 Lynch, 'Bringing Technology to Bear,' 22.
5 Fancott, '*Project Grizzly*.'
6 See Bhabha, *The Location of Culture*, and Irigaray, *Speculum of the Other Woman*.
7 Irigaray, *Speculum of the Other Woman*, 76.
8 Hutcheon, *Irony's Edge*, 12.
9 Lynch, quoted in Gilday, 'Liberating the Real,' 21.
10 While Hurtubise has been courted for years by David Letterman, Jay Leno, and Howard Stern, who appear desperate to get him on their shows, he has declined each time (*Ottawa Citizen*, 6 October 1998).

11 Generously pointed out to me by Keir Keightley. The movie version was released as *The Extreme Adventures of Super Dave: Accidents Happen* (Peter MacDonald, 2000).

12 Penley, 'Crackers and Whackers,' 103.

13 Hutcheon, *Irony's Edge*, 2.

14 Ibid., 54.

15 Ibid., 18.

16 Ibid., 20.

17 See Bourdieu, *Distinction*.

18 Blewitt, 'Film, Ideology and Bourdieu's Critique,' 371.

19 Blewitt, 'Book Review,' 398–9.

20 Pevere and Dymond, *Mondo Canuck*, 196.

21 Ibid., iii.

22 Dorland, *So Close to the State/s*, 17.

23 Bourdieu, *Distinction*, 33.

24 Doane, 'Film and the Masquerade.' The danger of this too-close identification and confusion between the real and fantasy is horrifyingly proven by Hurtubise's Uncle John's off-hand remark that he went to Vietnam 'for the fun and adventure' and spent his time playing dodge the grenade because he got bored.

25 De Certeau, *The Practice of Everyday Life*, xv.

26 Hurtubise, quoted in *The Vancouver Sun* (17 October 1996).

27 Bourdieu, *Distinction*, 387.

28 Hurtubise, quoted in *Hamilton Spectator* (24 January 1997).

Sympathetic Understanding in
Tu as crié Let Me Go

JANINE MARCHESSAULT

The many films of Anne Claire Poirier are distinguished by their exploration of women's pain. Her films are unique for the way they use facts, interviews, and poetic narrative to consider childbirth and rearing, prostitution, war, rape, and most recently drug addiction. Many have commented on the emotional aspects of her work, combining the conventions of the melodrama with counter-cinema politics as André Loiselle has put it.[1] Certainly, Poirier's films are striking for their engagement with female suffering, an engagement that often uses the properties of the film medium to elicit physical responses from audiences.

The most remarked upon example of this is the rape scene that opens *Mourir à tue-tête* (1979). Shot in subjective camera from the point of view of the victim, the scene is highly realistic. It is emotionally charged and shocking in the way it forces viewers to identify with a woman being raped in the back of a van. Ron Burnett's insightful account of this scene has highlighted the way the film creates multiple subject positions.[2] Through the filmmaker-character in the film, Poirier spends much time considering the politics of this representation and the kinds of identification it allows. The film, rightly, brought her international acclaim and set her apart from other feminist documentary filmmakers working at the National Film Board. Poirier's documentaries are visceral, beautiful, didactic, and committed to social change.

Tu as crié Let Me Go (1998) is the starkest, most restrained, and perhaps even least inventive of all Poirier's films. It is a film about the murder of her daughter, Yanne, a heroin addict and a prostitute. The film seeks to understand heroin addiction from the point of view of a parent who has lost a child to it. It is also, arguably, Poirier's most powerful film. I must confess that I cannot watch the film without crying. My starting point for wanting to write about it is my interest in the relation between art, emotion, and ethics. As a filmmaker who has sought to make very emotional films, Poirier provides fertile ground for thinking about affective structures in relation to documentary and fiction. Moreover, her films, the work of a politically committed feminist filmmaker, provide a unique ground for thinking about the political and aesthetic value of emotion.

Over the course of this essay, I wish to consider not only the emotional structure of the film but the ethical ramifications of soliciting emotional responses in order to both raise consciousness and create politics. I argue that *Tu as crié* is unique for the way it allows us to experience and gain knowledge from Poirier's expressed pain. In so doing, the film utilizes a double structure that does not conflate emotion and reason but makes them contiguous. Before discussing the film, let me briefly review some of the work being carried out on emotion in film studies.

Emotion and Film Studies
To use one's feelings as the basis for interpreting the affects and value of a work of art is a practice that is common to traditional forms of textual hermeneutics in film studies. For over three decades, this approach has been characterized somewhat disparagingly as 'impressionistic' criticism. Changes in methodology made the discipline of film studies less solipsistic, more scientific and theoretically sophisticated. One of the repercussions of the theoretical turn that came to Canada from the British journal *Screen* in the mid-1970s was that work on the text and work on spectatorship were divided into separate kinds of projects. Much of the theory coming from *Screen* was deeply informed by Althusser's model of ideology, seeing human experience as uniform and ideology as working on an unconscious level. Using this model, theories of spectatorship and textual meaning could not account for the connection between specific texts and the particular emotional experiences of individual spectators.

Althusser's anti-humanist Marxism had a profound influence on another important intellectual enterprise in England, the Birmingham Centre for Contemporary Cultural Studies. Writers like Stuart Hall rejected the expressive humanism of earlier versions of cultural studies which, not unlike the humanist strand in film criticism, sought to interpret culture as experience. Raymond Williams famously defined culture as a 'whole way of life' that linked context with spectatorship, focusing in particular on working-class culture to understand community. While Hall was critical of this earlier approach, which he saw as undertheorized, he was also critical of *Screen's* lack of specificity. The overdetermination of textual meanings and spectatorial responses relied upon a concept of culture that was static, that is, devoid of history and people.[3] Hall's famous encoding/decoding model, as well as his theory of articulation, while not without problems, offered more flexible possibilities for common understandings and differentiated interpretations.[4] It is precisely this stress on audiences, in many instances an ethnographic and sociological emphasis, that has always differentiated cultural studies from film studies. Yet what is often missing in cultural studies' analysis of film culture is the text and aesthetics – that is, the encoding.

Several new books devoted to studying film and emotion have appeared over the past five years, reinvigorating work on cinematic identification and emotions through the insights of cognitive psychology and philosophy.[5] Some of this new work is useful for the way it brings emotions back into the picture of screen studies. The shift from psychoanalysis to psychology allows many of these scholars to explore a nuanced and precise understanding of emotional responses to specific kinds of films. These accounts go beyond the more general categories of 'pleasure' and 'desire,' which have in the past been somewhat limited by a psychoanalytic taxonomy.[6] A cognitive approach to analysing emotions breaks down the opposition between emotions and reason to show that emotions are intricately tied to if not based in reason. Film cognitivists reject much of 1970s *Screen* theory, arguing that when we are watching a film, we are not simply passive dupes but are very much in control of the emotions and pleasures we are experiencing. Carl Plantinga and Greg Smith have summarized the cognitive perspective in the introduction to their anthology *Passionate Views*:

> Instead of conceptualizing emotions as formless, a cognitive scholar emphasizes the structure of emotions. They are processes that may be broken down into component processes, thus revealing their underlying structures. These structures might include scripts or a set of distinguishing characteristics or descriptions of typical goals and behaviors. This close analysis, we believe, will be invaluable in gaining a more precise understanding of how films cue emotions.[7]

Thus, cognitivist approaches to film analysis tend to confine their interpretation of specific texts to physiological or cognitive processes. Films
are more often than not generalized in order to make statements about
'how films cue emotions.' For this reason, much research is focused on
'the paradox of fiction,' on the way that a fiction film can elicit emotions
about characters that we know are not real. While this is a fascinating
problem, it is certainly not new. As with most 1970s and 1980s film
theory, the examples are drawn from formulaic Hollywood films whose
standardized forms enable scholars to describe in more precise ways
how spectators respond to certain cinematic conventions.

While cognitivist approaches stand in direct opposition to the context based study of reception that we find characteristic of cultural
studies, these suffer from some of the same limitations. Whether it is
the social character of a community of spectators or their physiological
processes that drive the study of reception, it is all too often the distinctive quality of the text as a work of art and/or description which is left
unaccounted for. Even though, as all good propagandists know, the
best way to the head is through the heart, very little work in cognitive
film studies has focused on nonfiction films. I would speculate that this
is so because nonfiction films are less standardized and emotional cues
are more difficult to discern.

What follows is not a new model for a cognitive description of
nonfiction films, but rather some ideas that might help us to better
understand the need for a methodology to study the emotional dimensions of documentary films.[8] Thus, my remarks around the complexity
of the emotional structure in *Tu as crié* are intended to underscore the
important role that interpretive paradigms centred on affect may play
in our understanding of nonfiction films.

Tu as crié ...

While most of Poirier's films have some autobiographical component,
Tu as crié is entirely autobiographical. How do we identify with Poirier,
who narrates the film and who has lost a daughter? How are our
emotions and sympathies intensified when the person before us and
the events recounted are real? How does the film invite us to make
judgments about the world it is representing? My analysis will focus
for the most part on the first five minutes of the film because these set
up the emotional structure of the entire work.

Tu as crié opens with high-contrast, black-and-white shots of an iceberg. It is photographed from the water and slowed down so that we

Tu as crié Let Me Go (1997), directed by Anne Claire Poirier. Courtesy of the National Film Board of Canada.

experience the iceberg out of time just slightly. It appears devoid of human presence. On the soundtrack we hear violins, women's chants, and the sound of seagulls mixed together in a dissonance that foregrounds intervals of silence. Poirier's voice follows. This voice-over, exquisitely written by Poirier and Marie-Claire Blais, will guide us through the film. At times it speaks to us directly of facts that meld into poetry and sorrow:

> 18 October 1992. Sunday morning of the end of the world. A young woman is dead, strangled in an apartment full of disorder. She was working as a prostitute; she was a heroin addict; she was pretty; she was my daughter.[9]

After a pause, Poirier continues. She is no longer addressing the viewer, she is speaking to herself and to her dead daughter: '*Yanne la forte; Yanne la fragile, Yanne, ma difficile.*' As the descriptions of her daughter unfold, she moves from '*la*' (the) to '*ma*' (my), from an objective description 'the strong' to a possessive noun, 'my difficult one,' that makes the description her own. It is a description of her own self, her identity so intricately – physically, emotionally, psychically – tied to her child.

A piece of the iceberg breaks off; it is white against black waters and a dark grey sky. It breaks off in a moment of drama and emotional intensity with *'Yanne, ma difficile.'* This is an image of nature as sublime. In an instant it signals chance and our inability to control the lifeworld. For as Kant maintained, the sublime is 'an outrage on the imagination' insofar as it exceeds the human capacity to imagine nature by means of reason. The iceberg both is outside human history and bears witness to its finality. According to Kant it is this nature that speaks to the limits of the law and of 'a higher finality.'[10] In *Tu as crié*, it is an image of mourning, a metaphoric gravestone, from which the filmmaker will attempt to imagine and make sense of her daughter's death.

From the spectacular image of the iceberg, we descend into the mundane, a back alley. Banal and generic, it could be any city in North America. While there is a striking contrast between the natural world and the cityscape, the camera movement and the black-and-white film stocks fuse them together. We are in front of a garage; an address scrawled on a post reads 3614. A band of sunlight crosses the pavement, and Poirier remembers this light from the police photographs: 'You were there in the morning light, I was not.' There is no body now, there is only the morning light. The scene is deserted. The camera floats unnaturally above the ground like a ghost; we hear footsteps on the pavement which are disconnected from the camera as it wanders down the street and, like the footsteps, goes nowhere. Poirier's voice-over speaks forcefully and with sadness to her daughter. For the moment, she has forgotten the audience; she remembers her daughter in child-hood, standing on the railway tracks to infinity, playing in the ocean swell, flying a kite: 'let it go, *maman.'* She remembers Yanne's new boyfriend, a heroin addict whom she wanted to save: 'let me go, *maman.'* This spoken memory over the scene of the death creates a space of mourning, a liminal space between past and present which I will address in more detail shortly. Poirier cues us to this liminality towards the end of the sequence when she says: 'Since your death I live in black and white. I live in the night ... In the cinema, black and white often signifies the past. Fine for me, time has stopped with you, *ma fulgurante* [lightning flash].'

In this first sequence, we are in an imaginary space, lost in time. From here we will travel back to night, to the apartment where Yanne was murdered. Through the empty hallways, Poirier searches for signs, traces, messages left behind from her daughter during her last hours. Poirier imagines Yanne's last words, her screams of 'Let Me Go.' We come to understand the double meaning of the film's title, which refers to both the daughter's drive for independence and her final words as Poirier imagines them. The mother's trauma is in arriving too late, in not being *there* for her daughter and thus, in her daughter's subsequent silence, her not being here to speak. This traumatic and eternal separation is enacted in the film's deceptively simple sound and image relations.

Fritz Lang represented this kind of violent separation masterfully in his early sound film *M* (1931). Recall the power of that opening scene when a mother calls out of the window to her daughter, Ilse, who has not returned home from school. The mother's cry is heard over a series of empty urban spaces, streets, alleyways, garages. She is too late; the sequence comes just after we know that the child has been abducted by a serial killer. I often show this sequence in my film classes to illustrate early uses of off-screen space and the power relations of voice and image. In *M* the voice is unable to control or to affect the visual spaces that contain the child's body because it is located elsewhere.

In Poirier's film, however, the voice is both inside and outside the screen. It is separated from the child's body by the frame and by time. The narration is what Michel Chion calls an *'acousmêtre,'* which has 'the ability to be everywhere, to see all, to know all, and to have complete power. In other words ubiquity, panopticism, omniscience and omnipotence.' Of course Chion tells us, 'the sound cinema did not invent the *acousmêtre*, the greatest *acousmêtre* is God – and even farther back, for every one of us, the Mother.'[11] Yet the *acousmêtre* in *Tu as crié* fails in its maternal function to be everywhere, all-seeing. It presents an exception in the history of cinema in that it cannot see all. In this instance 'we find the panoptic theme in its negative form.'[12] When the camera stands outside the door of the apartment where Yanne was murdered, the focus is on a door handle that cannot be turned. In fact, this sense of being separated from and outside the space where the death took place permeates large sections of the film. As we move along hallways and barren walls in the apartment building, doors and windows are closed to us, just as later we will move down streets into different neighbourhoods that are vacant and seemingly empty. Finally at the end of the sequence, the camera leads us into the morgue. Its brightly lit halls and sterile walls shine into the lens with a piercing rationality that contrasts painfully with Poirier's voice as it catches in her throat. Poirier agonizes over her daughter lying in this place for five days alone. She pictures her daughter's fresh body, alive. She consoles herself by imagining that she will see her again: 'I wait for you my child who is very much alive.'

... Let Me Go

In an eloquent review of the film, Peter Harcourt points out that the film's narrational technique, using voice-over on top of present-day spaces of past traumas, is a familiar technique in Poirier's films. We find this in her earlier film *Les Filles du Roy* (1974) and in *Mourir à tue-tête*. It was famously employed by Alain Resnais in *Nuit et brouillard* (1955) to speak to historical trauma. 'Resnais's investigation of the Nazi extermination camps,' writes Harcourt, 'provides a locus classicus for the exploration of horror by creating images of emptiness while verbally evoking the atrocities that once took place there.'[13] Indeed, what is often remarked upon in Resnais' film is its discursive distance from the Holocaust, stressing not only our incapacity to go back in time to change the past but also to fully understand it. The present-day images of the concentration camp are in colour and give us little access to the past atrocities whose material geographies have been transformed by time. The trauma is that space between the present and the black-and-white photographs and films of the past. The film is about the trauma of remembrance and frames its investigation of the Holocaust as a reflection upon the limits of cinematic representation.

The representation of bereavement and loss is a central problematic in *Tu as crié*'s aesthetic structure as well. In the case of Poirier's film, the past exists only as memory spoken on the soundtrack. Poirier does not show us photographs of her daughter, and there is no image whatsoever of the past – a point to which I will return. In effect the stark empty spaces that Poirier constructs and that Jacques Leduc photographs are outside history yet stuck in time. Neither fully imaginary nor entirely real, this is a space of mourning. This sense of being stuck in time that the film conveys is perfectly commensurate with Freud's description of mourning. In 'Mourning and Melancholia' he describes 'the work which mourning performs' as a forceful resistance to 'the reality principle,' a resistance to the very reality of the death of a loved one. Immersed in grief and sadness, the individual in mourning continues to cling to the lost person through the 'medium of a hallucinatory wishful psychosis.'[14] The mourner will turn away from the outside world 'in so far as it does not recall' the lost object. While little is actually known about the economics of mourning, Freud attempts a conjecture:

> Each single one of the memories and situations which demonstrate the libido's attachment of the lost object is met by the verdict of reality that the object no longer exists; and the ego confronted as it were, with the question whether it shall share this fate, is persuaded by the sum of the narcissistic satisfactions it derives from being alive to sever its attachment to the object that has been abolished. We may perhaps suppose that this work of severance is so slow and gradual that by the time it has been finished the expenditure of energy necessary for it is also dissipated.[15]

Mourning is extreme and solitary pain. It is one of the least rational yet most common of emotional experiences. Freud tells us the mourner will simply pass through it; eventually for some unknown reason reality wins out and the mourner rejoins the world.

Tu as crié can be read as a documentary about the act of mourning. Poirier constructs an emotional trajectory that will bring her back out into the world, a journey that will move towards connecting emotion to cognition. She tells us that she is looking for 'sense' not 'certitude.' The question she asks is, not why her daughter was a drug addict, but why being a drug addict condemned her to a life of shame and danger, 'a life with few alternatives.'

A figure in a white lab coat is the first body we see in the film. The camera follows him into the morgue; he slides a cadaver out of a cabinet; it is covered by a white sheet. The inclusion of this body is a surprise. We know that it is not Yanne, who was murdered in 1993. It could be anyone's daughter. It is at this point in the film that the first interview begins. Shot in a straightforward manner in black and white, a father, who similarly lost a daughter to 'the war on drugs,' speaks almost directly into the camera of his experiences. The double structure of the film is introduced: on the one hand there is the space of mourning described above, and on the other there are Poirier's interviews with young women who were heroin addicts and with parents whose children are dead because of their addiction. There is, as Harcourt points out, a balance in Poirier's film between the general and the particular which never conflates the two.[16] On a formal level this is represented as a movement back and forth between the space of mourning and the space of the world, the reality principle that will eventually win out.

As the film unfolds, we experience what Chion calls a 'deacousmatization' as the *acousmêtre*, Poirier's voice, is increasingly located in the film. In the second half of the film, we begin to see Poirier on-screen as she conducts the interviews. Her voice is given a place, a mortal body, a limit and a connection to others. As noted above, Poirier chooses not to give us an image of her daughter. She refuses the cinematographic qualities of Freud's 'medium of a hallucinatory wishful psychosis,' and instead presents us with vacant and silent spaces. We have no face, no voice, no trace of this young woman except through her mother's recollection. In this way, Poirier records an absence (Yanne's) and she underscores the unrepresentable (Yanne's murder) in a manner that is devastating and uncompromising. Loiselle's insistence on the melodramatic aspects of Poirier's cinema seems particularly apt with regard to this film. The oppositions between black and white, presence and absence, life and death, good and bad (*'les méchants'*) is typical of Poirier's films and perhaps more so in this mother/daughter story. While she has been criticized for universalizing women's suffering by stressing gender differences, one must see her oppositions as rhetorical devices aimed at intensifying ethical forces. As Peter Brooks has defined it, the emotional excesses and expressive oppositions that we find in the de-sacralized world of the nineteenth-century melodrama are intrinsic to its moral idiom:

> Melodrama is indeed, typically, not only a moralistic drama but the drama of morality: it strives to find, to articulate, to demonstrate, to 'prove' the existence of a moral universe which, though put into question, masked by villainy and perversions of judgment, does exist and can be made to assert its presence and its categorical forces among men.[17]

Poirier strives not for certitude but to make sense of her daughter's death. Her starting point for sense-making is not in facts but in sentiment and it is from sentiment that she will come to a moral judgment. Yanne's absence from the film heightens both our emotional involvement as well as our sense of profound loss. We are forced to fill in the absent images of the daughter with our own images. This process brings us into the film, augments our sympathetic identification with Poirier, and through this sympathy we come to understand her emotional and political position.

Similarly, Claude Lanzmann's film *Shoah* (1985), which consists of interviews with surviving concentration camp prisoners, guards, and passive on-lookers, refuses to represent the memories described in the interviews, allowing human testimony to stand as memory. Lanzmann's film is structured around witnessing and is concerned with the limits not of cinema, as with *Nuit et brouillard*, but of human testimony and the reality of experience. For this reason, he chooses to interview only those survivors who touched death, who stood at the edge of the abyss, who went as far as one could go into the horror without dying. Thomas Elsaesser writes of the way the film 'make[s] one see things which are not on screen and listen to voices speaking from within oneself.'[18] As spectators, we, like Lanzmann, become witnesses to the testimony of witnessing and as such we become connected to it. The trauma enacted by the film is not the impossibility of knowing what happened during the Holocaust but rather of knowing. Lanzmann has said that the film was made for the dead, and it is indeed a film for the dead because it aims to remember how and why they died.[19]

It has always been Poirier's strength as a filmmaker to create sympathetic and empathetic structures of identification, utilizing formal strategies that entreat the imagination, precisely as Elsaesser describes it, to find 'voices or pictures from within oneself.' Poirier's approach to telling her own story is all the more touching then because of its pronounced absences. Unlike Lanzmann's work of political archaeology, Poirier's film is made for the living. While she does attempt to reconstruct the last evening of her daughter's life, retracing steps and moving through passageways, the film seeks some form of reconciliation between past and present, between life and death. The absence of an image of Yanne works to create an empathetic bond between those – Poirier and other parents – who have suffered a devastating loss and the film's spectators.

I would like to return to an earlier point in this essay regarding the different emotional registers of fiction and nonfiction films. The argument often made is that the division between the two is illusory. *Shoah* for example, is a film that is full of fiction in its recollections and reenactments. Likewise, *Tu as crié* contains large segments of imagined moments through the voice-over. Further, many narrative films are based on or incorporate actual events and real people. To a great degree then, and in the most textually rich films, the distinction is not straightforward. However, as spectators we do distinguish between films that are based on something that happened and those based on something that did not. Clearly, our emotional response differs in the two instances. I would not go so far as to state that we respond to the nonfiction film as we do to events in real life heard through the news or in everyday conversation. This would be to deny film's creative capacity to represent through sounds and images the internal dimension of emotional states. This specificity is arguably what enhances our ability to imagine another's pain, to imagine ourselves in their place.

Sympathetic Understanding

In all her films, Poirier has used emotion to create a common basis for entry into politics. She creates what the eighteenth-century philosopher David Hume called 'sympathetic understanding,' which was the basis for the theory of 'moral sentiment' (1757). Hume, famous for pairing passion with morality, saw sympathy as occupying a special place in the realm of sentiments: 'it is a feeling together' with another. It is a unifying force that binds individuals together in the lifeworld, allowing us to understand each other's experiences and to create a common life. Sympathy involves ideas and imagination: 'an idea of a sentiment or passion may by this means be so enlivened as to become the very sentiment or passion,' thus giving us more information through which to understand others.[20] Sympathy allows us to recognize the basic resemblances between people so that 'the minds of men are mirrors to one another.' It is expressly through sympathy, through our 'connexion' to others, that we can come to make informed judgments. According to Hume, sympathy makes a moral sense possible and from this sense arises the need for justice.[21]

Tu as crié's great strength is in materializing sympathetic understanding, in showing how it connects people and creates community. We sympathize with Poirier, just as we see her sympathizing with those parents she interviews. Through the interviews we come to understand the war on drugs as an immoral government campaign that punishes the users, and protects the suppliers – the only solution, Poirier tells us, is legalization. But what makes Poirier's argument so compelling is that it is grounded in the painful repercussions of criminalization. We come to understand these repercussions through the filmmaker's mourning and through the testimonies of young women who, like Yanne, worked in the sex trades in order to support their addictions and often their boyfriends. We sympathize with them. It is in Yanne's absence that these women represent her not as a single victim but as a community suffering in similar circumstances.

Hume had a decisive influence on the English Romantics and on Wordsworth in particular, who believed that the expression of emotion in literature and poetry could allow for a shared language, and for a new common culture. In 1810 Wordsworth wrote 'Essays on Epitaphs' in which he argued that epitaphs were the original form of poetry. This sad writing was able to link a universal experience – grief – with language to create a common ground for sympathetic understanding. *Tu as crié* ends with a return to the iceberg. This time Poirier is on the screen, her back to us looking out. She tells us that the image of the iceberg was with her throughout the film and wonders: was it the memory of her daughter 'that conjured it up? 12,000 years of ice back into the sea.' Sublime nature is not devoid of reason but provides a locus for the meeting of emotion and of rationality.[22] Poirier is located in time (rather than stuck in it) and we know that some form of reconciliation has been found: she will let her daughter go. Her documentary is an epitaph along the lines that Wordsworth described almost two hundred years ago:

> exposed to all – to the wise and the most ignorant; it is ... perspicuous, and lovingly solicits regard; its story and admonitions are brief, that the thoughtless, the busy and indolent, may not be deterred, nor the impatient tired: the stooping old man cons the engraven record like a second horn-book; – the child is proud that he can read it; – and the stranger is introduced through its mediation to the company of a friend: it is concerning all, and for all: ... it is open to the day; the sun looks down upon the stone, and the rains of heaven beat against it.[23]

While Poirier's film is, in its beautiful starkness, intelligible to all, it does not try to create the immortality that Wordsworth believed to be the ultimate function of all funeral monuments. It does, however, carry with it a certain permanence that is the record of an emotional experience that will no doubt endure. The film secures, through the expression of perhaps the most elementary and universal of emotions, a ground for common experiences, and with this the possibility of a shared sense of justice.

Notes

This essay first appeared in the *Canadian Journal of Film Studies* 10, no. 2 (2001).

1 Loiselle, 'Despair as Empowerment.'
2 Burnett, *Cultures of Vision*, 189–99.

3 Hall, 'Recent Developments in Theories of Language and Ideology,' 161–2.

4 See Hall, *Encoding and Decoding in the Television Discourse*; Hall, 'Cultural Studies: Two Paradigms'; and Sparks, 'Stuart Hall, Cultural Studies and Marxism.'

5 See Smith, *Engaging Characters*; Tan, *Emotion and the Structure of Narrative Film*; Grodal, *Moving Pictures*; Plantinga and Smith, eds., *Passionate Views*.

6 The insight that thinking and feeling are not separate activities is something that has always been at the heart of feminist epistemologies and philosophy. It should be remembered that feminists turned to psychoanalysis as a theoretical tool for analysing and specifying the emotional responses of spectators. Moreover, film spectatorship became an area of investigation expressly because gender difference was recognized as an important determination of emotional behaviour both on the screen and in front of it.

7 Plantinga and Smith, eds., *Passionate Views*, 4.

8 The notion that documentary films need to be analysed in terms of their emotional structures is not new. The relation between documentary film, epistemology, and emotion has been the subject of Trinh Minh-ha's films and writings, which for many years have sought to conceptualize new models of knowledge through documentary. Ron Burnett's *Cultures of Vision* seeks to develop a model of spectatorship that relies on the psychoanalytic notion of 'projection' to recognize a creative role for the viewer. Burnett analyses how documentary images and the spectator's imagination commingle to form meaning and identification. Catherine Russell's study of the relation between autobiography and ethnography in personal films has analysed presentations of self as epistemological activity. Russell's work draws out the central place of emotional experience rather than essence in contemporary experimental autobiographical films and videos; see her *Experimental Ethnography*.

9 The translation of this text is mine. An English version of the film does exist, but at the time of this writing it was not in distribution.

10 Kant, *The Critique of Judgment*, 91–2.

11 Chion, *The Voice in the Cinema*, 24–5.

12 Ibid., 27.

13 Harcourt, 'Screams from Silence,' 23.

14 Freud, 'Mourning and Melancholia,' 253.

15 Ibid., 265.

16 Harcourt, 'Screams from Silence,' 25.

17 Brooks, *The Melodramatic Imagination*, 21.

18 Elsaesser, 'Subject Positions, Speaking Positions,' 174.

19 Lanzmann, talk delivered at York University, Toronto, 1 November 2000.
20 Hume, *Treatise*, II.I.xi.
21 Ibid., II.II.v. For in-depth considerations of Hume's philosophical works in relation to feminist epistemology, see Baier, *A Progress of Sentiments*, and Jacobson, ed., *Feminist Interpretations of David Hume*.
22 For a wonderful discussion of the relation between emotion and reason in the Kantian sublime, see Freeland, 'The Sublime in Cinema.'
23 Owen, ed., *Wordsworth's Literary Criticism*, 183.

Filmography

Paul Tomkowicz: Street-railway Switchman (1954)
Director: Roman Kroitor
Cinematographer: Lorne Batchelor
Editors: Tom Daly, Roman Kroitor
Music: Robert Fleming
Narrator: Tom Tweed
(black and white, 9 minutes)

The Days before Christmas (1958)
Director: Terence Macartney-Filgate, Wolf Koenig, Stanley Jackson
Cinematographers: Michel Brault, Georges Dufaux
Editors: Roman Kroitor, Wolf Koenig
Sound: John Locke, George Croll, Kathleen Shannon
Narrator: Stanley Jackson
Producers: Tom Daly, Roman Kroitor, Wolf Koenig
(black and white, 29 minutes)

Lonely Boy (1961)
Directors: Wolf Koenig, Roman Kroitor
Cinemtographer: Wolf Koenig
Editors: John Spotton, Guy L. Coté
Sound: Marcel Carrière
Narrator: Stanley Jackson
Producers: Tom Daly, Roman Kroitor
(black and white, 27 minutes)

Bûcherons de la Manouane (*Manouane River Lumberjacks*, **1962**)
Director: Arthur Lamothe
Cinematographers: Guy Borremans, Bernard Gosselin
Editors: Arthur Lamothe, Jean Dansereau
Music: Pierre Lemelin, Maurice Blackburn
Narrator: Victor Désy
Producers: Fernand Dansereau, Victor Jobin
(black and white, 28 minutes)

Pour la suite du monde (*Moontrap / Of Whales, the Moon and Men*, **1963**)
Directors: Pierre Perrault, Michel Brault
Cinematographer: Michel Brault
Editor: Werner Nold
Sound: Marcel Carrière
Music: Jean Cousineau, Jean Meunier
Producers: Fernand Dansereau
(black and white, 105 minutes)

On est au coton (*Cotton Mill, Treadmill*, **1970**)
Director: Denys Arcand
Assistant Director: Gérald Godin
Cinematographer: Alain Dostie
Editor: Pierre Bernier
Sound: Serge Beauchemin
Producers: Marc Beaudet, Guy L. Coté, Pierre Maheu
(black and white, 159 minutes)

Waiting for Fidel (**1974**)
Director: Michael Rubbo
Cinematographer: Douglas Kiefer
Editor: Michael Rubbo
Sound: Jacques Sevigny
Producers: Tom Daly, Michael Rubbo, Colin Low
(colour, 58 minutes)

Volcano: An Inquiry into the Life and Death of Malcolm Lowry (**1976**)
Director: Donald Brittain
Cinematographer: Douglas Kiefer
Editor: John Kramer

Sound: James McCarthy
Music: Alain Clavier
Narrators: Donald Brittain, Richard Burton
Producers: Donald Brittain, R.A. Duncan
(colour, 99 minutes)

Not a Love Story **(1981)**
Director: Bonnie Sherr Klein
Cinematographers: Pierre Letarte, Susan Trow
Editor: Anne Henderson
Sound: Yves Gendron
Music: Ginette Bellavance
Producers: Dorothy Todd Hénaut, Kathleen Shannon
(colour, 69 minutes)

Voyage en Amérique avec un cheval emprunté (Travels in America with a Borrowed Horse, **1987)**
Director: Jean Chabot
Cinematographer: Jacques Leduc
Editor: Catherine Martin
Music: René Lussier, Robert Derome
Producer: Jean Chabot
(colour, 57 minutes)

Forbidden Love: The Unashamed Stories of Lesbian Lives **(1993)**
Directors: Aerlyn Weissman, Lynn Fernie
Cinematographer: Zoe Dirse
Editors: Cathy Gulkin
Music: Kathryn Moses
Producers: Rena Fraticelli, Margaret Pettigrew, Ginny Stikeman
(colour, 85 minutes)

Kanehsatake: 270 Years of Resistance **(1993)**
Director: Alanis Obomsawin
Cinematographers: Roger Rochat, Jean-Claude Labrecque, Philippe Amiguet, Susan Trow, François Brault, Barry Perles, Zoe Dirse, Jocelyn Simard, André-Luc Dupont, Savas Kalogeros
Editor: Turji Luhovy
Producers: Alanis Obomsawin, Wolf Koenig
(colour, 119 minutes)

Project Grizzly **(1996)**
Director: Peter Lynch
Cinematographer: Tony Wanamaker
Editor: Caroline Christie
Music: Anne Bourne, Ken Myhr
Producers: Michael Allder, Louise Lore, Gerry Flahive
(colour, 72 minutes)

Tu as crié Let Me Go **(1997)**
Director: Anne Claire Poirier
Narration: Anne Claire Poirier, Marie-Claire Blais
Cinematographers: Jacques Leduc, Pierre Mignot
Editors: Monique Fortier, Yves Dion
Music: Marie Bernard
Producer: Paul Lapointe
(black and white, colour, 98 minutes)

Works Cited

Abel, Marie-Christine, et al., eds. *Le Cinéma québécois à l'heure internationale*. Montreal: Alain Stanké, 1990.

'Accueil controversé au Québec du film sur la crise d'Oka.' *La Tribune* (Sherbrooke) (25 September 1993).

Adorno, Theodor W. 'On Popular Music.' In *On Record: Rock, Pop, and the Written Word*, ed. Simon Frith and Andrew Goodwin. New York: Pantheon Books, 1989. 301–14.

– *The Culture Industry: Selected Essays on Mass Culture*, ed. J.M. Bernstein. London: Routledge, 1991.

Aitken, Ian. *Film and Reform: John Grierson and the Documentary Film Movement*. London: Routledge, 1990.

Alioff, Maurie. 'Dream Magic: Alanis Obomsawin after Oka.' *Matrix* 33 (Spring 1991): 5–9.

Anderson, Benedict. *Imagined Communities: Reflections on the Origin and Spread of Nationalism*, rev. ed. London: Verso, 1991.

Anderson, Elizabeth. 'Studio D's Imagined Community: From Development (1974) to Realignment (1986–1990).' In *Gendering the Nation: Canadian Women's Cinema*, ed. Kay Armatage et al. Toronto: University of Toronto Press, 1999. 41–61.

Anderson, Walter Truett. *The Truth about the Truth: De-confusing and Re-constructing the Postmodern World*. New York: Putnam, 1995.

Arcand, Denys. 'La genèse du film: Une entrevue.' *Cinéma Québec* 1, no. 2 (June/July 1971): 32.

Arcand, Denys, and Gerald Godin. 'Un film didactique.' *Cinéma Québec* 1, no. 2 (June/July 1971): 33–4.

Armatage, Kay, et al., eds. *Gendering the Nation: Canadian Women's Cinema*. Toronto: University of Toronto Press, 1999.

Artibise, Alan. *Winnipeg: An Illustrated History*. Toronto: James Lorimer, 1977.

Atherton, Tony. 'CBC Aims to Revive Documentary.' *Citizen* (Ottawa) (1 November 1993).

Backhouse, Charles. *Canadian Government Motion Picture Bureau, 1917–1941*. Ottawa: Canadian Film Institute, 1974.

Bad Object Choices, eds. *How Do I Look? Queer Film and Video*. Seattle: Bay Press, 1991.

Baele, Nancy. 'An Eye on Oka: Obomsawin's Acclaimed Film Is Too Strong for CBC.' *Citizen* (Ottawa) (14 October 1993).

Baier, Annette C. *A Progress of Sentiments: Reflections on Hume's 'Treatise.'* Cambridge: Harvard University Press, 1991.

Barnard, Elissa. 'Filmmaker Explores Oka Crisis and Lets Mohawks Tell Their Story.' *Chronicle Herald* (Halifax) (1 October 1993).

Barnouw, Erik. *Documentary: A History of the Non-Fiction Film*. Oxford: Oxford University Press, 1993.

Barthes, Roland. *S/Z*, trans. Richard Miller. Oxford: Blackwell, 1990.

Beaucage, Marjorie. 'Aboriginal Voices: Entitlement through Storytelling.' In *Mirror Machine: Video and Identity*, ed. Janine Marchessault. Toronto: YYZ Books, 1995. 214–26.

Beckett, Samuel. *Waiting for Godot*. New York: Grove Press, 1954.

Bender, Frederic L., ed. *Karl Marx: The Essential Writings*. New York: Harper Torchbooks, 1972.

Benjamin, Andrew, ed. *The Lyotard Reader*. Oxford: Basil Blackwell, 1989.

Bercuson, David, and S.F. Wise, eds. *The Valour and the Horror Revisited*. Montreal: McGill-Queen's University Press, 1994.

Bernstein, Matthew. '*Roger and Me*: Documentaphobia and Mixed Modes.' *Journal of Film and Video* 46, no. 1 (Spring 1994): 3–17.

Bérubé, Renald, and Yvan Patry, eds. *Le Cinéma québécois: Tendances et prolongements*. Montreal: Éditions Sainte-Marie, 1968.

Bhabha, Homi K. *The Location of Culture*. London: Routledge, 1994.

Bidd, Donald W. *The NFB Film Guide: The Productions of the National Film Board of Canada from 1939 to 1989*. Ottawa: National Film Board of Canada, 1991.

Blewitt, John. 'Book Review of *Pierre Bourdieu* by Richard Jenkins.' *British Journal of Aesthetics* 33, no. 4 (October 1993): 398–9.

– 'Film, Ideology, and Bourdieu's Critique of Public Taste.' *British Journal of Aesthetics* 33, no. 4 (October 1993): 367–72.

Blumer, Ronald. '*Fields of Sacrifice*.' In *Donald Brittain: Never the Ordinary Way*, ed. Terry Kolomeychuk et al. Winnipeg: National Film Board of Canada, 1991.

Blumer, Ronald, and Susan Schouten. 'Green Stripe and Common Sense.'
   Cinema Canada 15 (August-September 1974): 36–40.
Bonitzer, Pascal. 'The Silences of the Voice.' In *Narrative/Apparatus/Ideology:
   A Film Theory Reader*, ed. Philip Rosen. New York: Columbia University
   Press, 1986. 319–34.
Bonneville, Léo, ed. *Le Cinéma québécois par ceux qui le font*. Montreal: Éditions
   Pauline, 1979.
Bourdieu, Pierre. *Distinction: A Social Critique of the Judgement of Taste*, trans.
   R. Nice. Cambridge: Harvard University Press, 1984.
Brooks, Peter. *The Melodramatic Imagination: Balzac, Henry James, Melodrama,
   and the Mode of Excess*. New Haven: Yale University Press, 1976.
Brûlé, Michel. *Pierre Perrault ou un cinéma national*. Montreal: Presses de
   l'Université de Montréal, 1974.
Burnett, Ron. *Cultures of Vision: Images, Media, and the Imaginary*. Bloomington:
   Indiana University Press, 1995.
Cartier-Bresson, Henri. 'The Decisive Moment.' In *Photography in Print*, ed.
   Vicki Goldberg. Albuquerque: University of New Mexico Press, 1981.
   384–6.
Cawley, Richard. 'Film Reminds Us of Failures and Broken Promises.' *Gazette*
   (Montreal) (21 November 1993).
Chabot, Jean. 'L'Hypothèse Marker.' *La Revue de la cinémathèque* (May-June
   1989): 4–7.
Chapple, Steve, and Reebee Garofalo. *Rock 'n' Roll Is Here to Pay: The History
   and Politics of the Music Industry*. Elmhurst, IL: Music Business Publications,
   1977.
Charland, Maurice. 'Technological Nationalism.' *Canadian Journal of Political
   and Social Theory* 10, nos. 1–2 (1986): 196–220.
Chion, Michel. *The Voice in the Cinema*, trans. Claudia Gorbman. New York:
   Columbia University Press, 1999.
Clandfield, David. 'From the Picturesque to the Familiar: Films of the French
   Unit at the NFB (1958–1964).' In *Take Two: A Tribute to Film in Canada*, ed.
   Seth Feldman. Toronto: Irwin, 1984. 112–24.
– 'Ritual and Recital: The Perrault Project.' In *Take Two: A Tribute to Film in
   Canada*, ed. Seth Feldman. Toronto: Irwin, 1984. 136–48.
– *Canadian Film*. Toronto: Oxford University Press, 1987.
Corner, John. *The Art of Record: A Critical Introduction to Documentary*. Manches-
   ter: Manchester University Press, 1996.
Cornwell, Ethel F. *The 'Still Point': Theme and Variations in the Writings of
   T.S. Eliot, Coleridge, Yeats, Henry James, Virginia Woolf, and D.H. Lawrence*.
   New Brunswick, NJ: Rutgers University Press, 1962.

Côté, Roch. *Québec 2000*. Montreal: Fides, 1999.

Coulombe, Michel, and Marcel Jean, eds. *Le Dictionnaire du cinéma québécois*. Montreal: Boréal, 1988.

Cuthand, Doug. 'Documentary on Oka Standoff Is a Must-See.' *Leader-Post* (Regina) (13 September 1993).

de Certeau, Michel. *The Practice of Everyday Life*, trans. Steven Randall. Berkeley: University of California Press, 1984.

de Lauretis, Teresa. 'Guerilla in the Midst: Women's Cinema in the 80s.' *Screen* 31, no. 1 (Spring 1990): 6–25.

– 'Queer Theory: Lesbian and Gay Sexualities.' *differences: A Journal of Feminist Cultural Studies* 3, no. 2 (1991): 3–18.

Deleuze, Gilles. *Cinema 2: The Time Image*, trans. Hugh Tomlinson and Robert Galeta. London: Athlone Press, 1989.

– *Pourparlers*. Paris: Éditions de Minuit, 1990.

Doan, Laura, ed. *The Lesbian Postmodern*. New York: Columbia University Press, 1994.

Doane, Mary Ann. 'Film and the Masquerade: Theorising the Female Spectator.' *Screen* 23, nos. 3–4 (September-October 1982): 74–87.

– 'The Economy of Desire: The Commodity Form in/of the Cinema.' *Quarterly Review of Film and Video* 11, no. 1 (1989): 23–33.

Dorland, Michael. 'Rule Brittania: The Filmmaking Saga of Don C. Brittain.' *Cinema Canada* 126 (January 1986): 11–20.

– *So Close to the State/s: The Emergence of Canadian Feature Film Policy*. Toronto: University of Toronto Press, 1998.

Druick, Zöe. 'Documenting Government: Re-examining the 1950s National Film Board Films about Citizenship.' *Canadian Journal of Film Studies* 9, no. 1 (Spring 2000): 55–79.

Dyer, Richard. *Stars*. London: British Film Institute, 1979.

Elder, Bruce. 'On the Candid Eye Movement.' In *Canadian Film Reader*, ed. Seth Feldman and Joyce Nelson. Toronto: Peter Martin, 1977. 86–93.

– 'Two Journeys: A Review of *Not a Love Story*.' In *Take Two: A Tribute to Film in Canada*, ed. Seth Feldman. Toronto: Irwin, 1984. 236–43.

– *Image and Identity: Reflections on Canadian Film and Culture*. Waterloo: Wilfrid Laurier University Press, 1989.

Elsaesser, Thomas. 'Tales of Sound and Fury: Observations on the Family Melodrama.' In *Movies and Methods*, vol. 2, ed. Bill Nichols. Berkeley: University of California Press, 1985. 165–89.

– 'Subject Positions, Speaking Positions: From *Holocaust*, *Our Hitler*, and *Heimat* to *Shoah* and *Schindler's List*.' In *The Persistence of History: Cinema, Television, and the Modern Event*, ed. Vivian Sobchack. New York: Routledge, 1996. 145–83.

Euvrard, Michel. 'Interview with Arthur Lamothe.' *Take One* 1, no. 2 (1966): 13–16.

Euvrard, Michel, and Pierre Véronneau. 'Direct Cinema.' In *Self Portrait*, ed. Véronneau and Piers Handling. Ottawa: Canadian Film Institute, 1980. 77–93.

Evans, Gary. *John Grierson and the National Film Board: The Politics of Wartime Propaganda*. Toronto: University of Toronto Press, 1984.

– *In the National Interest: A Chronicle of the National Film Board of Canada from 1949 to 1989*. Toronto: University of Toronto Press, 1991.

Fancott, Harriet. '*Project Grizzly*.' *Vancouver Echo* (9 October 1996).

Feldman, Seth. 'The Silent Subject in English-Canadian Film.' In *Take Two: A Tribute to Film in Canada*, ed. Feldman. Toronto: Irwin, 1984. 48–57.

Feldman, Seth, ed. *Take Two: A Tribute to Film in Canada*. Toronto: Irwin, 1984.

Feldman, Seth, and Joyce Nelson, eds. *Canadian Film Reader*. Toronto: Peter Martin, 1977.

Fischer, Lucy. '*Sherman's March*: Documentary Film and the Discourse of Hysterical/Historical Narrative.' In *Documenting the Documentary*, ed. Barry K. Grant and Jeannette Sloniowski. Detroit: Wayne State University Press, 1998. 333–43.

Florence, Penny. 'Lesbian Cinema, Women's Cinema.' In *Outwrite: Lesbianism and Popular Culture*, ed. Gabriele Griffin. London: Pluto Press, 1993. 126–47.

Foucault, Michel. *The History of Sexuality*, vol. 1, trans. Robert Hurley. New York: Random House, 1990.

Fourlanty, Eric. 'États de crise.' *Voir* (Montreal) (28 October–3 November 1993).

Freeland, Cynthia A. 'The Sublime in Cinema.' In *Passionate Views: Film, Cognition and Emotion*, ed. Carl Plantinga and Greg M. Smith. Baltimore: Johns Hopkins University Press, 1999. 65–83.

Freud, Sigmund. 'Mourning and Melancholia.' In *On Metapsychology*, ed. Angela Richards. Harmondsworth: Penguin, 1983, 245–68.

Frith, Simon, and Angela McRobbie. 'Rock and Sexuality.' In *On Record: Rock, Pop, and the Written Word*, ed. Frith and Andrew Goodwin. New York: Pantheon Books, 1989. 371–89.

Fuller, Cam. 'Documentary Probes Wounds of Oka.' *Star Phoenix* (Saskatoon) (5 October 1993).

Gaines, Jane M. '*Lonely Boy* and the *Vérité* of Sex.' *Canadian Journal of Film Studies* 8, no. 1 (Spring 1999): 102–18.

Gilday, Katherine. 'Liberating the Real.' *P.O.V.* 28 (Fall 1996): 18–22.

Grant, Barry Keith. ' "Across the Great Divide": Imitation and Inflection in Canadian Rock Music.' *Journal of Canadian Studies* 21, no. 1 (Spring 1986): 116–27.

Greer, Sandy. 'Mohawks and the Media: Alanis Obomsawin's *Kanehsatake: 270 Years of Resistance.'* *Take One* 4 (Winter 1994): 18–21.

Griffin, Susan. *Pornography and Silence: Culture's Revenge against Nature.* New York: Harper and Row, 1981.

Grodal, Torben. *Moving Pictures: A New Theory of Genres, Feelings and Cognitions.* Oxford: Oxford University Press, 1997.

Gwyn, Richard. *Smallwood, the Unlikely Revolutionary.* Toronto: McClelland and Stewart, 1986.

Hall, Stuart. *Encoding and Decoding in the Television Discourse.* Birmingham: Centre for Contemporary Cultural Studies, 1973.

– 'Cultural Studies: Two Paradigms.' *Media, Culture and Society* 2, no. 1 (1980): 57–72.

– 'Recent Developments in Theories of Language and Ideology: A Critical Note.' In *Culture, Media and Language,* ed. Hall et al. London: Hutchinson, 1980. 157–62.

Handling, Piers. 'The National Film Board of Canada, 1939–1959.' In *Self Portrait: Essays on the Canadian and Quebec Cinemas,* ed. Pierre Véronneau and Handling. Ottawa: Canadian Film Institute, 1980. 42–53.

– 'The Diary Films of Michael Rubbo.' In *Take Two: A Tribute to Film in Canada,* ed. Seth Feldman. Toronto: Irwin, 1984. 205–16.

Harcourt, Peter. 'The Innocent Eye: An Aspect of the Work of the National Film Board of Canada.' In *Canadian Film Reader,* ed. Seth Feldman and Joyce Nelson. Toronto: Peter Martin Associates, 1977. 67–77.

– *Movies and Mythologies: Towards a National Cinema.* Toronto: Canadian Broadcasting Corporation, 1977.

– 'Screams from Silence: A Discussion of Anne Claire Poirier's *Tu as crié/Let Me Go.'* *P.O.V.* 34 (Spring 1998): 22–5.

Hardy, Forsyth, ed. *Grierson on Documentary.* London: Faber and Faber, 1966.

Harkness, John. 'The Improbable Rise of Denys Arcand.' *Sight and Sound* 58, no. 4 (Autumn 1989): 234–8.

Higson, Andrew. *Waving the Flag: Constructing a National Cinema in Britain.* Oxford: Clarendon Press, 1995.

Hugo, Victor. *Les Contemplations,* ed. J. Vianey. Paris: Hachette, 1922.

Hume, David. *A Treatise of Human Nature,* ed. David Fate Norton and Mary J. Norton. New York: Oxford University Press, 2000.

Hutcheon, Linda. *A Poetics of Postmodernism.* New York: Routledge, 1988.

– *As Canadian as – Possible – Under the Circumstances!* Toronto: ECW and York University Press, 1990.

– *Irony's Edge: The Theory and Politics of Irony.* London: Routledge, 1994.

Irigaray, Luce. *Speculum of the Other Woman*, trans. G.C. Gill. Ithaca: Cornell University Press, 1985.

Jacobson, Anne Jaap, ed. *Feminist Interpretations of David Hume*. University Park: Pennsylvania State University Press, 2000.

Jagose, Annamarie. *Queer Theory: An Introduction*. New York: New York University Press, 1996.

Jennings, Sarah. 'An Interview with Terence Macartney-Filgate.' In *Terence Macartney-Filgate*, ed. Charlotte Gobeil. Ottawa: Canadian Film Institute, 1966. 1–16.

Johnston, Claire. 'Women's Cinema as Counter Cinema.' In *Movies and Methods*, vol. 1, ed. Bill Nichols. Berkeley: University of California Press, 1976. 208–17.

Jones, D.B. *Movies and Memoranda: An Interpretive History of the National Film Board of Canada*. Ottawa: Canadian Film Institute, 1981.

– *The Best Butler in the Business: Tom Daly of the National Film Board of Canada*. Toronto: University of Toronto Press, 1996.

Kant, Immanuel. *The Critique of Judgment*, trans. James Creed Meredith. Oxford: Clarendon Press, 1969.

Klein, Bonnie Sherr, and Persimmon Blackbridge. *Slow Dance: A Story of Stroke, Love and Disability*. Toronto: Alfred A. Knopf, 1997.

Knelman, Martin. *This Is Where We Came In: The Career and Character of Canadian Film*. Toronto: McClelland and Stewart, 1977.

Lafrance, André, ed. *Cinéma d'ici*. Ottawa: Éditions Leméac, 1973.

La Rochelle, Réal. 'Sound Design and Music as *Tragédie en musique*: The Documentary Practice of Denys Arcand.' In *Auteur/Provocateur: The Films of Denys Arcand*, ed. André Loiselle and Brian McIlroy. Westport, CT: Praeger, 1995. 32–51.

La Rochelle, Réal, ed. *Denys Arcand: Cinéastes du Québec 8*. Montreal: Conseil québécois pour la diffusion du cinéma, 1971.

Larouche, Michel, ed. *L'Aventure du cinéma québécois en France*. Montreal: XYZ, 1996.

Leach, Jim. 'Second Images: Reflections on the Canadian Cinema(s) in the Seventies.' In *Take Two: A Tribute to Film in Canada*, ed. Seth Feldman. Toronto: Irwin, 1984. 100–10.

Lockerbie, Ian. 'Le Documentaire auto-réflexif au Québec: *L'Émotion dissonante* et *Passiflora*.' *Cinémas* 4, no. 2 (Winter 1994): 119–32.

Loiselle, André. '"I Only Know Where I Come From, Not Where I'm Going": A Conversation with Denys Arcand.' In *Auteur/Provocateur: The Films of Denys Arcand*, ed. Loiselle and Brian McIlroy. Westport, CT: Praeger, 1995. 136–61.

– 'Despair as Empowerment: Melodrama and Counter-Cinema in Anne Claire Poirier's *Mourir à tue-tête*.' *Canadian Journal of Film Studies* 8, no. 2 (Fall 1999): 21–43.

Loiselle, André, and Brian McIlroy, eds. *Auteur/Provocateur: The Films of Denys Arcand*. Westport, CT: Praeger, 1995.

Lynch, Peter. 'Bringing Technology to Bear on *Project Grizzly*.' *American Cinematographer* 78, no. 1 (January 1997): 22–4.

MacDonald, Jake. 'Baby It's Cold Outside.' *Globe and Mail* (18 November 2000).

Maheu, Pierre. *Un Parti pris révolutionnaire*. Montreal: Parti pris, 1983.

Malpas, Jeff. 'Finding Place: Spatiality, Locality, and Subjectivity.' In *Philosophy and Geography III: Philosophies of Place*, ed. Andrew Light and Jonathan M. Smith. Lanham, MD: Rowman and Littlefield, 1998. 21–43.

Marcorelles, Louis. *Living Cinema: New Directions in Contemporary Film-making*, trans. Isabel Quigley. New York: Praeger, 1973.

Marcuse, Herbert. *One-Dimensional Man: Studies in the Ideology of Advanced Industrial Society*, 2nd ed. Boston: Beacon Press, 1991.

Marginson, Karen. 'Talking Heads: *Kanehsatake*'s Alanis Obomsawin.' *International Documentary* 12, no. 11 (December 1993–January 1994): 1, 10–11.

Marsolais, Gilles. *L'Aventure du cinéma direct revisitée*. Laval: Les 400 Coups, 1997.

Mathews, Ed. 'Immigrants and the NFB.' *Cinema Canada* 138 (February 1987): 22–7.

Melhuish, Martin. *Heart of Gold: Thirty Years of Canadian Rock Music*. Toronto: CBC Enterprises, 1983.

Michael Rubbo: The Man and His Films. Montreal: National Film Board of Canada, 1980.

Miller, J.R. 'Great White Father Knows Best: Oka and the Land Claims Process.' In *Out of the Background: Readings in Canadian Native History*, ed. Ken S. Coates and Robin Fisher. Toronto: Copp Clark, 1996. 367–90.

Miller, James P. 'Buffet Scoffs at Tech Share Prices.' *Wall Street Journal*, reprinted in *Globe and Mail* (1 May 2000).

Morris, Peter. 'After Grierson: The National Film Board, 1945–1953.' In *Take Two: A Tribute to Film in Canada*, ed. Seth Feldman. Toronto: Irwin, 1984. 182–94.

– *The Film Companion*. Toronto: Irwin, 1984.

– 'Backwards to the Future: John Grierson's Film Policy for Canada.' In *Flashback: People and Institutions in Canadian Film History*, ed. Gene Walz. Montreal: Mediatexte, 1986. 17–35.

Mulvey, Laura. 'Visual Pleasure and Narrative Cinema.' *Screen* 16, no. 3 (Autumn 1975): 6–18.

Nelson, Joyce. *The Colonized Eye: Rethinking the Grierson Legend*. Toronto: Between the Lines, 1988.

Nepinak, Doug. '*Kanehsatake: 270 Years of Resistance*.' *Weetamah* (Winnipeg) (5 July 1993).

Newman, Sidney. Interview. *Cinéma Québec* 1, no. 2 (June–July 1971): 35.

Nichols, Bill. 'The Voice of Documentary.' *Film Quarterly* 36, no. 3 (Spring 1983): 17–30.

– *Representing Reality: Issues and Concepts in Documentary*. Bloomington: Indiana University Press, 1991.

– *Blurred Boundaries: Questions of Meaning in Contemporary Culture*. Bloomington: Indiana University Press, 1994.

Nuovo, Franco. 'Les Cowboys et les indiens.' *Journal de Montréal* (28 October 1993).

Owen, W.J.B., ed. *Wordsworth's Literary Criticism*. London: Routledge and Kegan Paul, 1974.

Owens, Craig. *Beyond Recognition: Representation, Power and Culture*. Berkeley: University of California Press, 1992.

Patry, Yvan. 'Arthur Lamothe: Réalisateur.' In *Le Cinéma québécois: Tendances et prolongements*, ed. Renald Bérubé and Yvan Patry. Montreal: Éditions Sainte-Marie, 1968. 116–20.

– *Arthur Lamothe*. Montreal: Conseil québécois pour la diffusion du cinéma, 1971.

Peellaert, Guy, and Nik Cohn. *Rock Dreams*. New York: Popular Library, 1973.

Penley, Constance. 'Crackers and Whackers: The White Trashing of Porn.' In *White Trash: Race and Class in America*, ed. Matt Wray and Annalee Newitz. London: Routledge, 1997. 89–112.

Perrault, Pierre. *Discours sur la condition sauvage et québécoise*. Montreal: Lidec, 1977.

– *Pour la suite du monde*. Montreal: l'Hexagone, 1992.

– *Cinéaste de la parole: Entretiens avec Paul Warren*. Montreal: L'Hexagone, 1996.

Perreault, Luc. 'On est au coton refait surface.' *La Presse* (24 January 1976).

Pertusati, Linda. *In Defense of Mohawk Land: Ethnopolitical Conflict in Native North America*. Albany: State University of New York Press, 1997.

Petrone, Penny, ed. *First People, First Voices*. Toronto: University of Toronto Press, 1991.

Pevere, Geoff, and Greig Dymond. *Mondo Canuck: A Canadian Pop Culture Odyssey*. Scarborough: Prentice-Hall Canada, 1996.

Plantinga, Carl, and Greg M. Smith, eds. *Passionate Views: Film, Cognition and Emotion*. Baltimore: Johns Hopkins University Press, 1999.

Rapport, Nigel, and Andrew Dawson. 'Home and Movement: A Polemic.' In

Migrants of Identity: Perceptions of Home in a World of Movement, ed. Rapport
‍   and Dawson. Oxford: Berg 1998. 19–38.

Rich, B. Ruby. 'New Queer Cinema.' *Sight and Sound* 2, no. 5 (September 1992):
   30–4.

– 'Anti-Porn: Soft Issue, Hard World.' In *Gendering the Nation: Canadian
   Women's Cinema*, ed. Kay Armatage et al. Toronto: University of Toronto
   Press, 1999. 62–75.

Riches, Hester. 'Oscars in Sight: Don Brittain on Lowry's *Volcano*.' *The Peak*
   (Simon Fraser University) (25 March 1977): 6–8.

Rolling Stone editors, ed. *The Rolling Stone Rock Almanac*. New York: Collier, 1983.

Rousseau, Yves. 'Contre la fuite du monde.' *24 images* 100 (Winter 2000): 31.

Roy, André. 'Non réconciliés.' *Kanehsatake: 270 ans de résistance* d'Alanis
   Obomsawin.' *24 Images* 71 (1993): 74.

Russell, Catherine. *Experimental Ethnography: The Work of Film in the Age of
   Video*. Durham, NC: Duke University Press, 1999.

Shaw, Greg. 'The Teen Idols.' In *The Rolling Stone Illustrated History of Rock and
   Roll*, ed. Jim Miller. New York: Random House, 1980. 96–100.

Shuker, Roy. *Understanding Popular Music*. New York: Routledge, 1994.

Sinclair, Donna. 'Film Review: *Kanehsatake: 270 Years of Resistance*.' *United
   Church Observer* (Toronto) (October 1993).

Smith, Murray. *Engaging Characters: Fiction, Emotion, and the Cinema*. Oxford:
   Clarendon Press, 1995.

Sparks, Colin. 'Stuart Hall, Cultural Studies and Marxism.' In *Stuart Hall:
   Critical Dialogues in Cultural Studies*,' ed. David Morley and Kuan-Hsing
   Chen. London: Routledge, 1996. 71–101.

Spivak, Gayatri. *In Other Worlds: Essays in Cultural Politics*. New York:
   Routledge, 1988.

Staehling, Richard. 'From *Rock around the Clock* to *The Trip*: The Truth about
   Teen Movies.' In *Kings of the Bs: Working within the Hollywood System*, ed.
   Todd McCarthy and Charles Flynn. New York: Dutton, 1975. 220–51.

Steven, Peter. *Brink of Reality: New Canadian Documentary Film and Video*.
   Toronto: Between the Lines, 1993.

Suleiman, Susan Rubin. 'Feminism and Postmodernism: A Question of Politics.' In *The Postmodern Reader*, ed. Charles Jencks. London: Academy Edi-
   tions, 1992. 318–22.

Sweeney, Gael. 'The Face on the Lunch Box: Television's Construction of the
   Teen Idol.' *Velvet Light Trap* 33 (Spring 1994): 49–59.

Tan, Ed S. *Emotion and the Structure of Narrative Film: Film as an Emotion Machine*, trans. Barbara Fasting. Mahwah: Lawrence Erlbaum, 1996.

Tracey, Lindalee. *Growing Up Naked: My Years in Bump and Grind*. Vancouver: Douglas and McIntyre, 1997.

Tremblay, Odile. 'Alanis, Pascale et Antonin ...' *Le Devoir* (Montreal) (27 October 1993).

Trinh T. Minh-Ha. 'Outside in Inside Out.' In *Questions of Third Cinema*, ed. Jim Pines and Paul Willemen. London: British Film Institute, 1989. 133–9.

– *When the Moon Waxes Red: Representation, Gender and Cultural Politics*. New York: Routledge, 1991.

Véronneau, Pierre. *Résistance et affirmation: La production francophone à l'ONF, 1939–64*. Montreal: Cinémathèque québécoise, 1987.

– 'L'Américanité: Les Paradoxes d'une notion.' *Cinémas* 1, nos. 1–2 (Autumn 1990): 87–100.

– 'Alone and with Others: Denys Arcand's Destiny within the Quebec Cinematic and Cultural Context.' In *Auteur/Provocateur: The Films of Denys Arcand*, ed. André Loiselle and Brian McIlroy. Westport, CT: Praeger, 1995. 10–31.

Véronneau, Pierre, Michael Dorland, and Seth Feldman, eds. *Dialogue: Canadian and Quebec Cinema*. Montreal: La cinémathèque québécoise, 1987.

Véronneau, Pierre, and Piers Handling, eds. *Self Portrait: Essays on the Canadian and Quebec Cinemas*. Ottawa: Canadian Film Institute, 1980.

White, Jerry. 'Alanis Obomsawin, Documentary Form and the Canadian Nation(s).' *CineAction!* 49 (Summer 1999): 26–36.

White, Patricia. 'Governing Lesbian Desire: *Nocturne*'s Oedipal Fantasy.' In *Feminisms in the Cinema*, ed. Laura Pietropaulo and Ada Testaferri. Bloomington: Indiana University Press, 1995. 86–105.

Wiegman, Robyn. 'Introduction: Mapping the Lesbian Postmodern.' In *The Lesbian Postmodern*, ed. Laura Doan. New York: Columbia University Press, 1994. 1–20.

Williams, Linda. 'Mirrors without Memories: Truth, History and the New Documentary.' *Film Quarterly* 46, no. 3 (Spring 1993): 9–21.

Wilton, Tamsin, ed. *Immortal, Invisible: Lesbians and the Moving Image*. London: Routledge, 1995.

Winston, Brian. 'The Documentary Film as Scientific Inscription.' In *Theorizing Documentary*, ed. Michael Renov. New York: Routledge, 1993. 58–89.

Wise, Wyndham. '100 Great and Glorious Years of Canadian Cinema – The Sequel.' *Take One* 5, no. 15 (Spring 1997): 24–39.

Wright, Judy, and Debbie Magidson. 'Making Films for Your Own People: An Interview with Denys Arcand.' In *Canadian Film Reader*, ed. Seth Feldman and Joyce Nelson. Toronto: Peter Martin Associates, 1977. 217–34.

Wright, Ronald. 'Cutting through the Razor Wire at Mohawk Barricades.' *Globe and Mail* (25 September 1993).

'Writing for the Screen: Six Interviews with Canadian Writers.' *Pot Pourri* (Summer 1976): 2–12.

York, Geoffrey, and Loreen Pindera. *The People of the Pines: The Warriors and the Legacy of Oka.* Toronto: Little, Brown, 1991.

Zimet, Jaye. *Strange Sisters: The Art of Lesbian Pulp Fiction, 1949–1969.* New York: Viking, 1999.

Index of Film Titles

Films are listed under their original titles. The English titles are either the title under which the film was released in English or, when there was no English version, a literal translation of the original title.

Alias Will James, 149

L'Amour … à quel prix? / Love … at What Price? 148–9

À Saint-Henri le cinq septembre / September Five at Saint-Henri, 44

À tout prendre / The Way It Goes, 45

Le Bedeau / The Sexton, 17

Bethune, 116, 120–123

The Blair Witch Project, 45

Bûcherons de la Manouane / Manouane River Lumberjacks, 11, 61–8

Le Chat dans le sac / The Cat in the Bag, 9, 45

Chronique d'un été / Chronicle of a Summer, 31–2, 41, 44

Churchill's Island, 118

City of Gold, 13, 35–6

Corral, 7, 13, 35–6, 44

David Holzman's Diary, 44

The Days before Christmas, 10, 32–3, 38–45

Dimanche d'Amérique / One Sunday in Canada, 62

Dirty Harry, 203

Les Enfants du silence / Children of Silence, 62

Enthusiasm, 91

Fields of Sacrifice, 119–20

Les Filles du Roy / They Called Us 'Les Filles du Roy,' 218

Forbidden Love, 11, 164–80

Gina, 93, 97, 100

Golden Gloves, 62, 68

Le Grand Jack / Jack Kerouac's Road – A Franco-American Odyssey, 149

Un Jeu si simple / Such a Simple Game, 68

Jour après jour / Day after Day, 62, 64

Kanehsatake: 270 Years of Resistance, 11, 181–96

Lonely Boy, 11, 13, 44, 48–60, 118, 122, 136

La Lutte / Wrestling, 44, 62

M, 217

Manger / Eating, 62

La Maudite Galette / Damned Money, 100

Memorandum, 122

Le Mépris n'aurait qu'un temps / Hell No Longer, 64

Mildred Pierce, 139

Momma Don't Allow, 37

Mourir à tue-tête / Scream from Silence, 135, 142, 211, 218

Neighbours, 36

Nobody Waved Good-bye, 8, 45

Not a Love Story: A Film about Pornography, 11, 131–47

Nuit et brouillard / Night and Fog, 218, 221

On est au coton / Cotton Mill, Treadmill, 11, 88–100

Paul Tomkowicz: Street-railway Switchman, 10, 13–27, 118

Persistent and Finagling, 106

Pincers on Japan, 118

Portrait of Jason, 56

Pour quelques arpents de neige / Strangers for the Day, 62

Pour la suite du monde / Moontrap / Of Whales, the Moon and Men, 10, 44, 71–84

La Poursuite du bonheur / The Pursuit of Happiness, 148–9

Primary, 32, 41, 44

Project Grizzly, 11, 197–209

Québec: Duplessis et après ... / Quebec: Duplessis and after ..., 88, 100

Québec USA ou l'invasion pacifique / Visit to a Foreign Country, 62

Les Raquetteurs / The Snowshoers, 44, 67

Road to the Reich, 118

Robocop, 201, 203

Roger and Me, 105

The Romance of Transportation in Canada, 36

Sad Song of Yellow Skin, 106

Salesman, 56

Setting Fires for Science, 117

Sherman's March, 105

Shoah, 220–1

Springtime in Greenland, 26

Stella Dallas, 139

La Terra trema / The Earth Trembles, 68

This Is Spinal Tap, 44

Tu as crié Let Me Go, 11, 211–25

Universe, 35–6

The Valour and the Horror, 107

La Vie rêvée / Dream Life, 179

Volcano: An Inquiry into the Life and Death of Malcolm Lowry, 11, 115–30

Voyage en Amérique avec un cheval emprunté / Travels in America with a Borrowed Horse, 10, 148–61

Voyage au bout de la route / Journey to the End of the Road, 149

Waiting for Fidel, 11, 103–14

The War Game, 44

Women Are Warriors, 118

General Index

Adorno, Theodor, 54, 89–90
Allder, Michael, 197–8, 209
Anderson, Benedict, 22
Althusser, Louis, 212
Anderson, Elizabeth, 143
Anderson, Walter Truett, 107
Arcand, Denys, 87–100

Bailey, Cameron, 205
Bannon, Ann, 173
Batchelor, Lorne, 13
Beachell, Chester, 36
Beaucage, Marjorie, 195
Beaudet, Marc, 96
Beckett, Samuel, 105
Berton, Pierre, 23
Bissonnette, Sophie, 148
Blackburn, Maurice, 64–5
Blais, Marie-Claire, 215
Bobet, Jacques, 16, 20–1
Bonitzer, Pascal, 107
Bonnière, René, 71
Bourassa, Robert, 182, 192
Bourdieu, Pierre, 203–4, 206–8
Bourgault, Hélène, 151
Brault, Michel, 39, 44, 71, 73–4, 78, 81

Brittain, Donald, 115–30
Brooks, Peter, 220
Brûlé, Michel, 72
Burnett, Ron, 211,

Canada Carries On (series), 33–4, 118
Canada at War (series), 119, 120
Canadian Broadcasting Corporation, 6, 24, 32, 103, 105, 107–8, 113, 119, 183
Canadian Film Development Corporation, 8
Canadian Government Motion Picture Bureau, 3
Candid Eye, The (series), 6, 8, 32–4, 38, 41, 44–5, 64, 89
candid eye filmmaking, 32–41, 44, 89, 116, 119, 149
Carrière, Marcel, 80
Carson, L.M. Kit, 44
Cartier, Jacques, 73, 82
Cartier-Bresson, Henri, 37–8, 74
Castro, Fidel, 104, 105, 110–12
censorship, 62, 87–8, 103–4
Challenge for Change/Société nouvelle (program), 9, 95–8

Chapple, Steve, 51–2
Charland, Maurice, 23
Chiasson, Herménégilde, 149
Chion, Michel, 217, 219–20
Chronique des Indiens du Nord-est du Québec (series), 62
Cinema Canada (journal), 67
cinéma direct, 8–9, 71, 77–80, 82–4
Cinéma Québec (journal), 67
cinéma vérité, 31–2, 36, 44, 61, 64, 68, 105
Cité libre (journal), 62, 67, 96
Clandfield, David, 48, 64, 68
Clarke, Shirley, 56
cognitive film theory, 212–13
Cornwell, Ethel, 27
Croll, George, 39
Curtiz, Michael, 139

Daly, Tom, 6, 13, 17, 34–6, 38–9, 41, 48, 119
de Certeau, Michel, 207–8
de Lauretis, Teresa, 170
Deleuze, Gilles, 156, 158
Descartes, René, 16
Devlin, Bernard, 37
direct cinema, 32, 44, 64, 94, 118, 135–6, 149
Dirse, Zoe, 182
Doane, Mary Anne, 207
Dogme 95, 44
Drew, Robert, 32
Druick, Zöe, 19–20
Dufaux, Georges, 39
Duplessis, Maurice, 18, 20, 96
Dyer, Richard, 48
Dymond, Greig, 50, 205–6

Eastwood, Clint, 201
Elder, R. Bruce, 38, 133–4

Eliot, T.S., 27
Elsaesser, Thomas, 221
En tant que femmes (series), 9
ethnographic documentary, 62, 104–5, 132–5, 137, 141
Euvrard, Michel, 67
Evans, Gary, 18, 36, 97

Faces of Canada (series), 13, 17–18
Feeney, John, 39
Feldman, Seth, 113
Fernie, Lynne, 164–80
Fish, Stanley, 178
Florence, Penny, 175
Ford, John, 201
Foucault, Michel, 169, 175
Fraticelli, Rina, 165
Free Cinema, 37
French Unit, 21, 44, 67, 71, 81, 88, 94
Freud, Sigmund, 218–20
Frith, Simon, 53

Garofalo, Reebee, 51–2
Godbout, Jacques, 95–6, 149
Godin, Gérard, 94, 99
Greene, Lorne, 7, 33, 35
Grierson, John, 5–10, 33–4, 38, 48, 77, 87, 97, 115, 135, 137, 197
Griffin, Susan, 135, 137–8, 141
Groulx, Gilles, 9, 45, 68, 116

Hall, Stuart, 212–13
Handling, Piers, 103, 110
Hansen, Christian, 132
Harcourt, Peter, 8, 25, 35, 218–19
Harkness, John, 98
Higson, Andrew, 5
Hugo, Victor, 84
Hume, David, 222–3
Hutcheon, Linda, 166, 178, 201, 204

Images (journal), 62, 67
Irigaray, Luce, 199
Irwin, Arthur, 17–18

Jackson, Stanley, 7, 13–14, 19, 32, 39–40, 43
Jones, D.B., 13–14, 17, 35, 49, 93
Jutra, Claude, 45

Kane, Michael, 122
Kant, Immanuel, 216
Klein, Bonnie Sherr, 131–47
Koenig, Wolf, 32, 34, 36–40, 44, 48–9, 56, 116, 122
Kramer, John, 115–16, 129
Kroitor, Roman, 13, 17, 19–20, 34, 39–41, 44, 48–9, 58, 116, 122

Lafonde, Jean-Daniel, 149
Lamothe, Arthur, 61–2, 64, 67–8
Lanctôt, Micheline, 148
Lang, Fritz, 217
Lanzmann, Claude, 220–1
La Rochelle, Réal, 88–91, 93, 98
Leacock, Richard, 32, 64
Leduc, Jacques, 218
Lefebvre, Jean Pierre, 67
Legg, Stuart, 34
Lesage, Jean, 96
Liberté (journal), 62, 67
Locke, Jack, 39
Lockerbie, Ian, 150
Loiselle, André, 211, 220
Low, Colin, 9, 34, 36
Lowry, Malcolm, 115–30
Lynch, Peter, 197, 199, 201
Lyotard, Jean-François, 175

Macartney-Filgate, Terence, 32, 34, 37, 39, 41, 44

Maddin, Guy, 26
Malpas, Jeff, 16
March of Time (series), 7
Marcuse, Herbert, 90, 98–100
Marker, Chris, 149
Marsolais, Gilles, 79
Maysles, Albert and David, 56
McBride, Jim, 44
McElwee, Ross, 105–6
McLaren, Norman, 6, 36
McLuhan, Marshall, 58
McPherson, Hugo, 95–6
McRobbie, Angela, 53
Melodrama, 139, 167, 169, 171–6
Michel, Eric, 148
Miller, Eric, 36
Millett, Kate, 140
Montaigne, Michel de, 150
Moore, Michael, 105–6
Morgan, Robin, 137, 144
Morin, Edgar, 31, 41, 64
Morris, Peter, 17–18, 36–7
Mulroney, Brian, 192
Mulvey, Laura, 166
myth, 8, 25–7, 62, 48–9, 74, 82–3, 108

National Dream, The (series), 23
Needham, Catherine, 132
Newman, Sidney, 94–7
Nichols, Bill, 104, 106, 108, 113, 132, 166, 169, 177

Objectif (journal), 67
Obomsawin, Alanis, 10, 181–96
On the Spot (series), 37
Owen, Don, 8, 45
Owens, Craig, 178

Paizs, John, 26
Parti pris (journal), 67, 88, 96

Patry, Yvan, 64
Peellaert, Guy, 58
Pelletier, Gérard, 97
Penley, Constance, 203
Pennebaker, Donn, 64
performance, 56–7, 72–4, 78–80, 112–
    13, 139–40, 201
Perrault, Pierre, 44, 71–5, 77–8, 80,
    82–4
Perron, Clément, 62
Perspective (series), 37
Pevere, Geoff, 50, 205–6
Plantinga, Carl, 213
Poirier, Anne Claire, 9, 135, 142, 211–
    25
Proulx, Abbé, 3

queer cinema, 169–75

Reiner, Rob, 44
Reisz, Karel, 37
Resnais, Alain, 218
Rich, E. Ruby, 133–4, 142
Richardson, Tony, 37
Riel, Louis, 23
Rochat, Roger, 182
Rouch, Jean, 31–2, 41, 71
Rousseau, Yves, 72
Roy, André, 194
Rubbo, Michael, 103–14, 143
Ruspoli, Mario, 71
Russell, Catherine, 224

Sadoul, Georges, 31
Said, Edward, 104
Screen (journal), 212–13
Sedgwick, Eve, 178

Séquences (journal), 67
Shannon, Kathleen, 9, 39, 56, 143
Sinclair, Lister, 122
Smith, Greg, 213
Spivak, Gayatri, 178
Staehling, Richard, 50
Studio D, 9, 131–2, 139, 143–4, 164
Sulieman, Susan Rubin, 178
Super Dave (series), 203

Take One (journal), 67
Temps présent (series), 62
Tonight Show (series), 51
Tracey, Lindalee, 131, 136–42, 144
Trudeau, Pierre, 96–7
Tweed, Tom, 14, 20

Unit B, 6–8, 13, 32, 34–8, 45, 48, 49,
    71, 88, 94, 118, 119

Verhoeven, Paul, 201
versioning, 16, 20–1, 67
Vertov, Dziga, 91
Vidor, King, 139
Visconti, Luchino, 68

Watkins, Peter, 44
Weigman, Robyn, 175–6
Weissman, Aerlyn, 164–80
White, Patricia, 170–1
Williams, Linda, 105–6
Williams, Raymond, 212
Winnipeg Film Group, 26
Winston, Brian, 5
Wordsworth, William, 222–3
World in Action, The (series), 33, 118